History and Criticism
of the Marcan Hypothesis

Hans-Herbert Stoldt

Translated and Edited by
Donald L. Niewyk

Introduction by
William R. Farmer

Mercer University Press
Macon, Georgia

T. & T. Clark Ltd.
36 George Street, Edinburgh

Originally published in 1977
as
Geschichte und Kritik der Markushypothese
by
Vandenhoeck und Ruprecht
Göttingen

Mercer University Press
ISBN 0-86554-002-0
Library of Congress No. 80-82572

T. & T. Clark Ltd.
0 567 09210 7

First printed . . . 1980

Acknowledgements

Special recognition is due to Gerda Neel, who assisted with the translation of the long first section of the book; to Heidrun Coleman, who helped with Parts II, III, and IV; and to Dr. Jack K. Jeans, whose generosity made their assistance possible. I should also like to thank Professor Eugene Van Ness Goetchius of the Episcopal Theological School, Cambridge, Mass., who aided with the translation of Chapter XIII. Father Bernard Orchard, O.S.B., of Ealing Abbey, London, rendered the Latin quotations into English. Professor John E. Steely of Southeastern Baptist Theological Seminary kindly read the entire translation and offered a number of valuable suggestions for improvement. Dr. Charles E. Wolfe of Hampstead, Md., prepared the text-critical notes in the appendix. Assistance with the technical terminology came from Professors William R. Farmer and Joseph B. Tyson of Southern Methodist University. Catherine Wilson helped polish the English prose, and Sally Snow, David Barrett Peabody, Martha Peabody, and Kurt Boggan assisted in the preparation of the manuscript. Furthermore, I must acknowledge the excellent editorial work by John Riches of T. & T. Clark, Edinburgh. Edwin D. Johnston of Mercer University generously undertook responsibility for preparing the indexes. Finally, Dr. Stoldt himself checked the accuracy of the translation, identified a few minor errors in the German edition, and provided three long paragraphs of new material on Bultmann in Chapter XIV.

D. L. N.

Table of Contents

Introduction

by
William R. Farmer

I was first introduced to the work of Hans-Herbert Stoldt by Bo Reicke in Basel the summer of 1977. He had recently received a copy of Stoldt's work for review in *Theologische Zeitschrift*. Stoldt was, he said, a retired school administrator who lived in Flensburg. His manuscript had once passed through the hands of Professor Reicke. He thus was able to provide me with Stoldt's address. We agreed that I would review the book for *T. Z.* [see "Kritik der Markushypothese," May/June 1978]; A few months later, at a meeting of the Society of Biblical Literature, Lamar Cope recommended a debate on Stoldt's book. This took place in November of 1978 during the meetings of S.B.L. in New Orleans.

Stoldt himself was present as a guest of the society and took part in the discussion which followed. David Dungan and Howard Kee presented prepared papers, pro and con, respectively. An evaluation of Stoldt's work by Kee appeared subsequently in a review for *J.B.L.* [March, 1979, pp. 140-143]. While he was in the United States, Stoldt lectured on his book to an audience of New Testament scholars from the greater Boston area. Preceding a dinner in his honor in Dallas, Texas, Stoldt was presented a copy of an English translation of his book by Donald Niewyk. Stoldt carried this copy back to Germany and has authorized all changes from the German original which are chiefly three in number: 1) a few paragraphs illuminating the relationships between form criticism and the Marcan hypothesis, which were omitted from the German edition, have been restored in the English edition; 2) In certain places in the German text, specifically at the close of some of his discussions of arguments used by earlier German New Testament critics, Stoldt has used the weapon of ridicule. The most obvious of these uses of ridicule have been eliminated from the English edition; 3) In order to improve the readibility of the book for a larger public, the extensive lists of words and phrases from the Gospels which Stoldt presents as part of his argument in the opening section of his book have been supplied in English and the evidence from the Greek text is given in an appendix. Many of the more important alternate readings in the text, utilized by Stoldt, are discussed by Charles E. Wolfe.

Concerning Stoldt's work, I have written as follows:

> Hans-Herbert Stoldt has made an important contribution to the world of New Testament studies. His book is an original contribution that will have far-reaching consequences. It will not go unnoticed that a distinguished German publishing house has made the results of Stoldt's research available. Since the Marcan hypothesis was born in Germany, it is not inappropriate that it there be put to rest. This is the import of Stoldt's book.

> What actually happened in the last century has become a matter of dispute. (Cf. Walter Schmithals, *Theologische Literaturzeitung* 92 [1967] 425, and the reply by William R. Farmer in *Biblica,* 54 [1973] 429.) New Testament scholars are not expected to be specialists in the history of German literature, and consequently, few know firsthand much about the history of their discipline. In order to accomplish in a decisive manner the task of writing a history of the Marcan hypothesis and in the same book offer a critical evaluation of that hypothesis, it helps if the author is both a New Testament critic and a student of nineteenth-century German literature. Stoldt brings both of these competencies to bear in his work.

> In his opening paragraph Stoldt defines his task in terms of 'Intellectual History.' He recognizes that the synoptic problem is one of the most difficult problems that has engaged the human mind. The ground of source analysis has been plowed so often during the past two centuries that Stoldt can understand that many would think it useless to attempt to rework it.

> In the light of this opening statement, the observation in the closing paragraph of Stoldt's book takes on added meaning: 'We stand not at the end of Gospel research. I think we stand rather at a turning point.' However we proceed, says Stoldt, we should do so with the understanding that so far as we can tell (we can only speak in terms of probability), the sequence in which the Gospels

were written was (as Griesbach and many other N.T. critics have held), first Matthew, second Luke, and third, making use of both of the other two, Mark.

Stoldt justifies this conclusion in part by reference to the history of the Marcan hypothesis. The fact that Mark was not encumbered by mythological and legendary birth narratives or resurrection stories made it appear, in the period of gospel research prior to form-criticism, to offer a more acceptable historical basis for Christian theology than either Matthew or Luke. How the consensus for Marcan priority grew in the absence of proof in this period is documented by Stoldt in two ways. First, he covers the ground historically by dealing with the relevant literature (the works of Wilke, Weisse, Holtzmann, Wernle, and Bernhard Weiss) in chronological order. On the basis of this historical analysis he then approaches the matter systematically, noting that there have been seven arguments for Marcan priority. Each is analyzed comprehensively and the contributions of different scholars are discussed. In this way, Stoldt guards himself against the danger of dealing with any particular argument in a piecemeal fashion as it might appear in the work of a single scholar. This 'double check' is a noteworthy feature of Stoldt's work.

Stoldt next takes up the question of the ideological background of the Marcan hypothesis, and asks how, in the absence of proof, belief in Marcan priority arose.

In a penultimate chapter Stoldt discusses the question of how, having come into being in the absence of proof, the Marcan hypothesis has maintained its existence to the present. He notes that there has never been a time when there have not been some scholars who were conscious of the critical difficulties with the hypothesis. At the same time, however, there have been many influential scholars who have put the weight of their scholarship behind belief in Marcan priority by assuming this hypothesis in their research. This is particularly the case with the form critics. Stoldt thinks it is tragic that this has happened, in view of the fact that the leading exponents of form criticism, Dibelius and Bultmann, were well aware that the two-document hypothesis was only a hypothesis and that there were continual difficulties with it. Stoldt notes that especially during the past fifteen years, Catholic scholars in Germany have been adopting Marcan priority. Stoldt further notes that in English-speaking circles since Butler, the consciousness that there are serious problems with the two-document hypothesis has been growing and he gives brief attention to some of the various alternatives that have been proposed in recent years.

In a final chapter, after opting for a qualified form of the Griesbach hypothesis, Stoldt notes that there is now much work to be done. For example, he recognizes that this new development is going to give to Matthew and Luke the source prominence that Mark and "Q" have had. [Cf. Perkins *Journal,* Spring, 1980, pp. 46-48]

Professor Hans Conzelmann, in a survey of some books about the Synoptic Gospels prepared for the readers of *Theologische Rundshau* [43/1978, pp. 321-327], has briefly reviewed Stoldt's work. Stoldt composed a lengthy reply to Conzelmann's review which was published in *Bibel und Gemeinde* [79/1979, pp. 283ff.]. Stoldt's reply to Conzelmann was quickly recognized as a text which raised profound questions about the ethics of scholarship. Professor Virgil Howard prepared a translation of Stoldt's reply, including Conzelmann's review which Stoldt had included in full. This translation was published in the 1980 summer issue of the Perkins *Journal.* I made use of a briefer form of Stoldt's response to Conzelmann in a paper prepared for the Pacific Coast Sectional meeting of S.B.L. in Berkeley, March, 1980, entitled "The Stoldt-Conzelmann Controversy." This paper was published in the summer, 1980 issue of *Perspectives in Religious Studies.*

Because of the importance of Stoldt's reply to Conzelmann, it is best to cite a selection of some key passages from Howard's translation; including the whole of what Conzelmann said about Stoldt's book.

"Reflections on Legitimacy and Limits of Theological Criticism:
A Fundamental Response to a Specific Case"

by

Hans-Herbert Stoldt

Principles

1) It belongs to the vocational hazards of the scholar that one is capable of error.

2) It belongs to the vocational ethos of the scholar that under certain circumstances one must acknowledge: "I have erred." Such an acknowledgement can only serve to enhance the honor of a scholar.

3) It is incompatible with the vocational ethos of a scholar to suppress by silence or by violence new findings which might challenge one's own on the grounds that "what should not be, cannot be."

Specifics:

The conclusion reached in my book, *History and Criticism of the Marcan Hypothesis* reads as follows:

> The Marcan hypothesis, for more than a hundred years almost universally regarded as the solution of the synoptic problem, is untenable.

A dedicated representative of the Marcan hypothesis, Hans Conzelmann, Professor of New Testament in Gottingen, has taken a critical position regarding my conclusion . . . In his recent discussion of literature dealing with the synoptic gospels he summarizes his judgment of my book in the following few sentences:

> The project is daring: the investigation of the synoptic sources has not reached a conclusion, but rather a turning point and the change of direction is to be here initiated. This is to be achieved by reviewing the most significant originators of the notion of Marcan priority and subsequently of the Two Source Theory and recounting their subjective motives. As is customary among those who dispute the Marcan hypothesis, the author does not engage in philological investigation of the texts. Indeed, he explicitly rejects this. He sees himself at that point "where we should view our subject from a distance, summarize the findings of our individual critical analysis of sources, and view the Marcan hypothesis as a whole in its theological context as a phenomenon in the history of ideas"(p. 232). In plain language: It is to be finished off by demonstrating its "ideological background" (p. 206ff.). A scientific discussion is thereby carefully precluded.

Thus Conzelmann. The main point of his objections to my criticism of the Marcan hypothesis is the claim that "the author does not engage in philological investigation of the texts."

Remarkable how one can simply overlook 205 (two hundred and five) pages of a book comprising only 236 pages altogether! In any case, Conzelmann does not even mention them. *Now, I am a professional philologian*—even if I have 'studied theology as well with passion'—and, accordingly, I pursue through 205 pages of my work a purely *philological* investigation in órder 'to examine thoroughly one more time, with the original text in hand, *sine ira et studio,* all the theories of sources that have become relevant in historical research.' This is stated programmatically on the first page of my book!

Following the completion of these 205 pages of philological analysis I write as the opening sentence of my chapter, "The Conclusion" (in which, by the way, I once more expressly affirm that 'the Marcan hypothesis is in any case philologically untenable' [p. 233/259] as follows:

> We have *now* reached the point in our deduction where we should view our subject from a distance, summarize the findings of our individual critical analyses of sources, and view the Marcan hypothesis as a whole in its theological context as a phenomenon in the history of ideas [232/257].

What does Conzelmann make out of this: He allows my entire philological investigation simply to disappear, picks up my quotation from p. 232/257, eliminates the opening words which are essential for a correct understanding of the context—'We have *now* reached the point . . .,' and inserts in their place before the remaining words of my sentence—'where we should . . . summarize the findings of our individual critical analyses of sources . . .' his own words—'He (Stoldt) sees himself at that point,' and then continues—'where we should . . .etc.' And now, in order to confirm and make credible that this is really my intended meaning, Conzelmann places *before* this the sentence—"Indeed he explicitly rejects this (i.e., the philological investigation of the texts)."* His evidence for this then reads—'He sees himself at that point where . . .' "

---

*Rainer Reisner concludes that Conzelmann's review contains a misstatement of fact about Stoldt's book on the point in dispute. *Theologische Beitrage,* Vol. 11, No. 2, 1980, pp. 80-83.

In response to Conzelmann's penultimate sentence: "In plain language: It [the Marcan hypothesis] is to be finished off by demonstrating its 'ideological background,' " Stoldt replies as follows:

> In truth, the ideological background plays absolutely no role in my critical analysis of the Marcan hypothesis. I have refuted this source theory exclusively through the two parts of my argument referred to above. At the end of this 205-page investigation—*notabene!*—*prior* to the chapter dealing with the ideological background I summarize the results of my critical analysis: 'Accordingly we can state that *the second Gospel does not possess priority over Matthew and Luke and was not their source.* Therefore, the result of our critical examination is that *the Marcan hypothesis is false—false in view of design, execution, and conclusion'* (p. 202/221) This shows without the slightest possibility of objection or doubt that my scientific conclusion was reached without drawing on or taking recourse to the ideological background of the Marcan hypothesis.

Stoldt's work represents a cutting edge of current Synoptic scholarship. His refutation of the reasons that were given for belief in Marcan priority in the nineteenth century are equally valid today. For example, neither of the two most competent defenders of Marcan priority, Werner Georg Kümmel, nor Franz Nierynck, claim to have found new arguments for Marcan priority. The basic arguments they present have been refuted by Stoldt. It is idle to complain against a woodsman ridding the forest of a diseased tree that he has only cut the roots or the trunk of the tree.

But Stoldt is more than a simple woodsman; he is an experienced forester in the domain of nineteenth-century German literature. He has spotted a sickly tree on the estate of theological studies. He has examined it and has decided that its illness is terminal. No amount of surgery, grafting, wiring, or propping up of sagging branches can save it. Here he offers for examination a well conceived, richly documented, and skillfully written report.

New arguments for Marcan priority may be found. But until they are, the case would appear to rest where Stoldt has found it. Meanwhile, enough time would seem to have elapsed to consider the long-term value of James M. Robinson's suggestion that: "the success of *Redaktionsgeschichte* in clarifying the theologies of Matthew and Luke on the assumption of dependence on Mark is perhaps the most important new argument for Marcan priority" ["On the *Gattung* of Mark (and John)," *Jesus and Man's Hope,* Vol 1, 1970 pp. 101-2]. The leading proponents of *Redaktionsgeschichte,* make no such claim for their work, and, indeed, acknowledge that their confident belief in Marcan priority rests upon arguments well established in synoptic literature. But these are precisely the arguments from the nineteenth century which Stoldt has refuted.

There is much evidence that can be said to *fit* the two-document or Marcan hypothesis. But such evidence as *fits* a hypothesis should not be construed as evidence *for* that hypothesis, unless it fits that hypothesis better than rival hypotheses. There is little evidence for Marcan priority that meets this simple but essential test. Every attempt to resolve the issue of priority in open discussion in both the Society of Biblical Literature and Studiorum Novi Testamenti Societas, by appealing to redactional considerations, has thus far failed to produce critical consensus. Individual scholars may be persuaded one way or the other. But no new scholarly agreement has been reached. This will probably remain the case until adequate research tools, objectively identifying the literary characteristics of each gospel, are available, and until more comprehensive reconstructions of the development of early Christianity, and more credible reconstructions of the development of the Gospel tradition, are ready for consideration.

Into this confusing, but exciting state of affairs in New Testament research Stoldt's book has come. What influence Stoldt's work may have upon the development of contemporary Gospel research remains to be seen. For the moment, however, it would appear that critical interest in Stoldt's work is going to be kept alive in North America, while scholars at German universities ponder how best to respond to this work of an "outsider," who, without the backing of a university chair in New Testament, with only the authority of reason and evidence, has weighed the dominant theory of contemporary Gospel research in the balance, and found it wanting.

The Marcan hypothesis, in light of Stoldt's research, appears increasingly problematic. It may live on in the minds of those who believe in "the 'Q' community," and it may thrive among those who are inspired by the vision of "Mark's Galileean community" resisting the authoritarianism of the Jerusalem (read Vatican) hierarchy. But sound criticism will seek a more secure basis for its work. Those interested in achieving a more adequate scholarly consensus in the discipline of Gospel studies will find reading Stoldt's book a demanding, but rich and rewarding, experience.

Chapter I

The State of the Problem

The critical analysis of the sources of the Gospels is justifiably regarded as one of the most difficult research problems in the history of ideas. Its difficulty is caused not only by the material itself but also by the almost unparalleled expenditure of conscientious attention to even the slightest detail over a period of the last 200 years. An entire army of scholars has employed its acumen and developed a high degree of philological precision and an almost detective-like sagacity; one can truly say that no other enterprise in the history of ideas has been subjected to anywhere near the same degree of scholarly scrutiny. The whole subject has been so thoroughly worked over — plowed and harrowed, one might say — that today we know how frequently every single important word appears in any one of the Gospels, how often in the others and, finally, how often it is used in the entire New Testament. This was done, not for the sake of the word itself, but in order to construct a theory of sources, building block by building block.

As a result of this incomparable expenditure of scholarly diligence, the labor devoted to the study of sources has become more and more time-consuming and troublesome. One would now presume that there was nothing new to be discovered, not even the smallest detail. What has been explored by a hundred thousand eyes can no longer be *terra incognita*, and what *they* have not seen will also not be visible for those who follow. As for repeated and further examinations, one would have to say: "Je n'en vois pas la nécessité." But has there ever been a time when new scholarly perceptions have not had their origins in doubts about old truths?

From such a doubt I shall proceed—not for the sake of doubt itself, but because I have found reason to doubt. This doubt was aroused above all by the fact of the strong, emotion-charged engagement that can be discerned in the history of Gospel research for the last hundred and forty years. This has induced me to inquire critically into all of the results of that research and to examine thoroughly one more time, with the original text in hand, dispassionately and carefully, all the theories of sources that have gained prominence in historical research—regardless of whether they are looked upon today as "out of date" or as "generally accepted."

I was driven not only by a theoretical scholarly interest but also by a consideration of elemental pragmatic importance, namely that all statements about the Gospels and about Jesus which are based on an erroneous source-hypothesis must inevitably go astray. There is only one key to the exploration of the Gospels and their contents: the correct solution of the problem of sources. It is the *condicio, sine qua non*, even though it is not yet the *condicio, qua*.

The present work does not approach a critical analysis of the *whole* problem of the Gospels, but for the time being examines only its most highly controversial and therefore most essential feature, the synoptic problem.

In all of world literature, the sacred, as well as the profane, our four canonical Gospels present not only a more or less singular literary phenomenon, but they comprise an absolutely unique problem of sources, the like of which is to be found nowhere else. As is well known, the first three Gospels are so closely related that their text can be presented in parallel columns to give an overall view, as was first done by Johann Jacob Griesbach, who coined the term "synopsis":

> *Synopsis Evangeliorum Matthaei, Marci et Lucae una cum iis Joannis pericopis, quae omnino cum caeterorum Evangelistarum narrationibus, conferendae sunt.* Textum recensuit J.J. Griesbach [*A Synopsis of the Gospels of Matthew, Mark and Luke, together with those pericopes of John which must certainly be compared with the narratives of the other Evangelists. J.J. Griesbach ... edited the text.*] Halle 1776, 1797[2], 1882[4] (text already in 1774 in the first edition of Griesbach's Greek New Testament).

Along with the striking measure of agreement between the first three Gospels there is at the same time an abundance of dissimilarities which, in turn, diverge sharply among themselves and which in part extend through whole chapters. This peculiar relationship of concordance and discrepancy constitutes the "Synoptic Problem".

The fourth Gospel not only exhibits a completely different diction in the discourses of Jesus, but also presents a chronologically and topographically divergent representation of his external activity as well as his internal attitude. Researchers in the last century looked at things as if there were only an either/or possibility, and they postulated the alternative: Either the synoptics, or John. For themselves they chose the synoptics. It is noteworthy that this decision was most difficult for David Friedrich Strauss. He was too clear-sighted not to see that this extraordinarily difficult problem could not be dismissed so lightly, but he allowed his judgment to vacillate. In the third edition of his *Leben Jesu* he retracted his extremely negative first opinion of 1835 concerning the value of the Gospel of John as a source, but in the fourth edition he recanted his previous recantation:

> In all these passages the earlier versions have now been restored, so that, if one likes, my labour in this new edition has consisted preeminently in grinding away the nicks in my good sword, which were made not by my enemy, but by myself (Introduction).

As a result of this negation of the scholarly usage of the Gospel of John for research into the life of Jesus, the synoptic authors and the synoptic problem have occupied the dominant position in the study of the sources.

There are only two basic solutions to the synoptic problem. In 1794, Johann Gottfried Eichhorn, who was highly praised in his time (1752-1827), had already posed the famous alternative: "Either the three Gospel writers made use of one another, or they depended upon a common source" ("Über die drei ersten Evangelisten," in: Eichhorn's *Allg. Bibliothek der biblischen Literatur,* First edition p. 766). The first possibility aims at an inner synoptic solution, the second at a pre-synoptic solution. Eichhorn himself endeavored to prove that no reciprocal utilization of the synoptic gospels could have taken place, and he decided in favor of the written ur-gospel hypothesis. This hypothesis was opposed by the oral ur-gospel hypothesis, which was established by Carl Ludwig Gieseler (1792-1854) with his work "Historisch-kritischer Versuch über die Entstehung und die frühesten Schicksale der schriftlichen Evangelien" (1818).

The difficulties and, correspondingly, the argumentation of these two contrary hypotheses were exactly opposed: the differences between synoptic authors did not pose any difficulty for the followers of the oral ur-gospel hypothesis; they explained the divergences by referring to the wide dissemination of the tradition, to the "destiny of all traditions," and they compared this with "a point which extends in several directions in straight lines, diverging more and more as it progresses" (Gieseler, p. 110). But the exact correspondence of the wording in whole sentences as well as in some individual, rarely-used expressions could not be explained in a satisfactory manner by the oral ur-gospel hypothesis; still less could it lend certainty to this hypothesis.

This state of affairs posed no problem for the proponents of the written ur-gospel hypothesis, since it supposed that all three synoptic authors had the same original written text. But this text, according to the proponents' unanimous opinion, was written in the Aramaic language; the verbal correspondence, on the other hand, was contained in the Greek text of the New Testament—and an Aramaic text could not be found! Apart from that, the main difficulty of the written ur-gospel hypothesis was how to offer a credible explanation of the extensive divergences, which at times cover complete chapters, while still insisting on a *common* written basic text, namely the ur-gospel. If the representatives of this theory were going to solve these manifold problems, there was no other way than to take refuge in numerous auxiliary hypotheses in the form of several assumed revisions or translations of the alleged Aramaic original text. What this ultimately meant was that they had to construct an artful, ingeniously-reasoned super-structure of hypotheses that embraces about twenty auxiliary theories. With their aid it was then possible to "explain" almost all of the phenomena of concordance and of discrepancy between the individual synoptic Gospels. "Exceptions" were acknowledged which were made to appear harmless, but, due to the real impossibility of the over-refined pyramid of hypotheses, this approach to the problem generated its own *reductio ad absurdum*. Thus research of the previous century rejected both the oral and the written ur-gospel solutions — and justifiably so. They belong to the misinterpretations of the Gospels.

Hence, Eichhorn's alternative also had been disposed of. This, in turn, brought about a new insight: the synoptic problem can be solved only by a "usage-relationship" of some kind or other between the three Gospels of Matthew, Mark and Luke. *But what kind of relationship? This question was and has remained the disputed issue and the unsolved puzzle.*

Until now it has been generally accepted that there were, in all, six different possibilities of utilization, calculated according to the law of permutation theory. But that hardly exhausts all of the potential combinations of the three Gospels: of these, there are not six, but over thirty (see below, p.144ff). It can be said that almost all of the theoretical relationships have been represented experimentally, or have at least put in an appearance, during the course of research. However, only two of them have received the concentrated attention of scholarly discussion, and thus taken on true historical importance; the Griesbach hypothesis, and the Marcan hypothesis.

Both of these theories proceed from the assumption that the key to the solution of the synoptic problem must lie in the Gospel of Mark. Without a doubt, the Gospel of Mark occupies a central position, and its relationship to the first and third Gospels is different from the relationship between those two. One may also reverse the situation and say: each of these two Gospels has for its very own a special relationship to Mark which cannot be compared with the one that relates it to the other. Both hypotheses, therefore, start from the same alternative: Either Matthew and Luke are dependent on Mark, or Mark is dependent on them. In a chronological sense this would mean that the Gospel of Mark is either the first or the last of the synoptic Gospels. Griesbach's hypothesis asserts the latter, and the Marcan hypothesis the former.

Johann Jacob Griesbach (1745-1812), who is the true founder of scholarly textual criticism, presented in 1789-90 the source-hypothesis which was named in his honor, in a clear-sighted, analytical inquiry in the Latin tongue:

> Commentatio, qua Marci Evangelium totum e Matthaei et Lucae commentariis decerptum esse monstratur. Jenae 1789. 1790. (reprinted in: *Commentatt. theolog.* ed. Velthusen, Kuinoil et Ruperti. Vol. 1 Lipsiae 1794 with the remark "iam recognita multisque augmentis locupletata"). [The Dissertation in which it is demonstrated that the whole Gospel of Mark is derived from the works of Matthew and Luke. Jenae 1789. 1790. (Reprinted in *Commentatt. theol.* ed. Velthusen, Kuinoil and Ruperti. Vol. 1 Leipzig 1794, with the remark "now revised and enriched with many additions").]

This, Griesbach's masterpiece, had been preceded by a smaller investigation regarding the sources of the resurrection accounts, in the form of a Jena University Easter program:

> Paschatos Solemnia pie celebranda civibus indicit Academia Jenensis: Inquiritur in fontes, unde Evangelistae suas de resurrectione Domini narrationes hauserint. Jenae 1783. [The University of Jena proclaims to the citizens for the pious celebration of the Easter Festival: An "Inquiry into the Sources from which the Evangelists drew their narratives of the Lord's Resurrection."]

The primary thesis of Griesbach's source theory then ran:

> The Summary of the opinion we are defending is this: that when Mark wrote his book he had in front of his eyes not only Matthew, but Luke as well, and that he excerpted from them whatever he

intended to preserve of the deeds, words and destiny of the Savior (Section 1).

In presenting this view Griesbach already had a forerunner in the Englishman Henry Owen, Rector of St. Olave in Hart-Street and Fellow of the Royal Society, with his work: *Observations on the Four Gospels*, (London, 1764). Owen characterizes the Gospel of Mark as a compilatory "abridgment of St. Matthew and St. Luke":

> That St. Mark followed this plan, no one can doubt, who compares his Gospel with those of the two former Evangelists. He copies largely from both: and takes either the one or the other perpetually for his guide. The order indeed is his own, and is very close and well connected. (p. 50)

This Owen-Griesbach source theory found immediate general recognition with the appearance of the "Commentatio", especially since Griesbach was indisputably a savant of high scholarly rank; and it was recognized and propagated by most of the leading theologians of the first half of the nineteenth century. In the same manner, the theory furnished the foundation for Heinrich Eberhard Gottlob Paulus's influential commentary on the three Gospels (3 Vols. 1800ff) as well as for De Wette's *Einleitung in das N.T.* (1826); and for Fritzsche's Latin Commentaries on Matthew (1826) and Mark (1830); which were praised by David Friedrich Strauss as constituting the best preliminary study for a critical presentation of the works of Jesus, in the introduction to the first volume of his *Leben Jesu*. Completely in harmony with Griesbach, Fritzsche states: "Throughout his whole book Mark relates nothing that is not contained in the commentaries of Matthew and Luke, apart from a few verses" *(Comment. prolegg,* 36). Others who concurred with Griesbach were: K. G. W. Theile, *De trium evangeliorum priorum necessitate* (1825) as well as the prematurely deceased Heinrich Saunier *Über die Quellen des Marcusevangeliums* (1825), H. Aug. Schott *Isagoge hist. crit. in libros novi foederis sacros* (1830), and above all, the "Anonymous Saxon" (Hasert), who preceded Ferdinand Christian Baur as the founder of the "tendence-theory" of Gospel research with his essay "Die Evangelien, ihr Geist, ihre Verfasser, ihr Verhältnis zu einander" (1845). The most emphatic representatives of Griesbach's hypothesis were F. C. Baur himself and his school, the so-called "Second Tübingen School."

But the most decisive and crucial event was the fact that David Friedrich Strauss, F. C. Baur's keenest pupil, based his work *Leben Jesu*, (1835) on the Griesbach hypothesis. Strauss had not produced his own theory of sources since he regarded the problem as solved by Griesbach: "Thus . . . the assertion that Mark based his writings on Peter's oral account and hence possessed a source of his own, cannot be reconciled with our second Gospel, which apparently is compiled from Matthew and Luke."

Strauss added the following in a footnote: "This has been conclusively demonstrated by Griesbach in the *Commentatio*, qua . . . cf. Saunier, *über die Quellen des Evangeliums des Marcus*, 1825 (Vol. 1, p. 65). In the third edition of Strauss's *Leben Jesu* the original "a source of his own" was changed to "his own original source," and instead of "apparently" he used "demonstrably" (I., p. 78).

Strauss first took a stand on the question of sources in his "popular edition" of the *Leben Jesu* (1864), Part II: *Die Evangelien als Quellen des Lebens Jesu*—again in agreement with Griesbach.

This Owen-Griesbach source-theory had the attractive advantage that it could function without auxiliary theories. Its founders arrived at their result solely on the basis of an internal analysis of the synoptic Gospels; they did not have to be on the lookout for earlier gospels or search out supplementary explanations. The hypothesis "tested out". They were of the opinion that, in view of the texts, the Gospel of Mark had to be considered as an abbreviated compilation of the kerygmatic work of Jesus drawn from Matthew and Luke, in which the prehistory (the nativity legends, *Evangelium infantiae*, and genealogy) was deliberately foregone. Moreover, only a fraction of the extensive sayings material that can be found in the first and third Evangelists had been presented by Mark who refrained in particular from reproducing the Sermon on the Mount.

Griesbach's basic theory is expressed with particular clarity in his explanatory amplifications in which he states and more closely illuminates the quintessence of his hypothesis, namely, that Mark represents an excerpt from Matthew and Luke:

In such a manner however, that . . .

4) *he sought brevity*, as one who wanted to write a book of small compass; and therefore

5) he not only omitted things that did not pertain to the office of Teacher that the Lord publicly performed, Mt 1 and 2, Lk 1 and 2, but also,

6) *passed over* several of the longer sermons of Christ, e.g. Mt 5, 6 and 7; 10:16-42; 11:20-30; 12:33-45; 13:37-54; 18:10-35; 20:1-16; 22:1-14; 23: 2-39; 24:37-51; 25:1-46; Lk 6:17-49; 19:11-28, and indeed, Lk 10:1-18:14, where he has omitted almost one-third of Luke's gospel in its entirety, since it consists almost wholly of discourses of Christ (Sect. 1. Edition Velthusen 1794, p. 365ff.).

In spite of its quantitative brevity, the Gospel of Mark is qualitatively more detailed in numerous single features than the corresponding parallel accounts in the first and third Gospels. Griesbach had correctly recognized this fact, and he had explained it in the same context:

so that (Mark)

13) expresses not infrequently by paraphrase and expounds more plainly and distinctly what they had handed down to him in briefer form.

14) adds to the stories of Matthew and Luke many special details which he thought would please his readers...(p. 368 f.)

10) adds for the sake of illustration matters which he thinks either useful or necessary for better understanding the narrative, e.g. Mk 7:3, 4, 5; ll:13; 12:42 (page 368).

Prior to Griesbach, these short but numerous passages of the second Gospel had been interpreted in quite a different way by Johann Benjamin Koppe in his treatise *Marcus non Epitomator Matthaei* (1782; new edition 1789); Mark could not be an *Epitomator* [Abbreviator], because he was a *Locupletator* [Expander]. From this Koppe drew the following conclusion:

It is probable that the shorter gospel was chronologically earlier, and that the longer ones, in which the Evangelists supplied and amplified matters that had been either omitted or else related too concisely, were composed at a later date (p. 9).

Griesbach responded with this well-aimed counter-argument:

We answer: It depends entirely on the intention of the author whether it is preferable to add to, or to subtract from, what others wrote before him (p. 396).

Now, besides the numerous small passages that go beyond the parallel text of Matthew and Luke, Mark has two more detailed pericopes which have no corresponding text in either the first or the third Gospel: the healing of the deaf-mute (Mk 7:32-37) as well as the healing of the blind man from Bethsaida (Mk 8:22-26). Griesbach acknowledges them as Mark's own composition:

Mark compiled the whole of his volume, if you except some twenty-four verses that he added on his own account, from the writings of Matthew and Luke (p. 369f.).

Griesbach had already substantially qualified this assertion that Mark "compiled his whole book," or, as is stated in the title of the *Commentatio*, "the whole gospel of Mark has been excerpted from the works of Matthew and Luke," by stating in his explanatory amplifications that Mark loved "to express periphrastically" or, as he also states, "to paraphrase the text,"

What is more, Griesbach did not fail to observe that the Gospel of Mark had to be regarded as a new version of the Gospel even if Mark did make use of Matthew and Luke as sources:

> because his aim was neither to copy out their books nor to summarize them, but with their guidance to compose a *new* narrative adapted to his readers (p. 402 in Latin text).

It is important to make this absolutely clear, because the advocates of the Marcan hypothesis, in their century-long polemic against Griesbach, have almost without exception ignored this fact. In 1910, the first edition of the *RGG¹* stated:

> The hypothesis that the Gospel of Mark arose out of the *slavish* use of Matthew and Luke by Mark has at times found considerable approval, but according to our present judgment it would put things upside down (II., 702 Bousset; author's italics).

In 1928, the second edition of the RGG played the very same tune:

> For a time this theory was favored in a form put forward by Griesbach himself which can scarcely be grasped today; according to this Mark, as the *last* synoptic gospel, *arose out of the slavish use of Matthew and Luke* (II, 423, Klostermann; author's italics).

And, even in 1931, Jülicher and Fascher still maintained that according to Griesbach's hypothesis Mark "appears in the end as a feeble compiler of Matthew and Luke" (p. 327). So much for Griesbach.

If the originators of the Marcan hypothesis now set about proving the opposite, namely, that Matthew and Luke had used the Gospel of Mark as a source, they did not find themselves in a particulary enviable situation. In order to clarify this, it may be appropriate at this point to stress first, in a general way, *the problems and the fundamental difficulties which face researchers who attempt to make the Marcan hypothesis seem convincing.*

A mere glance at the extent of the first three Gospels reveals that the quantitative aspect of the synoptic Gospels is strongly divergent and different. Mark comprises only sixteen chapters, and in the last chapter only the first eight verses are considered genuine. The Gospel of Luke, on the other hand, contains twenty-four chapters, and the Gospel of Matthew twenty-eight. Of course, in both instances their first two chapters have no counterpart in Mark,

---

¹*Die Religion in Geschichte und Gegenwart*

since they contain the so-called prehistory, while the Gospel of Mark starts only with the public ministry of Jesus. But, even if one subtracts this part, the other two still provide a surplus of ten and six chapters respectively.

On the other hand, Mark also exhibits a whole series of additional textual details that go beyond Matthew and Luke, above all in three particular pericopes:

1) the miracle of the healing of the deaf-mute (7:32-37).

2) the account of the healing of the blind man from Bethsaida (8:22-26).

3) the parable of the growing seed (4:26-29), and further,

4) the brief, but in content significant note (3:21): "And when his friends heard it, they went out to seize him, for they said, 'He is beside himself'."

These four cases concern themselves with material in Mark for which there is no corresponding testimony in the Gospels of Matthew and Luke. The following must also be considered:

5) a quite surprisingly large number of passages in the second Gospel in which minor additional details extend *beyond the particular text parallels which Mark shares with Matthew and Luke*—180 in number.

Over against these places in Mark mentioned in 5, we find a series of passages where the first and third Evangelists agree and go beyond the parallel text in Mark. These consist of:

1) sections in which both Matthew and Luke contain material which goes beyond the parallel text of the second Gospel, thirty-five cases in all,

2) concurrence of the first and the third Evangelists in expressions and wording against Mark, also totaling thirty-five cases;

3) corresponding divergences of Matthew and Luke from Mark in twenty-two cases, each of which involves the use of the same word.

In the following we present all these minor divergences between Mark on the one hand and Matthew and Luke on the other, complete in number and length as in the original text, in order that their abundance and weight may be exhibited for evaluation of the hypotheses. The critical edition of the Greek text we utilize is that of Nestle-Aland *Novum Testamentum Graece* 26th edition, 1979. (See Appendix for Greek text.)

Minor additional details in Mark that extend beyond the text of Matthew and Luke, including passages where either Matthew or Luke are lacking.

	Markus	
1)	1:1	The beginning of the gospel of Jesus Christ
2)	1:7	to stoop down
3)	1:13	and he was with the wild beasts;
4)	1:15	and believe in the gospel.
5)	1:19	a little farther,
6)	1:20	with the hired servants,
7)	1:29	and Andrew, with James and John.
8)	1:33	/entire verse/ And the whole city was gathered together about the door.
9)	1:35	and there he prayed.
10)	1:36-37	/entire verses/ And Simon and those who were with him pursued him, and they found him and said to him, "Every one is searching for you."
11)	1:41	Moved with pity,
12)	1:43	/entire verse/ And he sternly charged him, and sent him away at once,
13)	2:2	/entire verse/ And many were gathered together, so that there was no longer room for them, not even about the doors; and he was preaching the word to them.
14)	2:3	carried by four men.
15)	2:9	take up your pallet,
16)	2:13	/entire verse/ (He went out) again beside the sea; and all the crowd gathered about him, and he taught them.
17)	2:14	the son of Alphaeus
18)	2:15	for there were many who followed him,
19)	2:16	"Why does he eat with tax collectors and sinners?"
20)	2:18	Now John's disciples and the Pharisees were fasting
21)	2:19	As long as they have the bridegroom with them, they cannot fast.
22)	2:23	as they made their way
23)	2:25	when he was in need
24)	2:26	when Abiathar was high priest,
25)	2:27	"The sabbath was made for man, not man for the sabbath;"
26)	3:5	with anger, grieved at their hardness of heart,
27)	3:6	with the Herodians

28)	3:7	to the sea
29)	3:8	and (from)* Idumea * ( ) = understood in RSV
30)	3:9	/entire verse/ And he told his disciples to have a boat ready for him because of the crowd, lest they should crush him;
31)	3:14-16a	to be with him, and to be sent out to preach and have authority to cast out demons; (so he appointed twelve,)* * ( ) = lacking in RSV
32)	3:17	whom he surnamed Boanerges, that is, sons of thunder;
33)	3:22	And the scribes who came down from Jerusalem
34)	3:30	/entire verse/—for they had said, "He has an unclean spirit."
35)	3:34	And looking around on those who sat about him,
36)	4:1	Again he began to teach
37)	4:2-3a	and in his teaching he said to them: "Listen!. . . "
38)	4:7	and it yielded no grain (=fruit)
39)	4:8	growing up and increasing
40)	4:10	And when he was alone,
41)	4:12b	lest they should turn again, and be forgiven
42)	4:13	"Do you not understand this parable? How then shall you understand all the parables? . . ."
43)	4:23	/entire verse/ "If any man has ears to hear, let him hear."
44)	4:34	but privately to his own disciples he explained everything.
45)	4:35	On that day, when evening had come, he said to them,
46)	4:36	/entire verse/ And leaving the crowd, they took him with them in the boat, just as he was. And other boats were with him.
47)	4:38	in the stern . . . on the cushion;
48)	4:39	"Peace! Be still!"
49)	4:40	"Why are you afraid? . . ."
50)	5:5	/entire verse/ Night and day among the tombs and on the mountains he was always crying out, and bruising himself with stones.
51)	5:6	from afar
52)	5:13	about two thousand,
53)	5:20c	and all men marveled.
54)	5:26-27a	and who had suffered much under many physicians, and had spent all that she had, and was no better but rather grew worse. She had heard the reports about Jesus, and came up. . . in the crowd
55)	5:29	and she felt in her body that she was healed of her disease.

56)	5:30	turned about in the crowd, and said, "Who (touched) my garments?"
57)	5:34b	and be healed of your disease."
58)	5:40c	and went in where the child was.
59)	5:41	"Talitha cumi"; which means,
60)	5:42	(she was twelve years of age),
61)	6:2	And on the sabbath
62)	6:5-6a	except that he laid his hands upon a few sick people and healed them. And he marveled
63)	6:7	and began to send them out two by two,
64)	6:12-13	and preached that men should repent. And they cast out many demons, and anointed with oil many that were sick and healed them.
65)	6:14	(The)* King * = not in RSV
66)	6:14	for Jesus' name had become known.
67)	6:17	because he had married her.
68)	6:19-20	/entire verses/ And Herodias had a grudge against him, and wanted to kill him. But she could not, for Herod feared John, knowing that he was a righteous and holy man, and kept him safe. When he heard him, he was much perplexed; and yet he heard him gladly.
69)	6:21	But an opportunity came when. . .gave a banquet for his courtiers and officers and the leading men of Galilee.
70)	6:23	even half of my kingdom."
71)	6:24	And she went out, and said to (her mother), "What shall I ask?"
72)	6:25	And she came in immediately with haste to the king, and asked, saying,
73)	6:26	he did not want to break his word to her.
74)	6:27	And immediately the king sent a soldier of the guard and gave orders to bring his head.
75)	6:30	and taught.
76)	6:31	/entire verse/ And he said to them, "Come away by your-selves to a lonely place, and rest a while." For many were coming and going, and they had no leisure even to eat.
77)	6:37	And they said to him, "Shall we go and buy two hundred denarii worth of bread, and give it to them to eat?"
78)	6:38	And he said to them, "How many loaves have you? Go and see." And when they had found out, they said,
79)	6:39	by companies upon the green (grass)
80)	6:40	in groups, by hundreds and by fifties.

81)	6:41b	and he divided the two fish among them all.
82)	6:47b	and he was. . .on the land.
83)	6:48b	He meant to pass by them.
84)	6:52	/entire verse/ for they did not understand about the loaves, but their hearts were hardened.
85)	7:2-4	/entire verses/ they saw that some of his disciples ate with hands defiled, that is, unwashed. (For the Pharisees, and all the Jews, do not eat unless they wash their hands, observing the tradition of the elders; and when they come from the market place, they do not eat unless they purify themselves; and there are many other traditions which they observe, the washing of cups and pots and vessels of bronze.)
86)	7:8	/entire verse/ You leave the commandment of God, and hold fast the tradition of men."
87)	7:13	And many such things you do."
88)	7:18-19	cannot defile him, since it enters, not his heart,. . . (Thus he declared all foods clean.)
89)	7:24	And he entered a house, and would not have any one know it;
90)	7:26	Now the woman was a Greek, a Syrophoenician by birth.
91)	8:3b	and some of them have come a long way."
92)	8:12	And he sighed deeply in his spirit, and said,
93)	8:14	and they had only one loaf with them in the boat.
94)	8:15	and the leaven of Herod."
95)	8:17-18	or understand? Are your hearts hardened? Having eyes do you not see, and having ears do you not hear?
96)	8:27	on the way
97)	8:32	And he said this plainly.
98)	8:35	and the gospel's
99)	9:1	And he said to them,
100)	9:3	glistening, intensely white, as no fuller on earth could bleach them.
101)	9:10	/entire verse/ So they kept the matter to themselves, questioning what the rising from the dead meant.
102)	9:14-16	scribes arguing with them. And immediately all the crowd, when they saw him, were greatly amazed, and ran up to him and greeted him. And he asked them, "What are you discussing with them?"
103)	9:25b	"You dumb and deaf spirit, I command you, come out of him, and never enter him again."

104)	9:26-27	/entire verses/And after crying out and convulsing him terribly, it came out, and the boy was like a corpse; so that most of them said, "He is dead." But Jesus took him by the hand and lifted him up, and he arose.
105)	9:28	(into) the house
106)	9:29	/entire verse/ And he said to them, "This kind cannot be driven out by anything but prayer."
107)	9:33-34	And they came to Capernaum; and when he was in the house he asked them, "What were you discussing on the way?" But they were silent; for on the way they had discussed with one another. . . .
108)	9:35	And he sat down and called the twelve; and he said to them,
109)	9:36	taking him in his arms,
110)	9:39	for no one who does a mighty work in my name will be able soon after to speak evil of me.
111)	9:48	/entire verse/ where their worm does not die, and the fire is not quenched.
112)	9:49	/entire verse/ For every one will be salted with fire.
113)	9:50b	Have salt in yourselves, and be at peace with one another."
114)	10:10	/entire verse/ And in the house the disciples asked him again about this matter.
115)	10:12	/entire verse/ and if she divorces her husband and marries another, she commits adultery.
116)	10:16	And he took them in his arms and blessed them,
117)	10:17	And as he was setting out . . . and knelt before
118)	10:19	Do not defraud.
119)	10:20	"Teacher, . . ."
120)	10:21a	looking upon him, loved him,
121)	10:24	And the disciples were amazed at his words. But Jesus said to them. . ."Children, how hard it is to enter the kingdom of God! . . ."
122)	10:29	and for the gospel
123)	10:32	and Jesus was walking ahead of them; and they were amazed, and those who followed were afraid.
124)	10:38b-39b	or to be baptized with the baptism with which I am baptized? . . . and with the baptism with which I am baptized, you will be baptized;
125)	10:46	Bartimaeus, . . . the son of Timaeus,
126)	10:49-50	And they called the blind man, saying to him, "Take

		heart; rise, he is calling you." And throwing off his mantle he sprang up and came to Jesus.
127)	10:52	on the way
128)	11:4	tied at the door out in the open street;
129)	11:11b	and when he had looked round at everything, as it was already late,
130)	11:13b	for it was not the season for figs.
131)	11:14b	And his disciples heard it.
132)	11:16	/entire verse/ and he would not allow any one to carry anything through the temple.
133)	11:17	for all the nations'?
134)	11:23	but believes that what he says will come to pass, it will be done for him,
135)	11:25	And whenever you stand praying,
136)	11:28	and do them?"
137)	12:5b	and so with many others, some they beat and some they killed.
138)	12:6	He had still one other, a beloved son;
139)	12:12b	so they left him and went away.
140)	12:13	and some of the Herodians
141)	12:15*	Should we pay them, or should we not?" * = 12:14 in Greek; 12:15 in RSV
142)	12:15	and let me look at it."
143)	12:21	and died, leaving no children;
144)	12:27b	you are quite wrong,"
145)	12:28	And one of the scribes came up and heard them disputing with one another, and seeing that he answered them well,
146)	12:32-34	that he is one, and there is no other but he; and to love him with all the heart, and with all the understanding, and with all the strength, and to love one's neighbor as oneself, is much more than all whole burnt offerings and sacrifices." And when Jesus saw that he answered wisely, he said to him, "You are not far from the kingdom of God."
147)	12:37	And the great throng heard him gladly.
148)	12:41	Many rich people put in large sums.
149)	12:42	which make a penny.
150)	12:43	And he called his disciples to him,
151)	13:3	Peter and James and John and Andrew
152)	13:34b	and commands the doorkeeper to be on the watch.

153)	13:35b-37	in the evening, or at midnight, or at cockcrow, or in the morning—lest he come suddenly and find you asleep. And what I say to you I say to all: Watch."
154)	14:5	for more than three hundred denarii, . . . And they reproached her.
155)	14:6	"Let her alone; . . ."
156)	14:7	and whenever you will, you can do good to them;
157)	14:8a	She has done what she could;
158)	14:13a	And he sent two of his disciples,
159)	14:30	(before) (the cock crows) twice
160)	14:36	"Abba, . . ."
161)	14:40b	and they did not know what to answer him.
162)	14:44	and lead him away under guard."
163)	14:54	warming himself at the fire.
164)	14:56b	and their witness did not agree.
165)	14:59	/entire verse/ Yet not even so did their testimony agree.
166)	14:65	And the guards received him with blows.
167)	14:68	and the cock crowed. *RSV margin
168)	14:72	(the cock crowed) a second time.
169)	15:8	/entire verse/ And the crowd came up and began to ask Pilate to do as he was wont to do for them.
170)	15:21	the father of Alexander and Rufus,
171)	15:24	what each should take.
172)	15:25	/entire verse/ And it was the third hour, when they crucified him.
173)	15:29	"Aha! . . ."
174)	15:41	and also many other women who came up with him to Jerusalem.
175)	15:43	took courage
176)	15:44-45	/entire verses/ And Pilate wondered if he were already dead; and summoning the centurion, he asked him whether he was already dead. And when he learned from the centurion that he was dead, he granted the body to Joseph.
177)	16:1	bought spices, so that they might go and anoint him.
178)	16:3	/entire verse/ And they were saying to one another, "Who will roll away the stone for us from the door of the tomb?"
179)	16:4b	—it was very large.
180)	16:8	fled (from the tomb); for trembling and astonishment had come upon them; and they said nothing to any-one, for they were afraid.

Of these 180 cases of additional details in Mark, more than half affect the text of Matthew and Luke simultaneously, while the rest of the cases touch upon only that Evangelist whose order Mark followed.

Minor additional details in both Matthew and Luke that extend beyond Mark:

	MK	MT	LK	
1)	1:5	3:5	3:3	the region about the Jordan
2)	1:8	3:12	3:16	and with fire
3)	1:40	8:2	5:12	Lord
4)	2:3	9:2	5:18	on (his) bed
5)	2:12	9:7	5:25	he went home
6)	2:23	12:1	6:1	to eat
7)	2:26	12:4	6:4	only (priests)
8)	3:5	12:13	6:10	your (hand)
9)	4:10	13:11	8:10	to know (the secrets)
10)	4:15	13:19	8:12	heart
11)	4:36	8:23	8:22	to enter the boat
12)	4:36	8:23	8:22	his disciples
13)	4:38	8:25	8:24	approaching (RSV = they went)
14)	5:27	9:20	8:44	the fringe
15)	6:7	10:8	9:1	and heal the sick
16)	6:44	14:21	9:14	about (five thousand)
17)	9:2	17:2	9:29	(the) face
18)	9:7	17:5	9:34	he was still speaking (Lk = as he said this)
19)	9:19	17:17	9:41	and perverse
20)	9:19	17:17	9:41	here
21)	10:22	19:22	18:23	when (he) heard
22)	10:26	19:25	18:26	when (they) heard
23)	11:27	21:23	20:1	as (he was) teaching
24)	12:3	21:35	20:10	the tenants
25)	12:7	21:38	20:14	seeing him (Mt: +the son)
26)	12:12	21:45	20:16	the chief priests
27)	12:12	21:45	20:16	hearing
28)	12:28	22:35	10:25	teacher
29)	12:28	22:36	10:25	tempting (RSV = to test)
30)	12:38	23:1	20:45	the disciples
31)	13:19	24:21	21:23	great
32)	14:37	26:40	22:45	to the disciples

33)	14:62	26:64	22:69	hereafter (Lk = from now on)
34)	14:65	26:68	22:64	Who is it that struck you?
35)	14:72	26:75	22:62	He went out and wept bitterly.

Concurrence of Matthew and Luke in expressions and wording, contrary to Mark:

	MK		MT	LK
1)	1:10	split (separated)	opened	
2)	1:10	into him (on)	upon him	
3)	1:13	Satan	Devil	
4)	2:9	go your way	walk	
5)	2:12	amazed	frightened	filled with fear
6)	2:16	that (why?)	why?	
7)	2:21	sews	puts (sews)	
8)	2:26	(in company) with (=*sun*)	(in company) with (=*meta*)	
9)	3:1	withered (hand) (participle)	withered (hand) (adjective)	
10)	4:41	they were afraid	they were astonished	filled with fear they were astonished
11)	5:14	they came (to see)	came out (to meet)	went out (to see)
12)	5:27	she came	she came close (approached)	
13)	6:11	dust (*chous*)	dust (*koniortos*)	
14)	6:32	they went away	he withdrew (*anachoreo*)	he withdrew (*hupochoreo*)
15)	6:43	full	left over	left over
16)	8:31	by (the elders)	from (the elders)	
17)	8:34	to follow after	to come after (aorist)	to come after (present)
18)	9:18	they were not able	they could not	
19)	10:51	Master (Rabboni)	Lord	
20)	11:2 +11:7	to bring (the colt)	to lead (the colt)	
21)	12:15	bring (to me)	show (to me) (*epideiknumi*)	show (to me) (*deiknumi*)
22)	12:18	they come (present)	approaching (aorist)	
23)	12:22	last (of all) (*eschaton*)	last (of all) (*husteron*)	
24)	12:37	says	calls	

25)	14:11	opportunely (adverb)	opportunity (noun)
26)	14:36	yet . . . but	nevertheless . . . but
27)	14:47	he struck (*paio*)	he struck (*patasso*)
28)	14:47	ear (*otarion*)	ear (*otion*)
29)	14:53	they assemble (come together)	they gathered/convened (collected)
30)	15:1	they carried him away	they led him away
31)	15:20	they bring out (Jesus)	they lead out (Jesus)
32)	15:39	centurion (*kenturion*: Latinized form)	centurion (*ekatontarchos*)
33)	15:43	he went in to (Pilate)	approaching (Pilate)
34)	15:46	he wrapped (him) in (*eneileo*)	he wrapped (him) up in (*entulisso*)
35)	8:31	after three days to be raised (*anistaemi*)	on the third day to be raised (*egeiro*)

Concurrence of Matthew and Luke in diverging from Mark's word form:

	MK		MT	LK
1)	2:22	otherwise (=but if not) (RSV = if he (it) does)	otherwise (=but if not *indeed*) (RSV = if he (it) does)	
2)	4:3	a sower went out to sow	a sower went out to sow	
3)	4:9	who is having ears (individual)	the one having (participle) ears	
4)	4:11	the secret (singular) of the kingdom	the secrets (plural) of the kingdom	
5)	4:41	the wind . . . obeys him	the winds (plural) . . . obey him	
6)	6:7	he calls near (the twelve)	calling near (the twelve)	calling together (the twelve)
7)	6:7	he was giving them	he gave them	
8)	8:36	does it profit (a man)	will it profit	is (a man) profited
9)	9:14	when they came	coming to, they	
10)	9:31	is being handed over	is *about to be* handed over	
11)	10:20	(all these things) I kept/observed	(all these things) I guarded (myself) against	
12)	10:28	we have followed	we followed	
13)	11:1	as they are drawing near	when drawing near, they . . .	when drawing near, he . . .

14)	11:1	he sends	he sent
15)	11:2	(you) loose/untie it (and bring it)	loosing/untying it, (bring it)
16)	11:3	(you) say (that)	you will say (that)
17)	11:8	into/upon the way/road	in/on the way/road
18)	12:17	they were greatly marveling	they were marveling marveled they
19)	13:2	that *is* not thrown down	that *will* not be thrown down
20)	13:25	the powers *in* the heavens	the powers *of* the heavens
21)	14:10	Judas Iscariot (*Iskarioeth*)	(the one called) Judas (the one Judas Iscariot called) Iscariot (*Iskarioetaes*)
22)	15:14	(You) crucify (him)!	Let him be (they insisted that) crucified! he be crucified.

That completes the compilation of the textual divergences and differences between the Gospel of Mark and the Gospels of Matthew and Luke.

The problems inherent in the Marcan hypothesis can be read between the lines of this general overall view. These problems define more precisely the task with which the protagonists of the Marcan hypothesis saw themselves confronted in trying to prove its validity. They were obliged to answer the following questions and to furnish a solution to the problem which they embraced—a solution which had to be more convincing than the one found by Griesbach:

1) Where did the extensive additional substantive material shared by Matthew and Luke alone come from?

2) How could it be that the additional substantive material in the Gospel of Mark failed to appear in Matthew or in Luke, if Mark had been their source?

3) How can it be explained that in 180 cases Matthew and Luke, independently and without knowledge of each other, joined in leaving out and ignoring the identical phrases and sentences of the Gospel of Mark—if this had been their source?

4) How was it possible that both the first and third Evangelist, without having contact with each other, and in spite of their separate style of work, nevertheless in thirty-five cases added to the text of Mark in exactly the same places and in exactly the same phrasing?

5) What caused both Matthew and Luke, in another thirty-five cases, independently to agree in replacing a word which, according to the hypothesis, they found in the text of Mark, with the same similar-sounding new word?

6) What caused the other two synoptic writers, independently and without personal contact, in twenty-two cases to make exactly the same small modification in an identical manner to a word they both had in common in the text with Mark?

It is apparent that the originators of the Marcan hypothesis took on a heavy burden when they tried to prove its validity without first considering these liabilities. Regarded purely in quantitative terms, without mentioning the monumental internal difficulties of the Marcan hypothesis, it is obvious that what they had set for themselves was a truly Sisyphean task.

Indeed, it may be doubted that they were fully aware of these difficulties. In any case, *the advocates of the Marcan hypothesis have never exposed its inherent problems in anything approaching their true dimensions*, even though it ought to be the primary task of the systematic scholar to assemble an overall view of the problem well before involving himself in details, and then to proceed according to the strategic principle: evalute the situation, form a resolution, and act.

One looks in vain among the founders of the Marcan hypothesis for such a preparatory balancing of the pros and cons of their theory of sources. Rather, one has the impression that they rush too quickly into the thick of the fray, and that their gaze is overwhelmingly turned toward questions of detail in the synoptic gospels in order to consider these questions from the perspective of the Marcan hypothesis and to bring them into harmony with it whenever necessary. But only if these parts were fitted together to form an unbroken chain of evidence without excluding any unsolved questions could it be said that the Marcan hypothesis had been proved, at all events from this point of view.

Therefore, in the following chapters we shall submit this source-theory to a severe ordeal by fire. In doing so it is of decisive importance to examine this fundamental question from its very beginning, that is, *from the laying of its foundation by its originators*. But for what reason? Is it not possible to object and say that all of this is "old hat"—old research results that have gathered dust for more than a hundred years? Have not these results again and again been scrutinized and confirmed by competent researchers? It does not seem to be necessary to repeat the whole process; for some time these conclusions have belonged to the "assured results of scholarship," and they have stood forth like a *rock of Gibraltar*.

But let us assume that this "assured result of scholarship" was false. Then it must have been, or at least could have been, false from the very beginning. Then it would be of *decisive importance to examine it as it comes to birth* and to discover its *peccatum originale*. This is what we shall undertake in the following chapters.

Part I:

Critical Analysis of the Genesis of the Marcan Hypothesis

Chapter II

Its Foundation

In its initial stages, the debate on the Marcan hypothesis was fraught with dramatic turbulence. Even the overture began with fraternal strife. Ever since then, Wilke and Weisse, who are acknowledged as the two originators of the hypothesis, have been named in one breath and actually looked upon as a pair of Dioscuri in the history of research. Jülicher and Fascher said of them that they had "brilliantly inaugurated the Marcan hypothesis," *(Einleitung,* 1931[7] p.329). This statement may well have been made because the fundamental works of both appeared in the same year (1838).

But in actuality, they agreed in only one point—that the Gospel of Mark had been the source for Matthew and Luke. Even here they differed in an essential modality. Weisse considered the Gospel of Mark to be a second-hand, indirect apostolic source inspired by Peter, while Wilke plainly called it the "Ur-Gospel." In regard to the basic leading question that necessarily had to arise—that of where Matthew and Luke acquired that part of the text common to them but absent from Mark—they and their followers remained deeply divided.

This question can be looked upon as the basic problem of the Marcan hypothesis, one that winds like a *Leitmotiv* through its entire history: where did the non-Marcan material that is held in common by the first and third Gospels come from? The originators of the Marcan hypothesis could not reconcile their differences on this fundamental question of their theory of sources, and in the first year following the publication of their works a profound controversy arose between Weisse and Wilke: Wilke advocated an "intra-synoptic" solution, Weisse an "extra-synoptic" solution.

Even though Wilke's work appeared several months after Weisse's, we shall turn our attention first to Wilke's establishment of the Marcan hypothesis and then proceed to Weisse's. We shall do so because Weisse's foundation of the theory of sources has had continuing historical impact and has remained influential to the present day.

The intra-synoptic solution (Christian Gottlob Wilke).

Christian Gottlob Wilke (1788-1854) was a Protestant field chaplain in the Saxon army for five years and then, for fourteen years, pastor in Hermannsdorf in the Erz Mountains. From 1836 he lived as a private citizen in Dresden. In 1838, he published his *Urevangelist;* in 1840-41 he published a dictionary for the New Testament, *Clavis Novi Testamenti Philologica,* which was revised by Wilhelm Grimm; and in 1845 he published an essay of apology, justifying his planned conversion to Catholicism: *Is it possible for a Protestant to convert to Catholicism with a clear conscience?* He was converted in the subsequent year, and then resided until his death in Würzburg.

The exact title of his principal work, which appeared in the year 1838, reads:

The Ur-Evangelist

or

Critical Examination of the Interrelatedness
of the first three Evangelists

by Christian Gottlob Wilke,

formerly Pastor at Hermannsdorf in the Erz Mountains of Saxony,
Dresden and Leipzig,1838.

Wilke precedes his work with a preface. We reproduce it in its entirety because it is informative about his basic attitude toward scholarship in general and his own research project in particular:

> The vast difficulties that are attached to solving the problem of the reciprocal relationships of the Gospels, or just to providing an investigation of this subject with a planned analysis and systematic order need not be stressed and debated in the presence of experts. For more than ten years I have studied this problem and that of how to structure this essay, and I publish here only the

result of the studies which I pursued tirelessly at first alongside the regular duties of my pastoral office, and then from 1832 in the midst of the most bitter experiences. I am truly glad that after these hard struggles I was able again to regain and maintain the peace of mind and spirit which was essential for the continuation of this work. Whether the issue in question has been resolved or brought closer to a final decision because of my endeavour, that may be decided by expert and unbiased judges; *but frankly speaking, I do not desire to have my effort judged by those who have made up their minds that Mark excerpted his Gospel from the works of Matthew and Luke because I feel that these men, although worthy of respect, can no more be expected to have the necessary objectivity of judgment than I can be expected to be won over to their point of view* (author's italics). Although I have tried everywhere to employ correct and precise expression, it was unavoidable that at times phrases would intrude which I would now change; therefore I can only hope that reasonable critics will keep in mind more the substance and content of my effort than its form and expression.

The result of the whole, I am quite convinced, will withstand any form of criticism, and objections which might be raised against particular statements would only provide me with an opportunity to increase the number of proofs. Besides the proofs stated in this essay, I could have added many more, had not my intent been focused upon brevity as well as thoroughness.

Still more precise inquiry should be initiated into where Luke obtained the materials with which he enriched the Gospel of Mark (author's italics); into what the purpose of each particular Gospel was; and, finally, into how and by what means the correspondence between John and the type of the other Gospels was brought about. I shall also undertake these further investigations, if my situation improves, as I wish and hope it will. How soon I shall be able to carry out my project, or how long I may have to delay it, I do not know. The one thing that will increase my courage and double my diligence is that this essay, which I present to my patrons and friends for their critical evaluation, should receive favorable acceptance. Dresden, April 12, 1838. Ch. G. Wilke.

For the time being we shall let Wilke's preface speak for itself as an indirect self-characterization and not impose a commentary. We shall return to its appraisal and evaluation after we have completed our overall criticism of Wilke's work.

He bestowed on his work the title *The Original Evangelist* (*Der Urevangelist*). His conclusion was brief and to the point: "*Mark is the original Evangelist. It is his work which serves as the foundation for that of Matthew and Luke*" (p. 684).

One has to visualize from the perspective of this particular time the impact that must have been made by the theory proclaimed in the title. Eichhorn had preceded it with his unconfirmed theory of a written ur-gospel, just as Gieseler has postulated an oral ur-gospel. Both had expended considerable effort and ingenuity on the construction of such a gospel. Now Wilke appeared and declared: You are looking for the ur-gospel? Why do you want to search any further? See, here it is—Mark!

It would be hard to exaggerate the surprise of his contemporaries. This was a genuine academic sensation. No one before had given a thought to the possibility that the sought-after ur-gospel, the foundation of the canonical Gospels, was in fact one of the latter. At most, one had hoped to find it among the fragmentary materials, as Lessing had done with his Nazarene gospel, the existence of which was revealed to us by Jerome (Lessing: "New Hypothesis Concerning the Evangelists Regarded as Merely Human Historians," *Lessing's Theological Writings*, Stanford, 1957, translated by Henry Chadwick). But one of the synoptic Gospels themselves? That exceeded the most daring expectations. Weisse's newly-published work, in which Mark was portrayed merely as the oldest Gospel, paled beside this basic idea of Wilke's and was forced into the background. The already fascinating effect of the title *The Original Evangelist* was further intensified almost to the point of agitation by Wilke's emphatic statement near the end of his work: "For all eternity we affirm with hand and seal that our conclusion is the correct one" (p. 684).

With that he bound himself to the duty of delivering, without further delay, compelling evidence to verify his basic thesis.

Now we shall turn our attention to Wilke's essential arguments in order to determine their value as evidence.

Wilke's work of 694 pages, which Hilgenfeld calls a "painstaking as well as tiresome investigation," is divided by the author into two main parts, preceded by an introduction. This introduction contains the decisive foundational part of his argument for the Marcan hypothesis. Its twenty-two pages consider "The reciprocal relationship of the three first Gospels in general." Here Wilke draws up three synoptic columns:

> The first column will present the particular narrative passages
> which all three Gospels have in common together with those

passages which Mark has in common with one of the other two Evangelists, since one of them is always parallel to Mark. The second column will consist of those passages which belong to Matthew and Luke. The third column will accept only those which are the property of a single author (p. 4).

Wilke bases the arrangement of the first column on the following principle:

> "*Since Mark is always the one accompanied*, so that one of the other two writers always adheres to the sequence he initiated, it seems most advantageous in surveying the material to put Mark first in a three-columned context" (p. 4; author's italics).

This prefatory notice reveals that Wilke, in his principle of arrangement proceeds from a *preconceived* opinion that had yet to be verified the Marcan hypothesis. Yet he proceeds as if the thesis were already validated: "Since Mark is always the one accompanied..." From this unverified presupposition Wilke draws the following conclusion: "so that one of the other two writers always adheres to the sequence he (Mark) initiated."

But precisely this presupposition is highly debatable, and leads directly into the center of the synoptic problem. For the time being we shall put aside the basic debate on this question and leave a definite judgment on it for the second part of our investigation, "Critical Analysis of the Evidence for the Validity of the Marcan Hypothesis."

The effect of Wilke's anticipation of yet-to-be proven results of research is apparent in his grounding of all three columns in the "mutual relationship" of the three Evangelists. One cannot help but ask: where does this "mutual relationship" begin, and where does it end?

Wilke has an answer: "The starting point of the mutual relationship is therefore the start of Jesus' public life" (p. 8). To this he adds a substantial qualification: "insofar as it is preceded by the baptism of John" (p. 8). But that means, in other words: *it is the beginning of the Gospel of Mark*. And where does the mutual relationship terminate? Wilke's answer: "The final point is the resurrection of Jesus" (p. 8). Hence Wilke holds Mark's spurious ending to be genuine. To this day he stands alone among scholars in subscribing to this interpretation.

Wilke also uses this Marcan framework as the basis for his second column, the one which contains only the common sections of Matthew and Luke. In doing so he omits the nativity legends as well as the *Evangelium infantiae* and the genealogies. With what justification? The fact that they are not recorded in Mark; for thematically they can certainly stand in the parallel columns where the first and third Evangelists are concerned. But Wilke does not accept this as the starting point of these two Gospels. Rather he says: "Both Matthew and Luke place a separate history of the birth and childhood of Jesus before this starting point" (p. 8). And which is this "starting point" that Wilke uses as a foundation? Nothing other than *the beginning of the Gospel of Mark!*

Even in the third column, the one that contains the special material peculiar to a single evangelist, Wilke does not list the "prehistory" of Matthew and Luke. On the contrary, he presents only the single-author accounts which are *within the structural frame of Mark.* Consequently right from the start, Wilke offers, not a complete picture of the synoptic authors, but only a compilation from the Marcan perspective!

In the argumentation for an hypothesis, the positive and negative proofs are intertwined. They are tied to each other, they even interpenetrate. i.e., if one wants to prove one's own opinion, one must reduce the contrary opinion *ad absurdum.* Wilke's theory that Mark was the original Evangelist is opposed by three other hypotheses: (1) Eichhorn's construction of a written ur-gospel, (2) Gieseler's assertion of an original version preserved in the oral tradition, and (3) the Griesbach hypothesis. To Wilke's correct refutation of the first two theories we shall give no further consideration, since they are not directly related to the questions of literary dependence raised here.

Wilke directed his most intensive and emphatic arguments against the Griesbach hypothesis. How seriously he took it can be surmised from the fact that he could not avoid conceding to it at least the appearance of validity. His seventeenth point states:

> Since Matthew and Luke have transposed the original text, each one in different places and admixed with different elements, Mark's text has taken on the appearance of a mixture and compilation of the versions of the other two authors (p. 28; author's italics).

This is indeed a remarkable admission by Wilke. How does he try to defuse it? By continuing in the following way: "*although Mark has none of the literary style which is peculiar to his fellow-writers*" (p. 28; author's italics).

Now if one asks what actually constitutes the "literary style which is peculiar to his fellow-writers," Wilke answers by characterizing it as that which cannot be found in the Gospel of Mark. And, if one asks further, just what is Mark's "peculiar literary style," Wilke responds that it is whatever Matthew and Luke have in common with Mark; for, as Wilke says later, "it is especially those sentences which are the substratum of the transformation that still exhibit their peculiar form in Mark" (p. 457).

And how does Wilke know that the "substratum of the transformation" is really Mark and not Matthew and Luke? Because Mark is the "Original Evangelist"! It is obvious that there is always the same *petitio principii* and always the same *circulus vitiosus*.

Wilke provided the "proof" that Mark had to be the original author by stating his subjective judgment that it was impossible for Mark not to have been the original author. His eighteenth point exposes Wilke's tendency with a negative sham-argument:

> Mark's text is so different from the other texts, and yet it unites their constituent parts in such a way that, if it were made out of a mixture of them, it would have to be either a fusion of the other texts done involuntarily in the writer's memory; or a jumbling of the two texts which occurred during the process of transcription; or, finally, the effect of an intentional castration of both texts. But the text itself is incompatible with every one of these postulates . . . (p. 438f.)

Having psychologically prepared the soil, Wilke prepared to strike the decisive blow. He employed a truly hyperbolic distortion, which had nothing in common with objective argumentation, in an effort to reduce Griesbach's basic theory *ad absurdum*:

> *Mark was not an abbreviator, nor an epitomator, nor an excerptor, but a castrator of the other texts, or what else could one call the mutilator of borrowed sentences and the mingler of the mutilated?* And this idea could be reconciled with the thought of a rational author? And could it be expressed without accusing the prudent author of blithering and levity, whereas he far surpasses his co-writers in exactitude? What could have led Mark to *play games with the expressions of his informants* and make the decision *to concoct a hodgepodge of their words?* Can it be that he was striving so hard for originality?" (p. 443 f.; author's *italics*).

Now, Wilke's hypertrophic expression requires no commentary. This and similar cases will receive special attention later in Part C, "The Ideological Background of the Marcan Hypothesis."

Wilke appeared satisfied that this emotional disqualification of Griesbach's hypothesis securely anchored his own theory—*but with one qualification:*

> Point 21: Considering the reciprocal relationship in which the parallel texts of the units of discourse are positioned, *nothing stands in the way of accepting Mark as the original source of these*

relationships except the additional materials which embellish his
text more richly than the others.

But, this is precisely the first basic problem which confronted the
originators of the Marcan hypothesis: Mark's additional material. Wilke then
had to demonstrate why Matthew and Luke "avoided" or "left out" Mark's
supplementary material, as must have been the case according to his
hypothesis. That was true not only of the special pericopes but also of the
multitude of smaller paraphrastic turns of expression which Mark contains
over and above the text of the other two synoptic authors.

How does Wilke manage this problem? His solution is as simple as it is
false: there are, he says, "interpolations." In connection with his main
conclusion that "Mark is the original evangelist" and "It is his work which is
the foundation of the other two," he explains on the same page: "A by-
product of the main result is the fact that Mark's work, *aside from a few
interpolations*, originally had no other plan or form than it has at the present"
(p. 684).

This is the decisive remark by which Wilke attempts to save himself from
admitting the insufficiency of his Marcan hypothesis. His efforts to make this
problem appear harmless are completely transparent: Mark's 180 additional
details become "a few interpolations" or even "eliminations."

In several cases even Wilke himself obviously experienced some hesitation
and doubt. Was it really proper to regard the minor additional details in Mark
as mere redactional "insertions" and "additions"—as he liked to say instead of
"interpolations"? Therefore, he employed yet another method of preserving
his Marcan hypothesis from the problems posed by these extra parts of
Mark's text, parts which caused even him a certain uneasiness. Without any
further ado he declared them "eliminations" (or, as he also says, "text
purifications" and "isolations") of the first and third Evangelists from the text
of Mark, which, according to his hypothesis, had been their model:

> But what appears (sic!) to be an addition to the text of Mark when
> it is compared to Matthew and Luke belongs in the text; it is easier
> to prove that the "additions" belong to the text of Mark, and that
> the others omitted them than it is to say that Mark added these
> parts (p. 674).

His doubts notwithstanding, two pages later he declared with apodictic
certainty: "[Matthew and Luke] left out what they unquestionably had before
them" (p. 676).

At issue are the following alleged interpolations and eliminations:

INTERPOLATIONS IN THE GOSPEL OF MARK
(According to Wilke)

1:2-3a	"Behold, I send my messenger . . . in the wilderness:"
1:7	to stoop down
1:13	"And he was . . . by Satan;"
2:14	the son of Alphaeus
2:26	when Abiathar was high priest
3:6	with the Herodians
3:17	whom he surnamed Boanerges, that is, sons of thunder;
4:7	and it yielded no grain (fruit)
4:10	with the twelve
5:13	about two thousand
6:9	but to wear (=to put on)
6:37	two hundred denarii
6:40	they sat down in groups of fifty and one hundred
7:2	that is, unwashed
7:3,4,13	/the whole of verses 3, 4, 13/
8:1-10 } 8:17 } 8:20 }	/The Feeding of the Four Thousand/
9:6	for they were exceedingly afraid
9:32,35,39	/the whole of verses 32, 35, 39/
10:16	he took them in his arms
10:32	and they were amazed . . . were afraid
10:46	Bartimaeus . . . the son of Timaeus
13:14	(let the reader understand)
13:21-23	/doublet to 13:5-6/
13:32	nor the son
14:51,52	/entire verses/
15:21	the father of Alexander and Rufus
15:24	and they crucified him
15:25	and it was the third hour
15:42	it was the day of Preparation, that is, the day before the Sabbath
15:43	who was also . . . kingdom of God,
16:7	Peter
16:9	/entire verse/

Wilke considers Mark's spurious ending to be partially genuine (See above, p. 31).

ELIMINATIONS FROM THE GOSPEL OF MARK
BY MATTHEW AND LUKE
(According to Wilke)

1:29	with James and John
1:33	/entire verse/
2:3	carried by four men
2:9	take up your pallet
3:32	and . . . was sitting about him
4:38	But he was in the stern
5:23	"My little daughter is at the point of death."
6:38	"Go and see." And when they had found out . . .
6:43	and of the fish
10:21	and Jesus, looking upon him, loved him,
11:16	/entire verse/
14:58	made with hands + not made with hands
15:44-45	/entire verses/

The seasoned campaigner recognizes at first glance that in every single case Wilke's "interpolations" and "eliminations" relate to main proofs and documentations of the Owen-Griesbach hypothesis. If Wilke were to disprove the hypothesis, he would have to refute its arguments. Since he was not in a position to do so, he preferred to cut the Gordian knot, i.e., he fell back on the last resort of the die-hard exponent of an hypothesis and produced a dual *Deus ex machina*: e.g. "interpolation," "elimination."

Further, a fundamental point needs to be made regarding these corrections of the original text. If the alleged additions and omissions are to have even the appearance of probability, then at least it should be possible to substantiate and verify them text-critically; i.e., some kind of variants would have to be found in the codices which would reflect the status asserted by Wilke, or give clues that point in this direction. But that is nowhere the case. This adds up to the fact that Wilke has made his assertions without textual proof and foundation.

Now, even Wilke realized that with these minor details in Mark that extend beyond Matthew and Luke, the problem of the extra material in Mark could not yet be considered "solved." For, now the question arises: What about Mark's *major* additional material, the two pericopes of the healing of the deaf-mute (Mk. 7:32-37) and the healing of the blind man of Bethsaida (Mk. 8:22-26)? Even Wilke cannot simply dismiss them as "insertions" or "text purifications." Thus, he declares these passages to be *genuine* and even undertakes to submit the proof: "Point 5: the redactor of the Gospel of

Matthew had before him the complete Gospel of Mark, i.e., also those chapters which are Mark's alone"(p. 680).

Later, Wilke maintains the same thing about Luke, but he concentrates his main arguments on Matthew in a very long-winded deduction from which we shall call special attention only to the crucial point:

> Why did the compiler of Matthew refrain from assimilating the special narrative of Mark? If we look at his verse 15:30, we realize that he had found he had ample compensation for his omission. He had plenty of people who were healed, and finally he was compelled even to multiply their number, since he intended, as we have seen, to include the second feeding. Therefore, we can be certain that Matthew had Mark's narrative in front of him (p. 681).

Now, for us, it is not quite so easy to be this certain. It is not difficult to recognize that Wilke presupposes that which he intends to verify—that Matthew "had in front of him" Mark's pericope of the healing of the deaf-mute. For this purpose, Wilke places Matthew's summary report about the healing of many sick people (Mt. 15:30-31) in parallel to the *single* healing of the deaf-mute in Mark (7:32-37).

No words are necessary to explain that here we are confronted by neither a parallel case nor a comparable case. It would have been possible to compare an account in Matthew of an *individual* healing of a sick person with the case mentioned in Mark, but it is not possible to compare a collective representation with a special case. The two pericopes have essentially nothing to do with each other; neither of them constitutes a variant of the other. Wilke's allegation that the "compiler of Matthew" did not make use of Mark's special narrative because he "had found ample compensation" ("he had plenty of people who were healed") contains more imagination than proof. One might almost say that it is pulled out of thin air.

However, Wilke presents yet a second proof for his allegation: "...and finally he (Matthew) was compelled even to multiply their number, since he intended, as we have seen above, to include the second feeding" (p. 681).

As a matter of fact, Mt. 15:29-31 is followed by the "feeding of the four thousand." Wilke now asserts that Matthew transformed the single healing of the deaf-mute, which he found in Mark, into a mass-healing of a vastly different kind because he needed "people" for the subsequent feeding of the four thousand. Apart from the fact that here he makes, once again, a hypothetical assertion concerning Matthew's intentions which is neither proven nor provable, there is *clear counter-evidence*: Mark also follows the healing of the deaf-mute with the feeding of the four thousand. But, Mark does *not* prepare for the scene by producing people, nor does he make any effort to "multiply their number, since he intended to include the second feeding." On the contrary, without any further transition or motivation, he just lets the people be there immediately after the healing of the deaf-mute: "In those days, when again a great crowd had gathered, and they had nothing to eat" (Mk. 8:1).

But, Wilke is not troubled by that; he knows how to deal with such difficulties, and simply declares: "*The passage in question, the narrative of the feeding of the four thousand, had been transferred in later years from Matthew to Mark*"(p. 569; author's italics). Naturally, if one avails himself of such artful reasoning, it is certainly easy to hypothesize.

Wilke's argumentation for the second pericope in the special account in Mark, the healing of the blind man from Bethsaida, does not fare any better. Again we reduce his extensive demonstration of proof to the essential factors, especially in view of the simplicity of the basic thought. Mark's account of the healing of the blind man is sandwiched between the discourse about the leaven (Mk. 8:14-21 par Mt. 16:5-12) and the confession of Peter at Caesarea Philippi (Mk. 8:27-29 par Mt. 16:13-28). In his argumentation Wilke attempts to show that the topographical situation in Matthew also refers to Bethsaida, and then argues further:

> The words of Mk. 8:13 "he departed to the other side"[1] (to which Mk. 8:22 refers) and of Mt. 16:5 (which makes the mention of Bethsaida superfluous) stand in such relation to each other that one of the two authors must have changed the text that was at hand. We shall prove that Matthew made the change (p. 682).

To this end, Wilke again works with both interpolation and elimination, and now asserts:

> Also, according to Matthew, Jesus departed at the same time as his disciples when the sign was demanded of him (Mt. 16:4) and "to the other side"[2] belongs with "he departed"[3], (as in Mark) which Matthew omits here. Before the words "forgetting to take bread"[4], Matthew sets down artificially that which he omitted and

---

[1]ἀπῆλθεν εἰς τὸ πέραν.

[2]εἰς τὸ πέραν.

[3]ἀπῆλθεν.

[4]ἐπελάθοντο λαβεῖν ἄρτους.

writes "the disciples, coming to the other shore"[5]. *Just omit these words,* and you have the text of Mark (p. 683; author's italics).

The way Wilke argues here is a true piece of wizardry: "Just omit these words, and you have the text of Mark." With equal justification one could say of the text of Mark: Just add these words, and you have the text of Matthew.

So far, Wilke has attempted only to produce proof that Matthew was familiar with the two special pericopes of Mark, even though he "omitted" both. Now, the only thing missing is the corresponding "evidence" for Luke. This argumentation Wilke handles with even greater ease:

> The date that is given and that we, at least, firmly believe (sic!) to be established is of extreme importance. What are the conclusions that follow? The first is that, if the redactor of the Gospel of Matthew had the passages which we mentioned in front of him, then the very same passages must also have been available to Luke, who intentionally omitted sections 22-27. Therefore, we have to assume that the other Evangelists had before them the *complete* work of Mark with all of its parts intact (p. 683).

No, we most certainly do not have to assume this. Why should we follow Wilke in supposing that, just because Matthew knew the special Marcan pericopes, Luke must have known them, too? Now, for Wilke, this conclusion follows naturally from the Marcan hypothesis, which says that the Gospel of Mark functioned as a textual basis and source for Matthew, as well as for Luke, and that both of them were equally well acquainted with the entire text.

Again, without any doubt, we are confronted by a typical *petitio principii:* The validity of the Marcan hypothesis is to be proved by demonstrating that Matthew and Luke used the second Gospel. But now Wilke endeavors to prove the use of Mark by the first and third Evangelists on the basis of the "validity" of the Marcan hypothesis, and he concludes "that, if the redactor of the Gospel of Matthew had the passages which we mentioned in front of him, then the very same passages must also have been available to Luke...."

And, so Wilke, in his fashion, had "explained" the material in the Gospel of Mark which goes beyond the other two synoptic writers. But then, there still remained the much more extensive extra material common to Matthew and Luke, particularly the sayings material. Where did this material originate? And how can it be explained within the framework of the Marcan hypothesis? This was the other principal synoptic problem which confronted Wilke and would not go away.

---

[5]ἐλθόντες εἰς τὸ πέραν οἱ μαθηταί.

It is at the point of mastering this fundamental problem that we encounter the characteristic difference between the two contemporary originators of the Marcan hypothesis, Wilke and Weisse. Weisse looks for his salvation in an extra-synoptic solution. Wilke chooses an intra-synoptic solution with the aid of a second source. In his sixth "textual point," he formulates it in the following way: "Material occurring in the Gospel of Matthew that is similar to Luke's insertions into Mark, is derived from no other source than Luke" (p. 685).

Wilke's proof of this statement is brief. If it had taken him 684 pages to make it evident that Mark was the source of Matthew and Luke, he needed all of seven pages to demonstrate that Matthew used Luke as well as Mark. His principal support in this venture is the hardly disputable fact that Luke's Sermon on the Plain exhibits an older form than the Sermon on the Mount in Matthew. But the conclusion which Wilke draws from this is hardly convincing: "Luke's Sermon is not an abbreviated version of Matthew's Sermon on the Mount, but the reverse is true. Matthew's is an expanded version of Luke's" (p. 685).

This conclusion is not compelling, because from the very start, Wilke accepted only the alternative between these two possibilities. But there are several others. In any case it still has not been proven that either of the two authors knew and used the Gospel of the other; the divergences are greater than the correspondences. The possibility should at least be entertained that both authors obtained the convergent material from the same source and the divergent material from varying sources. Particularly where the Sermon on the Mount is concerned, there are good reasons for assuming that the authors did not avail themselves of the same source.

Therefore, according to Wilke, Matthew adopted and enlarged Luke's Sermon on the Plain. The entire sixth chapter is an insertion, says Wilke: "That which in Matthew might have the appearance of being the Logia (which Papias mentions as a composition by Matthew) has not been proven to be so" (p. 691). Also, the Sermon on the Mount was not written by the Apostle Matthew, but by the "redactor of the Gospel of Matthew," or, as he also often calls him, the "Matthean compiler" or the "Matthean interpolator" or the "Matthean transcriber." "Are we to suppose that the Apostle Matthew was actually such a compiler?" Wilke asks. "This we shall never believe, and thus we completely surrender our belief in the authenticity of the first Gospel" (p. 691 f.).

All in all, Wilke identifies Luke as *the sole source* of all the additional material common to Matthew and Luke which is not found in Mark. The text had been more frequently modified by Matthew either because, from time to time, this had seemed appropriate to him, or because the position of a particular pericope which he had requisitioned from Mark demanded special treatment, or for other reasons that Wilke sought to investigate in detail. Thus, he arrives at the utterly premature "conclusion": "Therefore we have seen that Matthew was acquainted with Luke's texts" (p. 691).

The question of where Luke obtained his extra-Marcan material—or, as Wilke calls it, "material with which he enriched the Gospel of Mark"—is left unanswered, as he himself mentions in his preface (see above, p. 5).

Wilke terminates his voluminous study with these words:

> We close our work with the assurance that after honest research and painstaking effort to clarify this controversial matter we could not have reached any other conclusions than those which, along with their supporting arguments, we have presented in this publication; we hope that it will win the applause of unbiased seekers of truth (p. 694).

Toward a Critique of Wilke

It is not without an element of scholarly and human tragedy that the most piercing criticism of Wilke came from none other than Christian Hermann Weisse, his fellow warrior in the cause of the Marcan hypothesis—and also, that it occurred in the same year in which both of them published their fundamental works. Wilke's *Urevangelist* had hardly left the press when his first and sharpest antagonist immediately leaped forward and subjected his book to merciless and annihilating criticism. It appeared in the *Berliner Jahrbücher für Wissenschaftliche Kritik* (1838, 595 ff.).

It cannot be denied that Weisse correctly chose the principal points from which to launch his objections to Wilke's argumentation; namely, the "textual purifications" in the Gospel of Mark, as well as the attribution of the additional material in Matthew and Luke to the alleged dependency of Matthew upon Luke. Of them, Weisse says that he had to fear

> that these elements will also prove to be a stumbling block for others, and it may be that this fact could substantially prejudice the success of the work. This is especially true of the first element mentioned, concerning the *multitude of violent textual alterations*, namely of eliminations that the author had permitted himself, particularly in the text of Mark (p. 613; author's italics).

And then, Weisse says something that hardly sounds attractive coming from an advocate of the Marcan hypothesis:

> Such a procedure is even more deplorable since it must unavoidably arouse suspicion among non-specialists and, even more, in those with evil intent; for if a hypothesis demands such acts of violence in order to be established, then such a hypothesis cannot possibly have a sound foundation.

Weisse designates Wilke's elimination of the second miracle of the feeding of the multitude as "probably the most daring example of all his arbitrary acts of this kind" (p. 616). He continues in the same manner: "Among the boldest of these alleged textual purifications is the repudiation of Mk. 14:47 and 51-52...among the most idle and unfounded, those of Mk. 3:6,...4:10,...and 6:7 ..." (p. 617).

Nor does Weisse neglect now and again to make Wilke and the reader properly aware of the merit of his own work:

> With regard to the words of Mk. 14:18...the writer of this paper is so bold as to direct the author's (Wilke's) attention to his (Weisse's) *Evangelische Geschichte* I, 601 ff. in the hope that the author will find there a satisfactory explanation of the matter that gives him such difficulty (p. 617).

Weisse's attitude towards the second item (dependence of Matthew on Luke) is no less sharply critical:

> The "Matthean compiler" (as [Wilke] likes to call the author of our first Gospel) was supposed to have obtained his material from Luke, while at the same time using Mark, and, with a minimum of personal additions, he was supposed to have compiled his narrations from the material of his two predecessors (p. 619).

And then, he brings up an argument against his comrade-in-arms for Marcan priority that, in conjunction with the preceding rebuke, could be regarded not only as treason but also as a stab in the back, especially coming as it does from a surpassingly ruthless and pitiless opponent of the Griesbach hypothesis.

> One can see that [Wilke] assigns the author of the first Gospel the same role which is allotted to the author of the Gospel of Mark in the *Griesbach hypothesis*, but with one difference. Matthew, says Wilke, did not assemble his narrative in every single case from that of the other two authors; on the contrary, he followed Mark whenever Mark led the way, while arbitrarily transferring Mark's narrations to different places and inserting at random supplementary material borrowed from Luke. Such proceedings are not in the least more probable than these imposed on Mark by

this particular hypothesis (Griesbach's)—*if Matthew had wanted to proceed in that way, why did he not just copy directly from Luke?* (p. 619; author's italics)

It is not difficult to recognize what Weisse alludes to here: Wilke's overly excited condemnation of Griesbach as the "castrator of the other texts" and as one who made "a hodgepodge out of their words." But one can also see why Weisse suddenly turns out to be Wilke's detractor rather than his defender: it is a genuine scholastic controversy over the Marcan hypothesis which appears right here at the very beginning, in the first year of its existence. Nothing less is at stake than the basic question, indeed the fundamental problem of the Marcan theory in general: How can one explain the extensive common material in Matthew and Luke for which there is no equivalent in Mark? This is the question that divides—then as now.

One might well have thought that, after Weisse's rigorous criticism, Wilke's intra-synoptic solution would have been laid to rest. But this was not the case. Three years later the theory was awakened to new and unexpected life by no less a figure than Bruno Bauer in his *Kritik der evangelischen Geschichte der Synoptiker* (1841-42). This publication suddenly brought Wilke more fame than he had dared hope for. Bruno Bauer gave his unqualified endorsement to Wilke's arguments as well as his results—at the expense of Christian Hermann Weisse. Bauer did give Weisse credit for his services in founding the Marcan hypothesis, but, with respect to the common additional narrative details in Matthew and Luke, he completely rejected Weisse's deduction that they came from a logia collection. Rather, he expressly defended Wilke's point of view that Matthew had drawn his material from Luke, and thus, he assigned the crown of immortality to *him*: "One part of Weisse's reasoning, and perhaps this very part, complete with its entire foundation, has already been refuted and overthrown by Wilke in his work—*which will be eternally remembered!*" (author's italics).

Now Weisse, for his part, did not receive Bruno Bauer's obvious preference for Wilke in total silence. He reacted immediately in the *Neue Jenaische Literaturzeitung*, and even 13 years later, in his second related work, the *Evangelienfrage* (1856), he still took revenge on Bruno Bauer by calling him "Wilke's uncalled successor" (p. 83).

But Wilke's "solution" of the Marcan problem had yet another effect, one which he scarcely intended or envisioned—an effect on the history of research. After all, he had advanced the point of view: "We therefore have to assume that the other Evangelists had the entire work of Mark...in front of them" (p. 684). However, he added a qualification which sounds harmless but nevertheless had serious consequences: "aside from a few interpolations."

One only needs to raise the question: What are the ultimate consequences of that statement? Now what else could it mean but that the Gospel of Mark does *not* exhibit quite the same form as our second canonical Gospel! In the technical terminology of later years that means that Wilke acknowledged the existence of an "ur-Mark"—only weakly and by way of suggestion, to be sure, but still in principle. In a weakened form, he calls it merely the "ur-type" (p. 674).

Concluding Remarks on Wilke

Now, if by way of summary we are to reach a general verdict on the fruits of Wilke's research, it can only be that he did not succeed in proving the Marcan hypothesis:

1) In his arguments Wilke presupposed that which he had yet to prove ("since Mark is always the one accompanied"). He always based the substance of his comparative synoptic columns on Mark. He could sustain his allegation that the Gospel of Mark formed the basic text and source of Matthew and Luke only by repeatedly resorting to a *petitio principii.*

2) His changes in the text (interpolations and eliminations) are arbitrary and not objectively justified since they are not textually documented and cannot be demonstrated in a single case. Already, they contain *in nuce* the assumption of an ur-Mark, functioning as an auxiliary hypothesis.

3) Wilke did not succeed in proving his thesis of Matthew's dependence on Luke. Wilke neither investigated nor answered the unavoidable question of where Luke obtained the narrative material that he holds in common with Matthew (see Wilke's preface).

We conclude that we cannot posthumously validate Wilke's pledge: "For all eternity we affirm with hand and seal that our conclusion is the correct one."

That much may be said with respect to the substance of the debate. But we cannot let matters rest there. An overall judgment of his achievements must also include a characterization of his scholarly disposition insofar as it influenced his investigation. And, in our opinion, there was such an influence here.

Two salient features will be recalled from Wilke's preface: his intense subjectivity, and his emotional involvement. His freely-voiced wish not to be judged by those "who have made up their minds that Mark excerpted his Gospel from the works of Matthew and Luke" cannot be reconciled with a scholarly attitude. It appears that he desires to be reviewed only by those who share his opinion. In other words, don't criticize!

Wilke's reasoning arouses even more suspicion: "...because I feel that these men, although worthy of respect, can no more be expected to have the necessary objectivity of judgment than I can be expected to be won over to their point of view." This implies nothing less than the assertion: in regard to this question we *both* have already made up our minds. Wilke is in no better position to impute partiality to other researchers than he is to turn this self-accusation into a self-recommendation. It gives rise to justifiable doubts concerning the sincerity and objectivity of his scholarly research.

His final words are equally subjective: "The one thing that will increase my courage and double my diligence is that this essay . . . should find favorable acceptance." This is a device to win approval which is uncommon in scholarly research and indeed incompatible with scholarly decorum.

Hence an intensely emotional accent is present in the main body of the argument as well as in the preface. When Wilke comes to discuss the so-called "intermediate form" which, according to Griesbach's hypothesis, Mark represents between Matthew and Luke, he writes: "Mark's passages 1:32 and 1:42 are held to be a mixture of the parallel texts. *One must not believe that....*The other passage....is supposed to be a mixture. *One should not believe that either*" (p. 475).

We meet this kind of emphasis again and again in Wilke's argumentation:

> It is an amply verified fact that Mark did not obtain material from the other Evangelists. That is as clear as day, and we humbly beg all those who are interested in our examinations first of all to convince themselves of the validity of these findings and to *believe not even one syllable, not even the smallest word* of those who try to prove the opposite (p 456, author's italics).

Wilke loved to cast doubts on the *bona fides* of those who thought differently from him:

> To be sure, now we are so bold as to believe that we have proved our case in the above inquiry....*Now only the good will to agree with us is lacking.* For ourselves we ask for nothing but this good will, since the object of our research will take care of itself by virtue of its innate power to convince (p. 375; author's italics).

On the other hand, Wilke is unwilling to grant his opponents' viewpoint any similar persuasive power:

> The contrary claim that this is not true and that Mark compiled his text solely from elements of the parallel narratives *is based on nothing more than a dictum* which tolerates no criticism and holds itself to be above mere reasons and results. One might as well give

such a dictum its due—by ignoring it and continuing the investigation without further concern. Now we shall proceed (p. 389).

This method of castigating his opponents' opinions by refusing to take them seriously is one that we encounter again and again in Wilke: "If they uphold their opinion in the face of clear evidence to the contrary, *that can remain a matter of complete indifference to us.* Nothing can be resolved by denials and authoritative decrees. Rather, here everything depends on criticism" (p. 427). Then he adds a footnote which sounds embarrassingly like an attack on his opponents' moral character:

> *Here we pronounce sentence justly and not on mere suspicion.* We have here the analogue of a case in which a person is condemned on suspicion by others who themselves do the very thing he is accused of doing. Their subjective suspicion even causes them to discount evidence in his favor, and they judge him guilty because they themselves are guilty (p. 428).

In this manner Wilke tries repeatedly to dismiss the arguments of his opponents. On one occasion he says of them: "We pay no attention to this kind of empty rhetoric and pseudo-sophistication" (p. 246); then again, he states: "Actually, very little intelligence is required in order to choose between these interpretations" (p. 419). Occasionally, with apparent sincerity, he assures his readers: "In all that we are doing, nothing shall be obtained surreptitiously" (p. 394).

Wilke is unable to convince on the strength of his objective arguments, nor does his subjective tone present a more positive image of his scholarly disposition.

Bruno Bauer numbered him among the immortals. According to Klopstock, immortality is a grand idea. That Bruno Bauer should have placed such high value upon research into the Gospels was hardly deemed inappropriate by his contemporaries. Even though such research is burdened by incomparable difficulties, it stands far above all other disciplines by virtue of its singular importance in intellectual history. But that he assigned immortality to one of the two originators of the Marcan hypothesis, Christian Gottlob Wilke, was not only a rash but also an unforgivable misjudgment; for Wilke had already been cogently refuted by the second originator of the Marcan hypothesis, Christian Hermann Weisse.

We shall now turn to Weisse.

The extra-synoptic solution (Christian Hermann Weisse)

Christian Hermann Weisse (1801-1866) is considered the principal founder of the Marcan hypothesis. Prior to taking up New Testament research, Weisse had travelled a varied path. He started out as a jurist, then moved on to philosophy, and, preferring religious philosophy, became a typical representative of the late resurgence of idealism. His books appeared almost yearly:

1833 *Die Idee der Gottheit*

1834 *Die philosophische Geheimlehre von der Unsterblichkeit des menschlichen Individuums,* furthermore *Theodizee*

1835 *Grundzüge der Metaphysik*

1836 *Von der Unsterblichkeit*

1837 *Kritik und Erläuterung des Goethe'schen Faust. Nebst einem Anhange zur sittlichen Beurteilung Goethe's.*

When the University of Leipzig refused him a full professorship in philosophy, he withdrew for several years from his academic activity and dedicated himself to private research. In 1837 he turned to theology, and one year later his principal work appeared in two volumes:

Die evangelische Geschichte
kritisch und philosophisch bearbeitet. 1838

Eighteen years later he again addressed himself to the same theme in a second work on the New Testament:

Die Evangelienfrage
in ihrem gegenwärtigen Stadium. 1856

The principal founder of the Marcan hypothesis now faced exactly the same unavoidable task as Wilke, that of explaining the origin of the textual materials common to both Matthew and Luke but not found in Mark. It was obvious to all that the Gospel of Mark was quantitatively insufficient to account for the derivation of these extra passages in the first and third Gospels. Since Weisse rejected the intra-synoptic solution, he had no other choice but to search for an auxiliary hypothesis. He believed that he had found a clue to such a complementary theory in the fragment of Papias that is to be found in the church history of Eusebius:[6] (Eusebius, *hist. eccl.* III 39: II 1n. 284, 290f.)

---

[6]Ματθαῖος μὲν οὖν ʽΕβραΐδι διαλέκτῳ τὰ λόγια συνετάξατο.

How did Weisse come to this particular solution to the problem of synoptic sources? The idea had been suggested to him by his reading of two of the most distinguished scholars of his time—Schleiermacher and Lachmann.

In 1832 Schleiermacher had published his discourse "Über die Zeugnisse des Papias von unsern beiden ersten Evangelisten" (in: *Theologische Studien und Kritiken*. (1832-WW I, 2 pp. 363-393). In it he had considered the more extensive Papias fragment regarding Mark, as well as the shorter one concerning Matthew, and commented: "Matthew has written a collection of statements made by Christ which may have been only single proverbs or extended ones, or most probably both. *Papias' expression simply cannot mean anything else* "(p. 365; author's italics). But Schleiermacher rejected just as firmly an identification of this logia compilation with our Gospel of Matthew: "Let us ask ourselves if it is really probable that this very same Matthew would still have written our Gospel after writing the collection of these speeches: my answer has to be entirely in the negative" (p. 367). And also: "Eusebius has not found a trace of two distinct works by Matthew in his Papias; thus it is probable that only the one existed, and it was not our Gospel" (p. 368). However, Schleiermacher also expressed the opinion: "*The Gospel of Matthew embraces this collection.*" Further he was of the view that "the reason it bears the name[7] is because it is based on this work by Matthew" (p. 372; author's italics).

Three years later Schleiermacher's interpretation was taken up by Karl Lachmann, who expressed his approval in the treatise "De ordine narrationum in evangeliis synopticis," also published in the *Theologischen Studien und Kritiken* (1835 pp. 570-590). In it he expressed his own view of Schleiermacher's opinion on the Gospel of Matthew:

> Matthaei autem evangelium illud intellego quod Schleiermacherus dixit (et sat fuit dixisse, vel sine argumentis: ita veritas rei primo aspectu patet; ut si Papiae testimonium aliter atque ille accipias, tamen debet concedi) illud, inquam, ex collectis et quasi domini Jesu Christi orationibus compositum primo, cui postmodum alii narrationes inferserunt (p. 577).

Hence Lachmann joins Schleiermacher in the opinion that Matthew's logia collection is contained in the canonical Gospel of Matthew and that it forms the basic core of the Gospel. According to Lachmann, others would later add historical reports to it. (verbatim: "soon after that other [people] stuffed it with narratives.")

---

[7]κατὰ Ματθαῖον.

Then Christian Hermann Weisse also took up Schleiermacher's idea and explicitly identified himself with it:

> As we can see, we are talking about the meaning of the word "logia" which has received so much attention recently because of Schleiermacher. Papias uses the word "logia" to describe the work of Matthew. *The word in its original sense, which is retained in all subsequent uses, indicates a collection consisting only of discourses and sayings of the Lord. This undeniable fact* was pointed out for the first time by Schleiermacher, who tried to use it as the basis of a new and divergent opinion about the original form of the Gospel of Matthew (*Ev. Gesch.* I p. 34; author's italics).

Now Christian Hermann Weisse believed himself capable of explaining every single additional detail in Matthew and Luke with the aid of this logia collection mentioned in the Papias fragment. That, he was sure, would solve the synoptic problem: "*It is our definite conviction that Mark is not the only common source of* [*Matthew and Luke*]. *There is also Matthew's sayings collection*" (I p. 83; author's italics).

Thus, Weisse becomes the originator of the two-source theory. He himself designates his basic idea as an "insight."

This interpretation of the Gospel of Matthew did not offer any particular problems for him. He felt supported by the authority of Schleiermacher and of Lachmann as well, since both stated that the logia text of the Apostle Matthew was contained in the canonical Gospel of Matthew. He called it the "genuine Matthew" and maintained that the Gospel of Matthew originated from the amalgamation of the "genuine Matthew" with the "genuine Mark."

But what about Luke? After all, Weisse had explained that the sayings collection was the "common source" of "these two," thus including Luke. How could he substantiate such a claim in relation to the third Gospel? Weisse emphasizes that Luke in his introductory dedication declared that already many had undertaken the same task; in this instance it can be assumed that the "many" embraced both the Gospel of Mark and Matthew's logia document. "The works of Mark and of the genuine Matthew were among the sources which he used. Given all that has been noted, it is so easy to accept this assumption that we would be quite surprised if that had not been the case."(I p. 56).

In reality, this opinion of Weisse's is in complete contradiction to Schleiermacner's authority (*Über die Schriften des Lukas, ein kritischer Versuch.* WW. 1836 1,2 pp. 1-220). But, nevertheless, C. H. Weisse knows how to produce Schleiermacher as the principal witness for his proposition. It is instructive to observe Weisse's characteristic mode of argumentation:

> There is no doubt that the distinguished theologian would himself have come to accept it (Weisse's opinion) had he been granted the opportunity to investigate further the excellent insight which he was later to formulate regarding the testimony of Papias and the nature of the Gospel of Matthew. In this insight Schleiermacher acknowledged that our Matthew embraced a large part of the sayings collection of the genuine Matthew. A more exact examination would unfailingly have brought him to affirm what he actually denied in the first treatise based on this insight: that Luke also must have used this collection, either directly or indirectly (I p. 84).

It is not necessary to dwell on the unscholarly nature of Weisse's mode of argumentation. Instead of admitting honestly and forthrightly that "Schleiermacher holds a different opinion," C.H. Weisse unjustifiably claims the authority of the "distinguished theologian" to support his own allegations! He insinuates that "a more exact examination would unfailingly" have brought Schleiermacher to his, Weisse's, conclusion. Weisse precedes the whole statement with an apodictic "There is no doubt that ...." That is how he gets Schleiermacher to "authorize" a logia source for Luke.

Now he possessed a historical source, the Gospel of Mark, as well as a sayings source—the logia collection. But this was not enough to free Weisse from the problems generated by his hypothesis. The Gospel of Mark was readily available, but what was known about the "logia"? The name, and nothing more! How could one find out about its substance and wording? There was no other way than inference, but from what? From the Gospels of Matthew and Luke, since, according to the hypothesis, both authors are supposed to have used the "logia" as a source.

Now this in itself would not have posed any great problem if the logia in these two Gospels were always in the same sequence and wording. But it is well known that this is not the case—quite the contrary! The Sermon on the Mount in Matthew comprises a unified block of logia embracing three interconnected chapters. On the other hand, in his Sermon on the Plain, Luke has only twenty-seven verses that are paralleled in Matthew's sermon, and not all of them with the identical wording. Also, an extensive portion of Matthew's Sermon on the Mount has no parallel in Luke at all; the remaining dominical sayings in Matthew's version of the Sermon are dispersed throughout Luke's entire Gospel.

But the dominical sayings were not restricted to the Matthean Sermon on the Mount and its Lucan pendant. There were still other extended discourses, numerous parables, and many individual logia. Not all of them were present in both Gospels, nor did they always appear in the same context and sequence. In view of such divergences, it was an eminently difficult problem to uncover and give form to the hypothetical second source of the first and third Evangelists.

But that was not all. At that point an additional question arose about the definition of the "logia." What did it signify? From the start, Weisse had identified himself with Schleiermacher's definition of the concept and had presented the substance of the logia collection in absolute agreement with Schleiermacher, "as a collection composed only of speeches and sayings of the Lord." But with regard to the question of who had access to the logia he distinctly distanced himself from Schleiermacher while unjustifiably laying posthumous claim to his presumptive agreement "that Luke also must have used this collection."

Now Weisse was completely trapped within the difficulties of the hypothesis. He knew no other way out of his difficulties in reconstructing the logia source than to suggest that it was to be sought and found in the material common to Matthew and Luke: "We are convinced that everything the two Evangelists have in common with each other, but not with Mark, is to be attributed to [the logia collection]" (Vol. II, p.4).

Everything that they have in common?! It seems that Weisse is starting to flounder. The additional material common to the first and third Evangelists consists not only of dominical sayings! There are within the text the following pericopes which unquestionably are not to be characterized as dominical sayings:

1) The words of John the Baptist (Mt. 3:7-12 par Lk. 3:7-9, 17),

2) The expanded form of the temptation story (Mt. 4:3-10 par Lk. 4:3-12),

3) The story of the centurion at Capernaum (Mt. 8:5-10; Lk. 7:2-10),

4) John the Baptist's inquiry (Mt. 11:2-6; Lk. 7:18-23),

5) Jesus' reply to the accusation of the Pharisees that he was in league with the devil (Mt. 12:22, 27, 28, 30 par Lk. 11:14, 19, 20, 23).

How will Weisse manage a state of affairs which completely contradicts his original definition of the logia concept? Right at the start of his critical review of the Gospels he is faced by the first problem in the form of John the Baptist's discourses. He attempts to apologize for them by saying: "They are the only example of a statement by someone else coming from a source which was otherwise said to contain only 'sayings of the Lord,' of a discourse, that is, by someone other than the Lord." (Vol. II, p. 5).

Weisse has no choice but to concede this initial weakness of his hypothesis:

> After what we have said about the composition of the Gospels of Matthew and Luke, it must be more than a little startling and puzzling that we encounter an apparent *contradiction to our postulate in the very first case* in which we attempt to apply it (Vol. II, p. 5; author's italics).

On this point one can only agree with Weisse. Since the hypothesis exposed its weakness at the very first citation, would it not have been wiser for him to reevaluate his hypothesis and draw the necessary conclusions? Then he would have been spared what was to follow—in an expanded pseudo-argumentation he attempted to transmute the words of John the Baptist into dominical sayings:

> Thus there is no other course of action (sic!) than to speak out for what is most probable (for in this case absolute certainty cannot be achieved): Matthew opened his work with a compilation of several statements which were spoken by Jesus, but which expressly referred back to John the Baptist, with the intention of underlining the meaning and activity of this prophetic man. Either that was the case, or Matthew understood the statements in this sense. (Vol. II, p. 8).

It is hard to believe that, deep within, Weisse was truly convinced of the validity of his allegation. The resigned remark "thus there is no other course of action" says a great deal. Actually the phrase ought to be continued with the words: "if we want to save the two-source theory."

The words of John the Baptist do pose a problem in themselves in that parallel expressions of Jesus can be found (Mt. 7:19; 12:34; 13:30; 15:13; 23:33; Mk. 10:28 par Lk. 12:50). But in this particular place it cannot be a problem, for here the words are expressly and explicitly identified as those of John. Thus they could not have been contained in a collection of dominical sayings.

The second example, too, poses quite a few difficulties for Weisse and his hypothesis. There is no doubt that the temptation story belongs to the historical or narrative presentations, and therefore, according to Weisse's postulate, could not have been found in the logia source.

Nevertheless, Weisse endeavored to remove this obstacle to his hypothesis by giving it a new interpretation. He rejected the view that the *tentatio Christi* was a historical narrative. Instead he bestowed a symbolic character on the entire account and explained the temptation as "something that Jesus himself had conceived and spoken."

Again it is instructive to observe (and typical of Weisse's pseudo-philosophical imagination) just what kind of symbolic meaning he attributes to Jesus in the temptation story: "It is essential," he says, "to dismiss all fear of a symbolic interpretation, even in the most minor details." The desert into which Jesus is led by the spirit was, according to Weisse, meant to be understood as "a spiritual desert." Fasting he interpreted as "consciousness of spiritual fasting." The number of forty days "seems to indicate that the length of the test was no accident but rather was ordained by a higher necessity." The wild beasts among which, according to Mark, Jesus found himself were interpreted as "the wild passions and desires which attempt to invade the consciousness of a highly gifted individual whenever there is a lack of spiritual satisfaction." The dialogue with Satan, the actual temptation of Jesus, is described as "not a common, nor simply a sensual temptation," but as "a temptation to commit spiritual sin, the sin of the man of genius" (pp. 18-25).

But let this matter rest. These examples suffice to show that Weisse attempted to save for his hypothesis evidence which clearly defies his definition of the logia document.

Moreover, this symbolic interpretation—which, according to Weisse, was "recorded in the notes of the Apostle Matthew, in all probability directly after he had heard it from the lips of the Master" (who told him that?!)—is reminiscent of Weisse's interpretation of Goethe's "Faust" ("with an appendix on the ethical appraisal of Goethe") (1837). In this work he interpreted Faust's intended suicide as "a symbol of spiritual self-annihilation"; Gretchen's fall as "a symbol for the poet's natural innocence and its downfall"; the desired and promised treasures of the imperial court as "treasures of the spirit . . . genius, the substance of science, art, religion, and of all forms of intense spiritual life—to gain all of these powers for the life of the state, and thus bring it refreshment and renewal"; the depth of the sea during the festival of Nereus as "the spiritual ocean of the world."

Karl Rosenkranz, in his review of Weisse's commentary, called this kind of analysis "hypersthenic exposition," and correctly said of these exaggerated interpretations: "Weisse has succumbed to a mania for elevating particular situations to a spiritual plane" (*Berliner Jahrbücher für wissenschaftliche Kritik*. 1837; with citations).

The third obstacle to Weisse's consistent logia theory was the pericope of the centurion at Capernaum, which in Matthew as well as Luke immediately follows the Sermon on the Mount. Since this story unquestionably belongs to the narrative reports, it could not have been part of Matthew's logia collection according to Schleiermacher's definition of the logia concept, which Weisse had adopted. But Weisse did not let even this diminish his conviction in the validity of his hypothesis. Rather, he provided this narration with "an explanation which emerges from our basic view of the synoptic Gospels quite without any strain and almost of necessity." In this "explanation," Weisse proclaimed the report to be a "parable":

> Hence there can be no doubt that in reality the Apostle Matthew, whose writings consist solely of the speeches and expressions of the Lord, comprehended this particular story as a *parable*. He repeated what he had heard and made it *sound like a historical report*. As we mentioned earlier, he treated the Temptation story similarly (Vol. II, p. 53 f.; author's italics).

Weisse saw the "true meaning and the substance of this parable" in the "spiritual miraculous power of Jesus working at a distance; his historical activity in the world unbounded by space and time was best expressed in the image of a corporeal healing miracle" (Vol.II, p. 56).

Simultaneously, this "parable" which sounded "like a historical report" offered Weisse the opportunity to conjecture about the text in the interest of his logia theory. It is quite out of character for a parable to conclude as in both Matthew and Luke with this realistic statement: "And the servant was healed at that very moment"(Mt. 8:13; Lk. 7:10). In Matthew this final statement is preceded by the saying about the people who would come from the east and the west to occupy the seats which were assigned "to the sons of the Kingdom." This saying is missing from the parallel report of Luke, but it can be found in Luke's "travel narrative" in connection with the threat of Israel's exclusion from the Kingdom of God (13:28-29).

Now Weisse argued that there was no possible reason why Luke should have made this change in position if in the "genuine Matthew" this saying had been "as closely associated with the narrative as it is in our Gospel of Matthew." On the other hand the procedure would be quite explicable if the logion of the sons of the Kingdom as a maxim had formed the conclusion of the parable in the logia document. This assumption poses no difficulties if one accepts the pericope as a parable.

Already Weisse's intent can be detected:

> The note about the actual success of the healing, which follows this saying in the first Gospel, but which takes the place of the saying in Luke, would have had to be missing from the original version. This note could be left out without any disadvantage to

the parable, for its point lies not in the demonstration of its success but in the dialogue between Jesus and the centurion (Vol. II, p. 55).

Hence, Weisse, with the aid of obviously unacceptable textual "conjecture," had happily "interpreted away" the obstacle to his view of this pericope as a parable. In doing so he transformed the first three major parts of the extra material common to Matthew and Luke—which were clearly not dominical sayings—into "words of the Lord." And he had done so in such a way that no one could challenge him.

But now we come to the points which even Weisse could not twist or turn—the extra material common to Matthew and Luke which not only consists of pure logia material, but is also clothed in historical form. On the subject of John the Baptist's inquiry (Mt. 11:2-19; Lk. 7:18-36), Weisse continued to ignore the historical framework and catalogued the pericope under the caption "Statements about John the Baptist." He did not feel obliged to justify his attribution of this segment to the logia source.

But the pericope in which Jesus replied to the accusations of the Pharisees that he was in league with the devil (Mt. 12:22-32 par Mk. 3:22-30; Lk. 11:14-23) posed an obvious hypothetical and exegetical dilemma for Weisse. Here the words of the Lord, which belong to the additional material common to Matthew and Luke, fall within a narrative framework which Mark also provides but, in his case, without the dominical sayings.

In view of this inescapable difficulty, Weisse gave way; and against all the presuppositions of his own hypothesis, asked his readers to believe:

1) that this pericope originally stood in the Gospel of *Mark*, minus the four verses which are in Mt. 12:22, 27, 28, 30 par Lk.; and

2) that the same pericope originally stood in the logia source, including the four verses which have no equivalent in Mark, and including the verses with purely narrative content which introduce this pericope (Mt. 12:22-24 par Lk.).

Weisse states accordingly:

> It appears that our Evangelist (Matthew) had also found in his source the story of the conversation between Jesus and the Pharisees regarding the driving out of the evil spirits, together with some additional modification and expansions. Here our Evangelist not only supplements Mark—he also must have found Mark's narrative together with the supplements in the original text of Matthew. I conclude this from his agreement with Luke and also from the fact that Luke presented the narrative at a different place than did Mark (Vol. II, p. 75).

It is evident that Weisse had no other means of escape than to surrender his own logia theory. What did he say at the beginning of his allegation of a second source of Matthew and Luke? "The word in its original sense, which is retained in all subsequent uses, always indicates a collection consisting *only* of discourses and sayings of the Lord." He had even called this an "undeniable fact." Now he had no choice but to include distinctly narrative reports in his "collection consisting only of discourses and sayings of the Lord" in order to keep his two-source theory alive. In doing so Weisse had betrayed his own principles and violated his own initial definition.

One has only to open the second volume of his *Evangelische Geschichte* for this suspicion to be aroused. Weisse began it with these words:

> In this volume we intend to enumerate a series of individual narrative accounts, in particular of sayings, discourses, and parables spoken by Christ. In all of these, the first and third Gospels generally follow Mark's thread of narration while also supplementing it.

Here we find some words which are incompatible with Weisse's own initial definition—"narrative accounts," and, quite unexpectedly, "*in particular of* sayings, discourses, and parables . . . ." An irksome phrase! Here we have for the first time the phrase which from that day forward would limit the definition of the logia source—from the establishment of the two-source theory to the present: "*a collection in particular of discourses and sayings of the Lord.*"

That meant that Weisse's consistent logia theory in Schleiermacher's sense, i.e., limiting it exclusively to unalloyed words of the Lord, ("Since Papias' expression cannot mean anything else") had proven itself inadequate to explain the extra-Marcan material common to both Matthew and Luke. Even Weisse himself could not sustain it.

It is not difficult to calculate the ramifications of what Weisse had done. Once a foot was in the door and it became permissible to assign to the logia source dominical sayings that had been framed and imbedded in narrative material, then all doors could be opened. After all, where in the Gospels, even in Mark's parallel text, can we find a single narrative pericope without the words of the Lord—if we exclude the report about the feast of Herod? Then practically everything can belong to the logia document. Thus the boundaries between the two major sources, which Weisse explicitly separated—an historical work, the Gospel of Mark, and a sayings source, the logia— became so thoroughly blurred that all real differences between them ceased to exist.

But there was worse to come for Weisse's two-source theory. Even if one understood the logia concept in its consistent sense as originally stipulated by Weisse, there still remained the question: is there no logia material in the Gospel of Mark? The answer is, most certainly! The Gospel of Mark, too, contains an abundance of logia in the pure form of dominical sayings, including spoken discourses, parables, and single logia:

1) Mark presents the great discourse on the parousia in thirty-two verses (13:5-37). As Bernhard Weiss observed, the pioneers of the Marcan hypothesis won themselves no laurels when they resorted to an auxiliary hypothesis in order to neutralize this fact. What they argued was that this eschatological discourse was added to the Gospels from a document concerning the last days which was in circulation at that time.

2) The Gospel of Mark contains the speech against pharisaism in an abridged version (12:38-40) as does Luke.

3) Mark provides the complete parable-discourse (4:1-34), including the parable of the sower (with its interpretation and the sayings about the purposes of parables), the sayings about the correct use of the parables, the parable of the seed growing by itself (Mark's exclusively!), and the parable of the mustard seed.

4) Mark presents the parable of the wicked husbandmen (12:1-12).

5) The sending out of the twelve (6:8-11).

6) The polemic against the Pharisees about the laws of men and the commands of God (7:6-23).

7) A profusion of single logia: 2:17; 2:21-22; 2:28; 3:24f; 4:21; 4:22; 4:24; 4:25; 8:12; 8:15; 8:34-38; 9:1; 9:37; 9:40; 9:42; 9:43; 9:45; 9:47; 9:50; 10:11; 10:31; 10:42-44; 11:24; 11:25; 12:35-37; 12:38. All of these individual logia have parallels in at least one of the other synoptic authors.

8) The following logia are unique to Mark:

   2:27. "The sabbath was made for man, not man for the sabbath."

   9:49: "For everyone will be salted with fire."

   9:50b: "Have salt in yourselves, and be at peace with one another."

The fact that the Gospel of Mark also contained logia thus proved to be indisputable. That inevitably raised the question of where Mark obtained his logia material. Christian Hermann Weisse gave this answer: from the Apostle Peter, whose interpreter Mark was. Once more Weisse relied on the note about Papias in Eusebius which said that Mark "wrote just as he remembered it"[8] (*hist. eccl.* III, 39).

This statement left itself open to a serious objection. The correspondence of the wording of the logia in Mark on the one hand and in Matthew and Luke on the other was too great for the latter two to have taken it from a written source and for Mark to have taken it from an oral source. Hence the two-source theory was left with only the possibility that Mark also must have used the logia document.

The man who first made this assertion—and he did it with apodictic certainty—was the most independently minded and unsparing theological critic of his time, Heinrich Ewald (1803-75), well-known as one of the "Göttingen Seven." Although Ewald was primarily an Old Testament scholar, he stated his opinion on the question of the Gospels in several articles in his *Jahrbücher der Biblischen Wissenschaft* (1849ff) as well as in a monograph *Die drei Evangelisten, übersetzt und erklärt* (1850). Having adopted the Marcan hypothesis as his point of departure, Ewald believed it to be irrefutable.

1) that Mark must have known the sayings collection,

2) that this collection consisted exclusively of logia without any kind of narrative content.

Moreover Ewald denied the originality of the "Two Sources." In doing research on the Pentateuch he had successfully employed the principle of "strata analysis." Then, transferring this principle to Gospel research, he came to a conclusion which, as always, he announced with a determination that left no room for doubt: in the synoptic writings nine different strata can be distinguished (although we shall not go into them individually here). Ewald advanced the view that the Gospel of Mark was not available to us in its original form. Earlier the Gospel of Mark had contained long discourse sections—most conspicuously the Matthean Sermon on the Mount—but also several additional accounts of a purely narrative character including, for instance, the pericope of the centurion at Capernaum.

---

[8]οὕτως ἔνια γράψας ὡς ἀπεμνημ.

Weisse's Self-Correction

Eighteen years after Christian Hermann Weisse published his first work on the subject of Gospel research, *Die evangelische Geschichte, kritisch und philosophisch bearbeitet* (1838), he produced a second book on the subject:

*Die Evangelienfrage in ihrem
gegenwaertigen Stadium (1856).*

Ewald's views had caused Weisse to doubt the validity of his own argumentation. He still rejected the idea that Mark had knowledge of or used the logia document, and he remained steadfast in his view that the sayings source and the Gospel of Mark are two *distinct*, original documents. But he had changed his mind about attributing *all* of the extra material common to Matthew and Luke to the logia collection, and hence withdrew his former opinion.

Weisse now said that the Gospels of Matthew and Luke showed "traces of sources that had been used in both" which were "different from the Gospel of Mark, which both had taken as their basis, and also different from the contents which we have to attribute to the sayings collection of the genuine Matthew. For our purposes, the characteristics of that content must be most carefully identified."

And then Weisse admitted:

> That such traces are actually present *cannot be denied any longer by this author. He recognizes it as a defect of his work in evangelical history that he assigned to the apostolic sayings collection,* without examining more closely their inner structure and constitution or evaluating their relationship to the whole composition, *all the narrative passages which were common to the first and third Gospels, but which they did not share with Mark.* The character of the sayings collection thereby becomes a great deal more problematical than it would be under other conditions. And yet, the possibility remains that all of these narratives originally belonged to the Gospel of Mark. (p. 88; author's italics).

Thus Weisse retracted the fundamental research premise that he had proclaimed eighteen years earlier (see above, pp. 49ff). Which of the sections that he had previously assigned to the logia source were affected?

He enumerated them explicitly:

1) The words of John the Baptist.
2) The expanded form of the temptation story.

3) Those parts of the Sermon on the Mount which the detailed version (Mt. 5-7) has in common with the shorter version (Lk. 6:20-49).

4) The story of the centurion at Capernaum.

5) The embassy of John, together with the discourses associated with it by both Evangelists (Mt. ll:12-19; Lk. 7:18-25).

6) Within the narrative passage (Mt. 12:22-32; Lk. 11:14-23), whose principal contents are common to both Gospels but not to Mark, there are several passages which the first and third Gospels share among themselves but not with Mark—Mt. 12:22 and Lk. 11:14; Mt. 12:27f. and Lk. 11:19; Mt. 12:30 and Lk. 11:23 (p. 156).

Then Weisse makes an assertion which is surprising for the decisiveness with which he now rejects his former convictions.

It is quite impossible to assign the first two sections which have been presented here to the sayings collection. To do so would be to transform the collection into an evangelical narration quite similar in character to our canonical Gospels. It would also surrender the entire gain which had been secured by the only correct interpretation of the word "logia," the one presented by Schleiermacher. Surely no attentive reader of my book has overlooked the difficulties caused by the erroneous presupposition that these two sections belong to the sayings collection, as stated in the first two parts of the fifth book. The same can be said, almost as emphatically, about the last three sections, or, at the very least, about the fourth. Here, too, it is not clear how they could have been included in a collection that was confined to sayings of the Lord, which, according to all indications, is what the writing of Matthew was (p. 156 f.; author's italics).

Very well, Weisse had recanted. He had reestablished the consistent logia character of the sayings collection which he himself had used as a basis and then abandoned. But this brought him face to face once more with the fundamental problem of the Marcan hypothesis: What is the source of the additional material which is shared by the first and third Evangelists, but not by Mark? Again Weisse had to clarify this cardinal question.

His new solution was even more remarkable than the first one, which he had just abandoned: *he attributed all those sections that are common only to the Gospels of Matthew and Luke to the Gospel of Mark, including the abridged version of the Sermon on the Mount:*

Ewald, supported by reasons which are worth careful scrutiny, had pointed out *(Die drei ersten Evangelien* p. 208 f.) the probability that there was a significant gap in the text of the Gospel of Mark c. 3:19, prior to the words "and he entered a house"[9]. Ewald suggested that this gap should be filled with nothing less than the Sermon on the Mount and the story of the centurion from Capernaum. He was led to this assumption by considering subjects other than those that I deal with here. He never had any doubt that the Sermon on the Mount belonged in its entirety to the sayings collection. According to Ewald's suppositions, Mark adopted the Sermon from this collection, and the other two followed suit. Thus, he was also inclined to presuppose that the whole Sermon, as it can be read in the first Gospel, had been an original constituent part of the Gospel of Mark. We are not permitted to agree with this supposition for reasons that are stated above. We can profit from Ewald's assumption only with respect to those parts of the discourse which are common to both Gospels (*Evangelienfrage,* p. 159f.)

But Weisse did agree with Ewald that the story of the centurion from Capernaum originally stood in the Gospel of Mark. To be sure, in his *Evangelische Geschichte* Weisse had attributed the story to the sayings collection with the explanation that it was "a parable, even though it sounds like a historical report."

By 1856, however, he had changed his mind: "We are accustomed to run across such transferences in Mark, and Ewald agrees that they occur; but to presuppose such a condition in a genuine apostolic document would be completely out of the question" (p. 161).

With that Weisse outdid himself. With the same excessive zeal with which he had previously attributed historical reports to the logia source, he then edited them out and reassigned them to the Gospel of Mark. Indeed, he went even further and assigned to Mark other sections which earlier he had *not* attributed to the logia source. The pericope of the centurion from Capernaum is followed—but only in Luke—by the story of the raising of the young man of Nain; following that is the pericope of John the Baptist's inquiry. Of this Weisse argued:

Ewald assumes that the Sermon on the Mount and the story of the centurion of Capernaum originated in a textual gap following

---

[9]καὶ ἔρχονται εἰς οἶκον.

> Mark 3:19. If we accept that as the most probable assumption among all the possible ones, *then there is nothing to keep us from including as well the narrative passages that follow immediately in Luke—the raising of the young man of Nain, and the mission from John* (p. 161f.; author's italics).

By this time Weisse had really developed a taste for this kind of thing. He wanted to incorporate other parts of Luke as well into the "original Mark," including the subsequent story of the penitent woman in the house of Simon (Lk. 7:36-50) and the following passage about the "ministering women" (8:1-3), which is found only in Luke. (*ibid.*)

But apparently Weisse did not feel too comfortable about violating his own hypothesis. Ewald's argument for a "Marcan gap" was a conspicuously convenient way for him to banish forever the calamitous situation which had resulted from his first hypothesis:

> Let us add to this the fact that Mk. 3:20-21 appears entirely out of place in Mark and would fit far better before 3:31. In that case we might be justified in taking the same point of view on this section, insofar as it conforms to what we have said before. *We would prefer to think that the correspondence which exists between the first and third Gospels was mediated by an earlier version of the Marcan text, now lost, whenever it could not have been mediated by the canonical Mark* (p. 162, author's italics).

Have we read correctly? We have. It is true, Weisse now accepted an ur-Mark! To be sure, he used only the word "prefer," but what is said is said! Now, toward the end of his deduction, Weisse had gone just as far as Wilke even though he had explicitly stated, when he established the two-source theory in his first Gospel treatise, the *Evangelische Geschichte* that

> the narrative which supplemented the logia was drawn in all its major aspects *from Mark—from the very same Mark that we still have as an independent Gospel document.* We have only to continue further, as far as Mark itself is concerned, to the assertion that . . . this makes it most likely that it is the product of a single process, *independent of written predecessors (Evangelische Geschichte*, Vol. I, p. 54; author's italics).

To this somewhat hesitantly-posited ur-Mark Weisse then assigned still other passages—with noticeably less hesitancy. His earlier assignment of these passages to the sayings source apparently had left him with a certain feeling of discomfort. That had been true, for example, of the temptation story, probably because of the fact that he had re-interpreted it symbolically:

It [the temptation story], too, is in every way typical of what we encounter whenever one of Mark's parable discourses has been transferred into the sphere of external reality. But we are by no means justified in assuming that the apostolic author of the sayings collection used the same style (*Evangelienfrage* p. 164).

In order to accommodate this story in the Gospel of Mark, Weisse assumed that there was a textual gap following Mk. 1:13: "*The words 'and the angels ministered to him*[10] *are and remain completely incomprehensible at this point unless we appropriate the detailed narration as we read it in the parallel presentation of the other two Evangelists*" (p. 163; author's italics).

That is certainly true, but it is exactly what the Griesbach school had always asserted!

Thus Weisse assigned to the ur-Mark everything which in his *Evangelische Geschichte* he had attributed to the sayings collection—except for the words of John the Baptist. Would he manage to assign these, too, to "an earlier version of the Marcan text, now lost"? This presented Weisse with a serious problem. It will be recalled that he had characterized the words of John as the authentic expressions of Jesus which had been transferred to John by the Apostle *Matthew*. (See above, p. 52). Now is Weisse wanted to transfer these words to the Gospel of *Mark* (the ur-Mark), he would simultaneously have to repudiate Matthew's authorship. That, in turn, would once more raise the question: Who projected the dominical sayings upon John the Baptist?

A serious question, indeed, and in a double sense, for eighteen years earlier, when he thought it was Matthew, Weisse had written: "Now if we ask who it is that has John the Baptist utter these expressions which are borrowed from the true Christ, the answer comes . . . not without difficulty" (*Evangelische Geschichte* Vol. II, p. 7).

Weisse had managed to overcome this difficulty and at the same time to credit Matthew with particular piety, for Matthew did it "with the intention of underlining the meaning and activity of this prophetic man."

Now Weisse decided on Mark—what else could he do? However, the motive that he attributed to Mark was rather less pious.

I have already explained how little such an assumption [the original authorship of Matthew] corresponds to the true character of the sayings collection; but it is different in regard to Mark. In any case he was guilty of confusion or of false attribution (sic!), even if we hold him to account only for what we read in the text of his canonical Gospel (p. 164).

---

[10]καὶ οἱ ἄγγελοι διηκόνουν αὐτῷ.

Now Weisse had to face the question of where in the Gospel of Mark to place the words of John which he had retrieved from the sayings source. Again a difficult problem for him, especially since he himself had to admit: "Finally, with respect to the words of John the Baptist, I do not presume to claim that, in the text of Mark that lies in front of me, one can actually sense a gap" (p. 164).

But after he had declared Mark the scapegoat who had become "guilty of confusion or of false attribution," Weisse felt justified in assuming that a *new* textual gap lay behind Mark's sayings of John:

> it is obvious, therefore, that the most natural way of explaining this peculiar phenomenon is to assume the existence of a gap following Mk. 1:5 or 6 that is similar to the ones following Mk. 1:13 and 3:19; and that we should fill this gap with the above-designated apothegms of the parallel gospel accounts (p. 165).

But that hardly freed Weisse from the problems caused by his transference. Now there was no place for the verses Mt. 3:12 par Lk. 3:17 (about the winnowing-fork; wheat and chaff) for in the order assumed by the Marcan hypothesis these verses came after Mk.1:7 and 8! What was Weisse supposed to do now? Should he, two verses after the third textual gap following Mk. 1:6, assume yet a fourth behind Mk. 1:8?

Weisse found a way out, even though it was not particularly elegant. He fell back on the same radical device that Wilke had used—all too often—in order to clear the path of textual obstacles: he eliminated them. "Consequently here, too, following Mk. 1:8, we must assume that words are omitted which in the first and third Evangelists follow the words we find in Mark" (*Evangelienfrage* p. 165).

This decision may have been difficult for Weisse, and he obviously did not enjoy this kind of transaction. At the end of his laborious argument he wrote:

> I do not fail to recognize that a certain appearance of violence is inescapable in a critical procedure of this kind. I gladly admit that I made the final decision only when I had clearly come to understand that any other possible attempt to explain the phenomenon in question would have entailed even greater violence. Since it is completely impossible to assert that an absolutely complete text of Mark has been transmitted to us—one has only to think of the obviously spurious conclusion—perhaps in this case, where there are such pressing causes and constraints for employing such a procedure, it is justified to reject the reproach of unwarranted violence (*Evangelienfrage* p. 165).

What was it that Weisse wrote in his review of Wilke's *Urevangelist* about the "multitude of violent textual alterations in the form of eliminations that the author had permitted himself, particularly in the text of Mark"? There the same Weisse wrote:

> Such a procedure is even more deplorable since it must unavoidably arouse suspicion among non-specialists and, even more, in those with evil intent; for if a hypothesis demands such acts of violence in order to be established, then such a hypothesis cannot possibly have a sound foundation (*Berliner Jahrbücher für wissenschaftliche Kritik.* 1838, col. 613).

Toward a Critique of Weisse

Both of Weisse's attempts to explain the *origin* of the common extra-Marcan material in Matthew and Luke within the framework of the Marcan hypothesis must be considered failures. The logia source has proved itself incapable of accommodating elements that do not consist of dominical sayings. The "lost" earlier form of the canonical Mark, the ur-Mark which Weisse had constructed in order to explain those elements, has proved to be non-existent, and attempts to document it have long since been abandoned.

But this objective statement alone is no more satisfying in the case of Weisse than in that of Wilke. In his case, too, any general evaluation of his achievements as a Gospel scholar cannot avoid setting forth his general methods of argumentation and characterizing his scholarly disposition. In his case, too, these methods and habits affected the manner in which he reasoned. Weisse was likewise influenced by powerful subjective and emotional forces.

This was especially obvious in his numerous formulas of assurance and affirmation:

> the most perceptible; the most eloquent; the most unequivocal in the world; in the most surprising and accurate way in the world; as we trust with the utmost assurance; according to our most certain conviction; we are not afraid to express it with the utmost confidence; this assumption explains them in the most simple and natural way, while any other assumption would have to attribute them to the unenlightened caprice of the Evangelists.

As early as 1839 Ferdinand Christian Baur had pointed to Weisse's objectionable method in a review of the latter's *Evangelische Geschichte*: "This predominance of Weisse's own subjectivity, so characteristically expressed in the repeated use of the unscholarly formula "according to our most sincere conviction," does distinguish Weisse's work unfavorably from that of Strauss" (*Jahrbücher für wissenschaftliche Kritik..* 1839, col. 161ff.).

In this we are not dealing with a general phenomenon of the time, as one might presume from Baur's allusion to Strauss's diction, but rather with a distinct peculiarity of the two originators of the Marcan hypothesis.

This peculiarity of emotional exaggeration was especially conspicuous in Weisse's self-correction. In it he condemned with almost frightening exaltation the very things which previously he had set forth with equal emphasis as categorically true. It was even more astounding that Weisse appended a statement of self-justification that ended in self-praise:

> I have been prompted . . . to abandon these opinions, but in such a manner as to make it apparent that this is in complete harmony with all the general principles and presuppositions of criticism which I, too, have followed and indeed, that they alone make this abandonment possible (*Evangelienfrage* p. 155 f.).

In addition to this exaggeration of expression, Weisse's scholarly mentality was characterized by a certain unscrupulousness in demonstrating proofs. One example of this was his inadmissible appropriation of the deceased Schleiermacher for the purpose of substantiating his own point of view about Luke's usage of the logia source. Another was the frivolity with which Weisse transferred pericopes from the sayings collection to the ur-Mark, even including parts which had never before been placed there.

Moreover, Weisse was not skilled at sustaining an argument. He constantly found himself in difficulties with his hypothesis, but he tried to surmount his difficulties by employing a pseudo-argumentation which, as a rule, was so transparent as to expose its vulnerability. Examples of this include the re-interpretation of the words of John the Baptist, the temptation story, and the pericope of the centurion at Capernaum as dominical sayings. Because of this Weisse repeatedly felt inclined to ask in advance for the indulgence of the reader, and to implore understanding of the decisions he had to make in regard to the hypothesis—even if these decisions were contrary to the facts:

1) "Thus there is no other course of action than to speak out for what is most probable (for in this case absolute certainty cannot be achieved) . . . ."(See above, p. 52).

2) "In that case we might be justified . . . ." "We would prefer to think . . . ." (See above, p. 62).

3) "Hence there is the possibility of other similar gaps . . . and it may be assumed whenever, as in this case, it is demanded by such pressing circumstances" (*Evangelienfrage* p. 163).

4) "After what we have said . . . it must be more than a little startling and puzzling . . ." (See above, pp. 52f.).

5) "I do not fail to recognize that a certain appearance of violence is inescapable in a critical procedure of this kind . . . where there are *such pressing causes and constraints* for employing such a procedure..(See above, p. 64; author's italics).

All this, together with numerous corresponding cases, makes it clear that, in reality, Weisse constantly found himself and his hypothesis on the verge of calamity. In this connection it is worth noting that almost every time he himself recognized the immediate difficulty confronting his hypothesis. He saw it clearly—and drew not a single conclusion from it! On the contrary, he tried again and again to get over the particular difficulty either by some very daring action, or at worst by glossing it over. In this manner, slowly but surely, his entire argumentation grew into a system of makeshifts. Would it not have been better for Weisse to draw a different conclusion from his difficulties—i.e., to reevaluate thoroughly the whole basis of his two-source theory? As it is, however, we can only count Weisse's failure to establish the Marcan hypothesis as another misinterpretation of the Gospel.

Albert Schweitzer, in his "Geschichte der Leben-Jesu-Forschung," evaluated the relative importance of Strauss and Weisse with these words: "Weisse deserves the seat to the right of the throne" (p. 125). But this singular praise hardly coincided with Strauss's view of Weisse; he called him a "dilettante" (*Leben Jesu, Volksausgabe* p. 50) and pronounced this fitting verdict upon his methods: "Had Weisse been a better exegete, he would not have found it so easy to make the objective information before him more palatable through arbitrary interpretations . . ." (p. 50). And Ewald in no way reciprocated Weisse's high esteem of him with equally high regard. He said of him, almost contemptuously: "Weisse and several other even less capable authors of the newest breed . . ." (*Geschichte Christus' und seiner Zeit* p. 128).

The findings of our critical analysis of Weisse's reasoning have also shown that there is absolutely no justification for Schweitzer's praise of Weisse. Weisse had failed as much as Wilke in proving the Marcan hypothesis. Jülicher and Fascher did hold that Weisse and Wilke had "brilliantly inaugurated" the Marcan hypothesis, but this verdict also belongs to the fallacies of historical research. Wilke did not deserve the crown of immortality, nor Weisse the throne at the side of David Friedrich Strauss. In the wake of Wilke's fiasco and Weisse's unsuccessful self-correction, it might have been expected that the Marcan hypothesis would have died a quick death shortly after its launching by these two authors. Whatever happened to keep it alive?

The man who saved Weisse from sinking into oblivion was the "new founder of the two-source theory," Heinrich Julius Holtzmann. He said of Weisse:

> His work provided the first evidence that it was possible to portray the life of Jesus in accordance with the highest demands of historical scholarship. In order to facilitate this presentation, he made use of an excellent critical "insight" (*Die synoptischen Evangelien,* 1863 p. 28).

And he praised him further: "It might be said that Weisse rediscovered the Marcan hypothesis and supplied it for the first time with a scholarly foundation" (p. 29).

Now we shall turn to Holtzmann.

Chapter III

The Refounding of the Marcan Hypothesis

Heinrich Julius Holtzmann

Heinrich Julius Holtzmann (1832-1910) is considered to be the man who brought virtually universal recognition to the Marcan hypothesis (in the form of the two-source theory) in his *Die synoptischen Evangelien* which appeared in the year 1863. In 1856 C. H. Weisse was still hardly able to name any scholars who agreed with his own source theory. Aside from Ritschl, only Hitzig, Reuss, Thiersch, and H. A. W. Meyer had come out in favor of the Marcan hypothesis.[1]

Holtzmann had a strong influence on the academic profession by virtue of his personality and his dedication to his subject: "He knew how to attract the younger generation, again and again, as a lecturer as well as a human being." (Arnold Meyer in *RGG²* 1928, col. 2000). He was greatly esteemed as a scholar by his contemporaries. Albert Schweitzer, his best-known student, said in praise of him that he had brought the Marcan hypothesis "so close to the point of certainty that it can no longer be regarded as a mere hypothesis" (*L. J.-Forschung* p. 202).

Holtzmann preceded his voluminous work with a motto, as many others had done before him; but he did so in a somewhat different way. He appropriated a polemical expression by Adolf Hilgenfeld which the latter had

---

[1]F. Hitzig, *Über Johannes Markus und seine Schriften* (1843); Eduard Reuss, *Geschichte der Heiligen Schriften Neuen Testaments* (2nd ed., 1853); W. Thiersch, *Die Kirche im Apostolischen Zeitalter* (1852); H. A. W. Meyer, *Kritischexegetischer Kommentar über das Neue Testament* (3rd ed., 1853).

used in his recently published book *Kanon und Kritik*: "Now everyone can see the real state of the Marcan hypothesis, behind which has concentrated the main opposition to recent criticism."[2] Holtzmann gave this sentence a positive meaning:

> For my part, I take the liberty of divesting these words of their negative connotation and placing them at the head of the following investigations in the hope that they will substantiate the radiant state of health of this particular hypothesis.

When he approached his task of refounding the Marcan hypothesis, he was sometimes able to draw upon the works of his predecessors, Weisse and Wilke—but not always. He took advantage of their preliminary work, and utilized it as far as possible, especially the individual arguments. Thus quite frequently his reasoning, directly or indirectly, conformed to that of Wilke and Weisse, and in many instances the contents of his book read like a repetition of his predecessors.

On fundamental matters, however, Holtzmann moved away from Wilke's intra-synoptic solution, in spite of Bruno Bauer's panegyric. He decided in favor of Weisse's version of the two-source theory—but with essential corrections or modifications. How could it have been otherwise, given Weisse's fluctuations and vacillations about his hypothesis?

Holtzmann proceeded in this manner: he did not say that Matthew and Luke used the canonical Gospel of Mark as a source. Rather, he posited two fundamental sources, a historical source and a logia source which he designated with the Greek capital letters alpha and lambda. For simplicity's sake we shall call them A and L.

Exactly what were these two fundamental documents? On the subject of Source A, which Holtzmann consistently called the "ur-Mark," he made the following unavoidable corrections of Weisse's views:

1) Rightly, Holtzmann reassigned the pericopes which in Luke, and in Luke alone, follow the "centurion at Capernaum," i.e., the pericopes of the "young man of Nain" and the "ministering women," from the ur-Mark to a special Lucan source. Weisse, in the last version of his hypothesis, had rashly and thoughtlessly attributed them to the ur-Mark.

2) In contrast to Weisse, he assigned the pericopes "John the Baptist's inquiry" and "Jesus' testimony concerning John" not to the ur-Mark, but to the sayings collection.

---

[2]Translator's note: One must recognize the irony intended by Hilgenfeld to appreciate the point Stoldt is making about Holtzmann's use of this motto.

3) He relocated the pericope of the adulteress, Jn. 7:53-8:11 in historical source A. This pericope had been placed after Lk. 21:38 by manuscripts belonging to the Ferrar group.

4) In a similar manner he reassigned verses 28:9, 10, 16-20 in Matthew's report of the resurrection to the ur-Mark.

Consequently Holtzmann's ur-Mark (historical source A) consisted:

1) of (almost) the complete canonical Gospel of Mark,

2) of the corresponding parallel passages in Matthew and Luke,

3) of the short form of the Sermon on the Mount, which Holtzmann believed to exist in its purest form in Lk. 6:20-49,

4) of the pericope of the centurion at Capernaum,

5) of the pericope of the adulteress, Jn. 7:53-8:11,

6) of the verses Mt. 28:9, 10, 16-20.

Clearly, Holtzmann began where Weisse had left off, with an assumed ur-Mark. This ur-Mark, which did not exist as an actual source but only as an "inferred" source construction, now underwent modification as an auxiliary hypothesis. One might say that, in contrast to Weisse, Holtzmann's modification was quite ingenious. One must seriously question whether it really still deserved to be called an "ur-Mark" if it included all the passages in Matthew and Luke that are parallel to Mark, Luke's short form of the Sermon on the Mount, and the pericope of the centurion from Capernaum, which appears only in Matthew and Luke.

It is not difficult to see that this is truly a fundamental departure from Weisse's original hypothesis. The tactical advantages of positing such a "historical source A" as a prop for the Marcan theory is quite obvious. Now it is no longer the canonical Gospel of Mark which serves as the basis for Matthew and Luke, but source A. But at the same time this source A was also the source of the canonical Gospel of Mark, even though the latter formed the core of source A and was included in its entirety, except for a few verses. Therefore, according to Holtzmann, all three synoptic Gospels, Mark included, used source A and therefore constitute variations of A, either by way of omission or of addition.

How does all this work?

1) The canonical Gospel of Mark used source A exclusively and was formed solely through the omission of
   a) all the parallel passages of the first and third Evangelists corresponding to this Gospel,
   b) the Lucan Sermon on the Mount,

c) the pericope of the centurion at Capernaum,

d) the pericope of the adulteress,

e) the verses Mt. 28:9, 10, 16-20. In addition Mark had appropriated two small supplements from another source.

2) The canonical Gospels of Matthew and Luke were formed by using source A as well as source L; and also by omitting certain passages from source A, and adding others which were not present there.

This extremely shrewd train of thought provided Holtzmann with a hypothetical construction that enabled him to transfer the common extra-Marcan material in Matthew and Luke to source A in which Mark's own special material is also found. Then he could explain: "The canonical Mark had omitted them"; or he could say about the special material in Mark: "Matthew or Luke or both had disregarded them."

In both principal cases Holtzmann had the obligation to explain *why* passages were added or omitted and to offer proof for his explanations. It was not hard to guess which method Holtzmann would use—the *argumentatio secundum hypothesin* (argumentation according to the hypothesis). As an example of this let us consider the case of Holtzmann's "Luke's omissions from A," since this appears to be especially instructive about Holtzmann's method of argumentation. In this instance we are concerned with Marcan texts in A which, according to the hypothesis, had been read by Matthew *and* Luke but have parallels *only* in the Gospel of Matthew. Therefore, likewise according to the hypothesis, Luke must have eliminated them. Holtzmann "explained" this phenomenon in the following terms:

No. 30 - Jesus walking on the sea—seemed superfluous when taken with the other narrative of the tempest.

No. 31 - The miracles in the land Gennesaret were passed over because in general Luke did not like summarized reports and believed that the earlier passages of this kind were sufficient.

No. 32 - The washing of the hands—was to be replaced by the longer castigation of empty legalism (11:37-52).

No. 33 - The Canaanite woman—this might appear to be doubtful, but it could appropriately be left out since it is covered on the one hand (insofar as the acceptance of the Gentiles formed the *tertium comparationis*) by 7:2-10, and on the other hand (insofar as the antitype of the deeds of Elias is the *tertium comparationis*) by 7:11-17.

No. 34 - The deaf-mute—is to have its parallel in 11:14.

No. 35 - The feeding of the four thousand—was of no interest alongside the feeding of the five thousand, which had just been related.

No. 36 - The signs of the time—is to have its parallel in 11:29-32 and 12:54-56.

No. 37 - The warning about the leaven of the Pharisees—is still to come (12:1).

No. 38 - The blind man of Bethsaida—seemed to be a superfluous prelude to the blind man of Jericho (p. 105 f.).

Holtzmann summarized his conclusion as follows: "Hence obvious reasons of economy led to the elimination of this series of pericopes"(p. 106).

These "reasons of economy" were not exactly as obvious as Holtzmann so casually—all too casually—suggested. They were unconvincing because they were provided with no proof whatsoever. In every one of the above cases there were questions that could not be sidestepped. Why did the same or corresponding causes not also apply to Matthew and Mark, or at least to one of the two? They had also just previously presented the feeding of the five thousand. How is it that the feeding of the four thousand held their interest when "alongside the feeding of the five thousand" it held no further attraction for Luke? This brings us to the heart of the problem! Mark also presented the pericope of the blind man of Jericho. How is it that for Mark the pericope of the blind man from Bethsaida was important when for Luke it seemed a "superfluous prelude to the blind man of Jericho"? And why should the pericope of the washing of hands be replaced in Luke by the longer castigation of empty legalism (11:37-52)? Matthew had it, too, but he certainly did not leave out the "washing of hands."

None of this had any rhyme or reason. To be sure, the absence of a parallel in Luke would be contrary to the Marcan hypothesis, but this is hardly sufficient cause to offer grounds for it which are contrary to reason.

In all, Holtzmann presented forty-seven minor texts (of a total of one hundred and eighty) from the Gospel of Mark that extend beyond Matthew and Luke. He attributed all of them to A, albeit with a remarkable qualification: "However, in some cases pure additions of Mark must be acknowledged. They were added either purely for clarification . . . or else they might be historical notes, authentic passages which Mark had drawn from the traditionally transmitted text."

Now, that was exactly what Griesbach had alleged. But in the same breath Holtzmann stated: "Matthew and Luke omitted material at least as frequently."

That had not been asserted by Griesbach, but rather by Wilke (cf. his eliminations, p. 35f.). Having assigned Mark and the appropriate parallel passages to source A, Holtzmann always had the choice of both possibilities: addition or omission. His alleged source A gave him *carte blanche*! Hence, whatever he did squared with his hypothesis.

Here the decisive error was already apparent, and Holtzmann and all the other advocates of the Marcan hypothesis had been forced into it by their theory of sources: the error of neglecting to give convincing reasons why the Evangelists made their alleged additions and omissions. There was a clear danger that unwarranted assumptions would be made about the moves and thoughts of the Evangelists. If one did not want to appear an "ignoramus-ignorabimus," there remains for the exegete no other choice than the *argumentatio secundum hypothesin*—which, as we have just seen, resulted in disaster. We shall give this problem more detailed attention in Chapter V of the second part of our work under the heading "The Proof from Psychological Reflection."

For the time being we shall leave the discussion of source A. Now we shall inquire into the structure of Holtzmann's second fundamental source, source "L," and into the interrelationships of both parts. Only then shall we be in a position to make a critical analysis of Holtzmann's whole hypothetical structure.

Anyone wanting to take a closer look at Holtzmann's source L is in for a great surprise. If such a logia source is to be found at all, there can be no doubt that it must be traced to Papias' note: "So then Matthew composed *ta logia* in the Hebrew language."[3] *This is the sole literary support for the presumption of a sayings source of any kind.* For Weisse, it provided the constitutive element of his establishment of the two-source theory. The Gospels contain only one section of material which can correctly be termed a completed "composition of *ta logia*," in full conformity with Papias' note—namely, Matthew's Sermon on the Mount and Luke's short version thereof. One could have various opinions about whether this is all that Papias' note refers to or whether it is more far-reaching in character, embracing other speeches, parables, and individual sayings. However, in no case could the Sermon on the Mount be excluded; on the contrary, it had to be considered the principal element.

Holtzmann was of a different opinion:

> In order to determine the contents of this second source, one
> usually proceeds . . . from those larger passages in Matthew which

---

[3]Ματθαῖος μὲν οὖν ῾Εβραΐδι διαλέκτῳ τὰ λόγια συνετάξατο.

disrupt the coherence of source A. These include the Sermon on the Mount (ch. 5-7), the instructions to the disciples (ch. 10), the discourse about the relationship of the Gospels to the generation in which they appear (ch. 11), the collection of parables (ch. 13), the fragments about the duties of the Christian community (ch. 18), the woes against the Pharisees (ch. 23), and the eschatological discourse (ch. 24 and 25) . . . (p. 128).

Then Holtzmann went into the subject in greater detail:

But, regardless of how it is approached, this whole conception of the sayings collection is untenable. To regard a composition consisting of Mt. 5-7, 10, 11, 13, 18, 23-5 as an original work would be absolutely incredible and unsupportable. It would be possible to do so only by depending, consciously or unconsciously, on the traditional priority of our supposedly apostolic Matthew with respect to the relationship of source L to our first Gospel . . . We, on the contrary, will demonstrate that the starting point for research into the second source may be sought with infinitely greater chances for success among these same passages as they appear in Luke (p. 129).

Later Holtzmann once more expressly emphasized this principle and praised his reconstruction of this sayings source as the product of his special scholarly insight: "In thus keeping primarily to Luke in our description of source L, we distinguish ourselves most decisively from previous attempts to reconstruct the sayings collection" (p. 141).

Thus the Gospel of Luke was supposed to form the nucleus of source L. But exactly what part of Luke was Holtzmann talking about? He had, after all, assigned the short version of the Sermon on the Mount (Lk. 6:20-49) to historical source A, the ur-Mark. Holtzmann decided in favor of the "travel narrative": "As such it is the great interpolation, in which the bulk of the material contained in the second source is preserved" (p. 141).

What other choice was there, after Holtzmann had assigned Luke's only coherent and fundamental section to the ur-Mark? Now it is really quite instructive to discover just why Holtzmann concluded that the canonical Mark passed over Luke's Sermon on the Mount and excluded it from his newly-formed Gospel. According to the hypothesis, Mark drew only upon source A [the ur-Mark] and he must have seen it there. Holtzmann offered the following reason:

The spoken discourses of Christ, which probably had been recorded first, are much less prominent in Mark than in Matthew and Luke. To be sure, at times Mark omitted longer discourses in A, or else he shortened them or left out transitional material, which rendered the discourse unclear. *The Sermon on the Mount in particular was too long for him* (p. 116; author's italics).

The weakness and untenability of Holtzmann's argument is already evident. It forces him to take refuge in a line of thought that is scarcely convincing. Are we to suppose that Mark left out the Sermon on the Mount because it was too long for him? Against this is the fact that the synoptic apocalypse (Mk. 13:5-37) and the parable chapter (Mk. 4:1-34) were not too long for Mark, even though they were, respectively, three and five verses longer than the Lucan Sermon on the Mount.

Moreover, Holtzmann betrayed his own insecurity in this matter when he later offered his readers the choice of yet another explanation: "Perhaps he (Mark) left out the Sermon on the Mount as much because of its *Ebionite exordium* as because of its length" (p. 386).

If that were the case, it would seem peculiar that the author of the ur-Mark, whom Holtzmann considered to be Mark, the pupil of Peter, did not object to this; otherwise he would not have included the Sermon on the Mount in his ur-Mark.

What, then, did Holtzmann think about the origin of *Matthew's* Sermon on the Mount? The first thing he said is that it is "not to be conceived of as a continuum" (p. 104). No doubt he was correct if he meant to say that it did not represent a coherent discourse. However, the Sermon on the Mount was recorded in the first Gospel as a "continuum," i.e. as an uninterrupted, coherent "composition of *ta logia*," the only one in the Gospel that genuinely fits this description.

Holtzmann's hypothetical construction then left him with only one avenue of escape, that of designating Matthew's Sermon on the Mount as a "compilation" (p. 174). Hence he envisaged Matthew having combined the subsections in the following manner: From the ur-Mark he extracted 5:12, 5:39-52; 7:12; 5:44-48; 7:1-2; 7:3-5; 7:16-21; 7:24-27.

From the sayings source, or else from "other sources," he extracted all of the remaining texts between 5:13 and 7:25.

In detail, then, the composition of Matthew's Sermon on the Mount looked like this: Holtzmann explained that Matthew had drawn the historical introduction and the general substance from A and then "modified" it. In his own words:

> . . . which source he expanded by anticipating some statements recorded in other sections of A and by working in a much larger

number taken from L and other sources, either by fitting them in as occasion arose or by grouping them according to thematic similarity (p. 174).

This, however, threw an obstacle in the path of Holtzmann's hypothesis. Neither in L nor in A could he accommodate those logia that are without parallel passages in Luke and Mark. He was left with no other choice than to ascribe them to the "other sources" of the Evangelists. At issue were the following words of the Master: Mt. 5:14, 16, 17, 19-24, 27, 28, 33-38; 6:1-8, 16-18, 34; 7:6, 15, 21.

To be sure, it was very convenient, but scarcely justifiable, for Holtzmann to ascribe these logia to "other" unidentified sources, just because he could not derive them from either of his alleged sources, A or L. Holtzmann left open the questions of which sources were involved and what their characteristics were: "Where Matthew obtained the material which formed the basis of Sermon on the Mount No. 4 remains unclear" (p. 161f). By "No. 4" Holtzmann meant the previously cited passages in Matthew that have no parallels in Luke or Mark.

In other words: his account of the sources of the Matthean Sermon on the Mount is incomplete. It was small consolation that he identified the Evangelist Matthew as the author of at least those logia about which he knew nothing more: "In these two points alone is the first Gospel truly original" (p. 162).

The second point was the discourse against the Pharisees. Here Holtzmann saw Matthew's Sermon on the Mount as having been formed by the following modifications: Luke's four beatitudes in A were brought up to seven by Matthew. Those in A that were specifically directed toward the disciples were "transformed into general sentences" (p. 175). The logia of light and salt (Mt. 5:13-16) showed a fusion of A and L "with special traditions." In regard to "Jesus' fundamental attitude towards the law" he recognized only verse 18 as originating in source L, while the remainder he ascribed "to Matthew's enlistment of a lesser, indeterminable (sic!) source."

According to Holtzmann, Mt. 5:21-48, which he called the "seven examples of the true fulfillment of the law," had been compiled "from A, L, and other traditions." The same was true of the "seven true means of virtue" in Mt. 6:1-7, 12. Holtzmann maintained that the conclusion of the Sermon on the Mount (7:13-27) was compiled by the author of the Gospel of Matthew as follows:

> Consisting primarily of a number of appropriately selected paraenetic segments from L Lk. 6:43-45=Mt. 7:16-20 which, how-

ever, appear to be extensively modified by the relationship that
Matthew gives them to the false prophets; specifically Mt. 7:19, 20
was an addition; A Lk. 6:46=Mt. 7:21; A Lk. 6:47-49=Mt. 7:24-27,
so that the independence is most pronounced in Mt. 7:13-15, 19-
23, where, moreover, Mt. 7:22, 23 is an adaptation of L Lk. 13:25-
27 (p. 178).

Of the closing statement (Mt. 7:28, 29) Holtzmann asserted: "Formed by
Matthew from A (Mk. 1:22=Lk. 4:32), although after such a long speech
directed against the Pharisees it was hardly the place for special remarks
about his manner of preaching or for an explanation of why he preached
differently from the Pharisees" (p. 178).

Furthermore, he stated that Matthew had relocated the Sermon on the
Mount. At first Holtzmann had placed it as No. 17 in A, following the
selection of the twelve (Mk. 3:13-19), but now he maintained that "Matthew
advanced it from the later context of A to the beginning of the public ministry
of Jesus."

In view of Holtzmann's assumption that Matthew composed the Sermon
on the Mount in this extraordinarily complex fashion, it is instructive to
compare this with the criticisms that Holtzmann had leveled at Ewald's thesis
that Mark not only knew the sayings source but also used it:

But Mark, who in our view expressed himself in such a simple
manner, came across in Ewald's work as presenting an extremely
artificial mixture, inasmuch as 1:9-20; 9:2-13, 30-32; 10:1-31; 11:1-
21; 12:13-37 supposedly originated in the earliest Gospel, our
source A while 1:4-8; 3:23-29; 4:3-32; 6:7-11; 8:27-9:1, 33-50;
11:27-12:12; 12:38-40; 13:1-14:2 were supposedly drawn from L
(p. 138).

If Holtzmann characterizes this as "an extremely artificial mixture," what
then was one to say about his view of the composition of the Matthean
Sermon on the Mount? One can see what discrepancies he was prepared to
accept in order to salvage the Marcan hypothesis. This was probably
Holtzmann's final and decisive reason for holding that the essential portions
of the logia document were found, not in the Gospel of Matthew but in Luke.
Thus, to him, it was Luke's travel narrative which was really to be regarded as
the place where source L would be found.

Apart from this, however, he ascribed no constitutive influence whatever
to source L in the development of the structure of the Gospels of Matthew and
Luke. That influence he assigned solely to source A: "On the contrary, in
Matthew as well as in Mark and Luke the outline of the whole is derived from

A. Only the additional discourse material that goes beyond Mark must be attributed to the use of L" (p. 137).

By this time Holtzmann's aim was already apparent. The fact that he accepted Mark alone as the determining element in the structure of all three Gospels had uncommonly important consequences for the discourse material: the entire considerable discourse material which Matthew and Luke had in common with Mark, all the speeches, parables, and single logia were supposedly derived, not from logia source L, but rather from historical source A! Any additional logia elements present were only interspersions in the framework of source A.

What was Holtzmann trying to achieve with this? He was attempting to counter the claim that Mark, too, must have used the sayings source if his Gospel contains so much discourse material. Clearly, Holtzmann was trying to out-maneuver Ewald. The latter had argued that the sayings source was the foundation for all three synoptic authors because he recognized that, even on the basis of the Marcan hypothesis, this assumption could not be circumvented.

This, however, was something that Holtzmann could not and would not admit any more than Weisse, since to do so would sink the entire Marcan hypothesis. Consequently he declared Ewald's assumption unnecessary, maintaining that Mark alone was completely adequate to explain the discourse material common to all three synoptic Gospels: "However, the situation neither supports nor justifies this (Ewald's) procedure, because—as has been shown—the passages which Matthew and Luke have in common with Mark require only a single common source" (p. 138).

At this point, however, Holtzmann's version of the hypothesis raised an unavoidable question. If source A had been used by all three synoptic authors, but source L had been used only by Matthew and Luke and not by Mark, was Mark entirely unacquainted with source L? Surprisingly enough, Holtzmann answered in the negative. This, in turn, led almost inquisitorially to a further question: why did Mark not also use source L, just as Matthew and Luke did?

To this question Holtzmann gave the following answer:

> But the relationship of our second Gospel (which embraces less discourse material than does source A) to source L is best explained by the assumption that Mark intended to do more than simply edit source A. At the same time he wanted to produce a work which would function as a complementary companion to a book containing the words of Jesus—our second source—which

was already in the hands of the community. Thus it must be assumed that Mark was acquainted with the words of Jesus (p. 385).

Then Holtzmann introduced Hitzig and Credner as his principal witnesses:

> Hitzig (*Über Johannes*, p. 122) remarked that the logia referred to in 8:38 were not further specified. Rather, the author who was acquainted with them presumed that his readers were, too. The author was completely aware that he had achieved little in a didactic sense, 4:22,23; 12:28, quite as if he intended to stimulate his readers to investigate further (Credner, *Einleitung*, p. 110). Mark retained only the parable collection, which was not present in L, and the eschatological discourse, which stood quite independently alongside the two eschatological discourses in L. Otherwise, Mark provided only as many of the words of Jesus as seemed absolutely necessary in any given situation, while he avoided everything which could have obstructed in any way the reader's view of the active ministry of Jesus. In Mark, Jesus always spoke in relation to historical events, present or future. His words were externally motivated, brief, and decisive expressions which further illuminated the actual situation which had occasioned them or pointed toward a real situation, usually without a hint of doctrine. All this leads to the conclusion that Mark knew that his readers were acquainted with the second source. That he himself had knowledge of this source is clear from what has been said above about Mark having combined the beginning of source A with the beginning of source L (p. 385).

Thus far Heinrich Julius Holtzmann. Can it be that he was trying to produce evidence against his own two-source theory? If ever anything were designed to reduce the theory *ad absurdum*, it was Holtzmann's first aid. Mark was supposed to have known the logia source as well as Matthew and Luke did. But why, then, this discrepancy in the ways in which they used it? By contrast to the others, are we to suppose that Mark did not make use of this source? Who would agree with Holtzmann? The first and third Evangelists faced exactly the same problem that Mark did. Why were the conclusions they drew from it entirely different from Mark's?

Holtzmann alleged that Mark wanted only to supplement L. Now what had Holtzmann himself said about the intentions of the other two Evangelists when they took a portion of L and combined it with A? He expressly affirmed that for Matthew and Luke, as much as for Mark, the outline was drawn from

A; only the "additional discourse material" not present in Mark had to be "attributed to the use of L."

But this hardly appears to make sense. Why did they not adopt the same time- and work-saving procedure as Mark? After all, Holtzmann himself said that Mark "knew that his readers were acquainted with" the logia source and cited it as the reason why Mark decided not to take full advantage of source L. If Mark did know this, as Holtzmann alleged, then inevitably Matthew and Luke could have surmised the same thing. Why did they go to the great trouble of combining the "additional discourse material," with which their readers were supposedly already acquainted, with A—especially since their efforts took such radically divergent directions, and required such extraordinarily complex methods that Holtzmann himself had trouble analyzing and differentiating them? The whole argument is riddled with inconsistencies.

In the second place: if Mark presumed that his readers had knowledge of the logia source, how does one explain the fact that he eliminated the religious and ethical heart of Jesus' preaching, the Sermon on the Mount, from A when he set down his canonical Gospel? Did he intend to withhold this sermon from his readers? According to the hypothesis, the Sermon was not included in the logia source L which "his readers were acquainted with." Nor was it present in the canonical Gospel of Mark. Consequently, his readers could not have been aware of the Sermon on the Mount. Or did Mark perhaps know that Matthew and Luke had retained it when they used A, and feel that it was therefore unnecessary for him to do so? The opposite was true. Holtzmann maintained unequivocally and explicitly: "Our investigation has proved that Mark could not have known Matthew or Luke" (p. 388).

It follows that the Sermon on the Mount must have been lost to the readers of the Gospel of Mark and the logia document; for if, according to the results of Holtzmann's investigations, Mark could not have known Matthew and Luke, they must have been even less accessible to simple readers.

In the third place: if Mark in editing A, in Holtzmann's words, "at the same time wanted to produce a work which would function as a complementary companion to a book containing the words of Jesus—our second source—which was already in the hands of the community," then the question is: "*Whatever happened to that book*?" Because if it was already "in the hands of the community" it could not have simply disappeared without a trace. Some kind of information about its whereabouts would have come down to us, or some sort of written evidence would have been preserved of its existence in the community.

Furthermore, if Mark was able to assume that his readers had knowledge of this work, as Holtzmann claimed, then this could mean only that it predated the Gospel of Mark. It would not only have commanded as much respect as the canonical Gospels which were transmitted to us, but it would have been even more venerated due to its greater antiquity and therefore most certainly would not have been lost. How, then, could it have become lost to the community? And how was it possible that not the slightest mention about its use in the community had ever been passed on to us? The answer was simple. Holtzmann's allegations about the use of the logia source in the community were utterly unsubstantiated. They served the purpose of supporting his version of the Marcan hypothesis—nothing more.

In the fourth place: Mark, according to Holtzmann, intended to produce a work which was supposed "to function as a complementary companion" to the logia document. And he "provided only as many of the words of Jesus as seemed absolutely necessary in any given situation." If one asks further: just how much was "absolutely necessary in any given situation," the answer would be: exactly what is in the Gospel of Mark. Here we have a classic *petitio principii* of the kind we have already encountered in Wilke.

Holtzmann's attempt to minimize the quantitative importance of the sayings material in Mark cannot be reconciled with his earlier assertion that the Gospel of Mark formed the core of the parable chapter, Mt. 13,

> which is nothing other than an expansion and elaboration of A (Mk. 4:1-20); as well as of the instruction discourse (A) Mk. 6:7-11=Lk. 9:1-6 (Mt. 10 appears to be a fusion of this with extensive information from L), as well as of the attack on the scribes and Pharisees (Mt. 23), which emerged from a combination of L with A (Mk. 12:38-40); as well as of the eschatological discourse (Mt. 24-25)—a vast superstructure compared to the simple memorial in Mk. 13 (p. 141 ff.).

The whole questionable manner of Holtzmann's argumentation becomes obvious when we add here all of Mark's individual logia, of which a few are his sole possession (see above, p. 57). He is justified neither by the general rules of objectivity nor by his line of reasoning to distinguish so sharply between a purely historical source and a pure sayings source, of which he stated:

> The differences in their contents were of a kind which demanded either an intensification of the differences by reducing A to purely historical material (since L contained nothing but sayings material); or a complete giving up of these differences by attempting to combine the sources, as was done by Matthew and Luke (p. 387).

But that is simply not correct. The Gospel of Mark was positively not the result of "reducing A to purely historical material" (see above, p. 57f.). Nor was he any closer to the truth about source L, his statements about its "uniform character according to which it should contain only authentic sayings of Jesus" notwithstanding. This can be exhibited by a striking example. When he attempted to reconstruct source L, Holtzmann pointed out that in order to determine its beginning, one of Weisse's previously held opinions had to be examined; i.e., that the speech of John the Baptist which was missing in Mark belonged to the logia source. Holtzmann noted that Weisse's decision to retract the opinion was fully justified, but then he added, surprisingly: "However, the mistake was based on correct intuition" (p. 142).

And now to our astonishment we read: "Because the first long section which not only Luke but . . . also Matthew drew from L referred, in fact, to John the Baptist."

Our astonishment increases as we read further:

> Just as A commenced with the appearance of John the Baptist, so L began with an expression of Jesus about the importance and value of John (the Baptist) with reference to the words "the beginning of the Gospel"[4] Lk. 7:18-35=Mt. 11:2-11, 16-19. *But since these words had to be motivated by John's inquiry, they constituted a historical introduction which Luke enlarged according to his custom* (p. 143; author's italics).

That is to say that Holtzmann reduced both himself and his definition of source L *ad absurdum.* He did exactly what Weisse had done, even though he had just finished congratulating him for withdrawing his first opinion. Now he portrayed his own source L, which he still acknowledged to consist "solely of discourse material," as beginning with a historical introduction of not inconsiderable size—to be specific, Lk. 7:18-21:

> The disciples of John told him of all these things. And John, calling to him two of his disciples, sent them to the Lord, saying, "Are you he who is come, or shall we look for another?" And when the men had come to him, they said, "John the Baptist has sent us to you, saying 'Are you he who is come, or shall we look for another?' " In that same hour he cured many diseases and plagues and evil spirits, and on many that were blind he bestowed sight. And he answered them. . . .

Now there are at least two opinions about the "logia." They may be viewed as consisting solely of "pure," i.e., unadorned words of the Master as we find

---

[4] ἀρχὴ τοῦ εὐαγγελίου.

them in Matthew's Sermon on the Mount. Or we might view them as including short historical introductions or transitional passages. Holtzmann frequently took the latter position and upheld it in principle:

> It is clear that these brief and general historical statements, which were attached only to a few fragments, could be combined without difficulty with the largely unchronological and loose topical order of these logia (p. 136).

That may be conceded. But without any doubt, the historical report about John the Baptist's inquiry did not conform to this. It could not be minimized as a "minor historical introduction," measured against Holtzmann's own postulate that such links had to be "restricted to only the most essential cases" and would be permissible only *"where the author of L would otherwise have had to omit the saying in question"* (p. 134; author's italics).

But the fact that this was not the case here can be deduced from the parallel passage in Matthew (11:2-3): "Now when John heard in prison about the deeds of Christ, he sent word by his disciples and said to him, 'Are you he who is to come, or shall we look for another?' "

That is all, and it would have been quite sufficient as a historical introduction. It also proves that in Luke we are not dealing with "a minor historical introduction" employed "where it was absolutely essential," or "where the author . . . would otherwise have had to omit the specific saying in question." That is not the case, as the parallel in Matthew shows. And it was a badly disguised pretense when Holtzmann added to his statement about Matthew's historical introduction the phrase "which Luke enlarged according to his custom." This "custom" is simply not to be documented in Luke. Actually, Holtzmann has only one other example in the form of the dominical saying: "He who loves father or mother more than me . . . ." In Mt. 10:37 this passage stands within the framework of the discourse on the mission of the Twelve, but in Luke it appears as a single logion (14:26). There it is introduced by a brief notice: "Now great multitudes accompanied him; and he turned and said to them."

Holtzmann labeled this "a brief transitional passage stemming from Luke's *horror vacui*, which we encounter frequently in his writing" (p. 155). A lovely phrase, but factually unconvincing. The fact is that unlike Matthew, Luke did not bring together the words of the Master into groups of sayings but preferred instead to present them as individual logia. Be that as it may, it was utterly impermissible to assign the Lucan report about John the Baptist's inquiry to sayings source L as "a short historical introduction" that had been "enlarged according to [Luke's] custom." Here Holtzmann unquestionably violated his own source hypothesis. Of L he said that it "contained only authentic sayings of Jesus" (p. 142); then, in the same context, he himself declared that to go beyond that principle would "require one to sacrifice the uniform character of the second source." Here, on the subject of John the Baptist's inquiry, Holtzmann's self-consolation could not gain acceptance. The only time it could possibly be conceded would be in regard to very small introductions: "The assumption must be restricted to only the most essential cases" (p. 133 f.).

Now that we have acquainted ourselves with the structure of Holtzmann's two fundamental sources, we are in a position to sketch out the "interrelationships" and the "interdependencies" of both parts. We shall demonstrate them with two striking examples. Then, in conclusion, we shall offer a comprehensive, overall judgment of the value, the justification and the evidential power of Holtzmann's version of the hypothesis.

The first example concerns the Sermon on the Mount. It represents a special kind of hypothetical difficulty, in addition to those already mentioned. Holtzmann had placed Luke's short version as part of the original contents of A (ur-Mark), adding: "revised by Matthew" (p. 5). Now, to be sure, Luke's Sermon on the Plain has its counterpart in Matthew's Sermon on the Mount, though by no means in exactly the same order. And yet, two verses of Luke's version (6:39 and 6:40) do not reappear in connection with Mt. 5-7. To be sure, they are in the first Gospel, not in the Sermon on the Mount, but in Mt. 15:14 and Mt. 10:24-25.

Thus Holtzmann, having assigned Luke's version of the Sermon on the Mount to the ur-Mark, naturally found his hypothesis confronted with calamity, and he had no one to blame but himself. Not that he found the difficulty the least bit insurmountable. His clever composition of the sources offered him the possibility of extricating himself. Holtzmann had only to juggle the contents of his hypothesis a bit, and for him the problem ceased to exist. To be specific, when he fitted together the sources in his hypothesis he had included Luke's version in A, but, as a precautionary measure, *without* the two verses which did not have a corresponding parallel in Matthew. And what did he do with them once he had removed them from A? He transferred them to L and disposed of them in proper order. Then it could be claimed that Matthew and Luke had extracted these two verses from sayings source L and placed them in different parts of their Gospels; Luke in the Sermon on the Mount, but Matthew elsewhere! Very clever of Holtzmann, but—even within the framework of a two-source theory—not especially credible.

The second example is even more instructive concerning Holtzmann's method of moving back and forth between the two sources, of making exchanges, first with one side, then the other, and of wriggling to and fro, always in the service of his hypothesis. The example chosen is the pericope about the sending out of the disciples. Luke gives the report in two parts. One speaks of the sending out of the Twelve (9:1-6 par Mk. 6:6-13), the other of the sending out of the Seventy (10:1-12). Matthew reports the delegation of the disciples in the form of the great missionary discourse (10:1-12).

Holtzmann brought all of this into line with his hypothesis in the following manner: Luke's report of the sending out of the Twelve, which has an equivalent parallel in Mark, he allocated to his source A, as was to be expected. On the other hand, the sending out of the Seventy, which Luke alone presents, he transferred to source L. And then he argued:

> For example, it was *simply a matter of literary composition when Matthew, shunning repetition,* merged Jesus' words to the Twelve, as Matthew found them in A, with the speech to the Seventy as presented in Luke 10:3-12 (p. 137; author's italics).

But immediately the question arises: How did Holtzmann know that Matthew shunned repetition? Luke, for his part, did not fuse the sending out of the Twelve with that of the Seventy. Therefore *he* certainly could not have shunned repetition. Perhaps, though, this was related to the *horror vacui* which Holtzmann would have liked to impute to him. But this cannot be true either, because Luke shunned repetition of the second feeding miracle, as Holtzmann has explicitly maintained. Why should Matthew have done so when Luke did not do so at this point?

It is not difficult to recognize how Holtzmann arrived at such an untenable position. He had transferred the sending out of the Twelve to A because it also appeared in Mark, but he had transferred the sending out of the Seventy to L because it did not appear in Mark. Since he regarded both A and L as sources of Matthew and Luke, and since Luke presents both reports but Matthew only one, Holtzmann was obliged to offer some reason. Without much ado Holtzmann constructed the previously mentioned assertion (". . . shunning repetition, merged . .") without being able to make it even slightly probable—not to speak of proving it. It is simply absurd that Matthew should have "shunned" the minor trouble of repeating something and then have burdened himself with the much more difficult, complicated, and time-consuming task of combining two reports. This is why Holtzmann resorted to psychologizing arguments to reconcile this with his hypothesis: at one time Luke felt no inclination to repeat material (the second feeding miracle); the next time it was Matthew (in the second missionary report).

Holtzmann had transferred Luke's version of the sending out of the Seventy to source L because it did not have a parallel in the Gospel of Mark. Now if source L, the "sayings source," were to make any sense at all, i.e., actually contained sayings, then there was no other logical conclusion than for Holtzmann to classify the entire great sending-out discourse as part of L! But that he did not do. Rather, he transferred the passage that has a parallel in Mark (verses 10:1, 9-11, 14) to A. Then Matthew was supposed to have taken the rest from L, where he had found it in the "sending out of the Seventy"!

Then Holtzmann said of this impossible merging of sources that it was "simply a matter of literary composition." In no way did he perceive this ingenious compilation to be an "extremely artificial mixture," which is what he had said about Ewald's assertion that Mark had used the sayings source (see above, p. 78). When it came to his own combinations of sources, as here, Holtzmann saw the matter in quite different light:

> Mark 6:11 ("for a testimony against them"[5]) brought Ewald to the conclusion that Matthew's great missionary discourse had come from L; although it was missing from Mt. 10:14 it had been added in 10:18. But on the other hand, how clear the situation becomes when Lk. 9:3 5 is seen to stem from A, as the entire context proves, while the passage Lk. 10:2-12 whose parallels in Mark show themselves to be insertions there too, is viewed as coming from a second source which only Matthew and Luke had in common (p. 138f.).

However, we cannot be convinced that Holtzmann's view of the situation is any clearer than Ewald's. If one is prepared to accept the logia document as one of the two sources in the two-source theory, then one cannot avoid the fact that Mark knew and used this sayings source, as Ewald correctly recognized.

But Holtzmann could not admit that without sacrificing the character of his source A as the supporting structure of both Matthew and Luke, thereby making Mark itself a secondary source. His rejection of the force of Ewald's logic showed that with respect to the Marcan hypothesis—he made the same mistake as Weisse when the latter explained: "We are not permitted to agree with his (Ewald's) supposition . . ." (see above, p. 61).

Toward a Critique of Holtzmann

Holtzmann's re-establishment of the Marcan hypothesis depended entirely upon the hypothetical structure which forms the basis of his complex theory. Wilke had sought a solution to the synoptic problem in existing sources, the canonical Gospels, which were subjected to critical textual

---

[5]εἰς μαρτύριον αὐτοῖς.

analysis in order to furnish an understanding of their reciprocal relationships. Holtzmann approached the subject from a different direction. He erected a theoretical superstructure with two imaginary entities which he endowed with the character of primary sources: A and L. He asserted that the first one corresponded to the ur-Mark, and that the second one was identical with the logia collection, the only literary proof of which was Papias' well-known note.

Although Holtzmann regarded these basic documents as the constituent factors of the two-source theory, he did not endow them with equal importance, as was the case with Weisse's two sources, the existing Gospel of Mark and the inferred logia document. In Holtzmann's theory there is a fundamental shift of emphasis to Mark, in a quantitative as well as in a qualitative respect.

In Holtzmann's view, the "ur-Mark" source is absolutely dominant. It embraces not only the canonical Gospel of Mark but also all of the corresponding parallel texts in the Gospels of Matthew and Luke, as well as the Lucan Sermon on the Mount.

In comparison, the logia source with its independent contents is quantitatively quite insignificant. Its only essential constituents are logia and a series of sayings from the Lucan travel narrative, since Holtzmann has excluded the extensive connected complex of logia of both Sermons on the Mount, as well as *all the logia in the Gospel of Mark*, including the discourses and parables. He maintains that Matthew and Luke drew this latter group in its entirety directly from the Gospel of Mark and not from the sayings source. During the process of transcription the first and the third Evangelists enlarged and partially modified the text by adding additional material from L.

As a consequence of this intra-synoptic shift of gravity, Holtzmann's sayings source is difficult to grasp in a concrete sense and has only minimal formative weight of its own. Moreover, it plays no role in influencing the structure and composition of the first and third Gospels, as Holtzmann himself had stressed (see above, p. 74f.).

And so, the balance between Mark and the logia, which was maintained in C. H. Weisse's formulation of the two-source theory, has been shifted so far in favor of Mark that their formative weight and relative influence are now in a state of radical disequilibrium. Here an unavoidable question arises: why did Holtzmann make this gravitational shift within the two-source theory, and why did he deprive the logia source of its formative weight? It is unmistakable that he created his entirely theoretical source construction in support of Marcan priority. And there was no doubt that his two fundamental sources in the form he gave them were neither provable nor even tangible. Rather, they were theoretical constructions and had never existed in an historical sense. With this, the whole structure of Holtzmann's hypothesis collapses.

The direct consequence of this faulty construction was that Holtzmann had to support the structure of his hypothesis by resorting to a series of moves of obvious academic impropriety such as we have observed again and again during the course of our investigations: the indefensible removal of Matthew's Sermon on the Mount from the logia source and its absolute dismemberment and emasculation; the dislocation of the sayings source from the Gospel of matthew to the Gospel of Luke, in sharp opposition to the only unequivocal literary foundation in Papias; the shifting of the Lucan Sermon on the Mount to the historical source ur-Mark; the recognition that Mark knew of the logia source, but the denial that he used it; the untenable argument that this was because Mark wanted to write only "supplements" to it because he knew that the logia were "used by the community"—all these are unambiguously self-serving assertions that are simply unarguable. Then, too, there are problems of proof that are part and parcel of the structure of Holtzmann's hypothesis, which unavoidably force constant shifting and changes of course because the textual facts could not be reconciled with the hypothesis, first on one side, then on the other.

One is justified in asking: why does Holtzmann burden himself with all these difficulties? What are his more profound reasons or motivations? If we are to expose the secrets of his theoretical source composition, we must track down, like a detective, his preliminary deliberations and calculations. In fact, we are dealing with a hypothesis whose strategy has been thoroughly thought through and worked out in its every detail—almost in the manner of a general staff, one might say—with the goal of affirming the validity of the Marcan hypothesis.

That can be demonstrated with the example of the "ur-Mark." Ever since the time of Griesbach's thesis and Wilke's and Weisse's counter-thesis, the basic synoptic problem could be summed up in a single cardinal question: did Mark use Matthew and Luke, or did they use Mark? That is the decisive point upon which everything else depends. That question must form the starting point—and its answer the final goal of any investigation.

How did Holtzmann tackle this life-or-death question? Far from confronting it, he avoided it by refusing to make the subject of his examinations the direct relationship of Matthew and Luke to Mark and the other way around. Rather, from the very start he gave the Gospel of Mark an assured place in his basic document, where, with all its mass and weight, it formed without interruption the principal part and the nucleus of that document.

On the other hand, Matthew and Luke still had to take shape. This took place essentially on the basis of Mark, who supplied them with a complete structure, a full narrative, and all his logia. The rest they extracted from L or "other sources." What had happened to the cardinal synoptic problem? Naturally, Mark was not affected by such a problem. Since Holtzmann had placed his Gospel in source A, it re-emerged unchanged and intact. But Matthew and Luke were demonstrably dependent on Mark, according to Holtzmann's hypothesis. Mark was their source. In this way Holtzmann "solved" the synoptic problem in his own fashion.

But was it really solved? No, Holtzmann had merely erected a theoretical stage-set which did not live up to its promises. It only created an illusion. For if one were to ask, "Does Mark possess priority or posteriority?" Holtzmann can reply: "unquestionably priority, since he comprises the real substance of source A from which the other two draw their material and at the same time provides their supporting structure." And if one were to ask further, "Is Mark then an original or a secondary source?" Holtzmann would again be able to answer: "Original certainly. From the very beginning Mark was part of source A, and he remains what he was then—unchanged and unchangeable. But the others, Matthew and Luke, are derived from him. Mark was the original source; the others are sources which follow him."

Holtzmann, having avoided the issue of direct verification by playing according to the rules of his hypothesis, could now attempt to "prove" indirectly the validity of his Marcan hypothesis with the aid of ingeniously constructed hypotheses. But this procedure was by no means meant to help solve the synoptic problem dispassionately and carefully from the perspective of pure objectivity. It was only a hypothetical construction in favor of Mark.

That Holtzmann was motivated by this intention can be deduced from the fact that he did not take issue with any other hypothesis—except for Griesbach's. To this purpose he devoted a special section thirteen pages long (p. 113-126) and placed at the head of part fifteen of his fourth chapter on "The Linguistic Usage of the Synoptic Authors" the polemic title "Against Griesbach's Hypothesis."

In this section he launched a general attack against Griesbach, and ended his argument by staking his whole painstakingly constructed hypothesis on a single card. In a surprising move he played his trump against Griesbach by apparently agreeing with him:

> In fact, Mark did have a text which seems to conform now with Matthew, now with Luke. Often it contains in the same verse elements of both texts, as, for instance, chapter 2:13-22, in which

verses 13-19 are closer to Matthew, while 20-22 come closer to Luke, and 18 and 21 represent a mixture (p. 344).

And further:

> Indeed, as a rule Mark agrees with both of them wherever the two are in harmony; with only one whenever the other diverged. This, to be sure, created the appearance that Mark copied the co-writer who had not deviated. What one writer leaves out of the text Mark appears to borrow from the other; or if one adds something, Mark joins the other in the omission (p. 344).

Holtzmann's use of the words "seems" and "appearance" shows that his extensive concession to Griesbach was not sincere, but a carefully calculated rhetorical trick. This became evident when he reached out to strike the decisive blow: "But such a relationship of Mark to the other two texts not only does not contradict our findings, rather, *given these findings,* it is exactly what we should expect" (p. 344; author's italics).

With this blow Holtzmann believed he had disarmed his opponent. But he was mistaken. In making this bald attempt at inverting the Griesbach theory and usurping it for his own benefit he found it necessary to attach a trifling-sounding, but in terms of content very significant, condition: "given these findings"—Holtzmann's "findings." And if they could not be accepted as given?! As we demonstrated, they could not be. Holtzmann had staked everything on one card—and lost! Since his "findings" could not be presupposed, then according to his own logic, they had to be reversed.

A little further on in his argumentation he himself had to admit this indirectly by stating:

> Once they had become accustomed to depend on the first source (A), nothing was more natural than for Matthew and Luke to be influenced in their independent works to a certain degree by the linguistic usage of A. It is this easily verified fact which has given rise to the *illusion* that here and there the epitomator Mark adopted or at least left in sayings from Matthew and Luke which otherwise would have been unknown to him (p. 346; author's italics).

And so, according to Holtzmann, Griesbach's hypothesis is based on an "illusion."

It is not without a certain element of tragedy that twenty years later Holtzmann had to admit—more or less covertly—that his ur-Mark hypothesis was based on an illusion; although he used not that expression but a more ambiguous one. In his *Lehrbuch der historisch-kritischen Einleitung in das Neue Testament* (1885) Vol. II, p. 339 he wrote the following:

> Quickly, one after the other these scholars finally interceded for Marcan priority . . . and Holtzmann, who in 1863 endeavored to sort through the existing material and pursue the critical process to a provisional conclusion in favor of the Marcan hypothesis. But since that time the controversy about the synoptic problem has moved decisively into the foreground of discussion. The intimate bond that links it with the quest for the "historical Jesus" has raised it to a question of crucial significance.

Below this it says in small print:

> For clarity's sake I shall list here the points where I have changed my previous position as the result of discussions with Strauss, Hilgenfeld, Weizsäcker, Keim, Weisse, Beyschlag and Simons:
>
> 1) Not everything in Matthew and Luke that goes beyond Mark can be accommodated in the sayings collection. At times elements from the collection are more highly modified by Luke than they are by Matthew. It is possible that it contained narrative sketches that formed undetachable frames for the sayings of the Lord.
>
> 2) Luke knew Matthew as well as Mark.
>
> 3) Consequently, at least most of the motives for distinguishing between an ur-Mark and Mark must be dismissed (p. 339).

One can sympathize with Holtzmann, since it must have been difficult for him to announce this "change of position," especially in regard to the third point. Neither was he spared the final death blow to the ur-Mark hypothesis, which was administered fourteen years later by Paul Wernle, the "consummator of the two-source theory":

> Evidence of a longer ur-Mark has never been produced and cannot be produced . . . I cannot see anything missing in the stories of John the Baptist and the Temptation; I would not know where to find a gap that would be fitting for the centurion from Capernaum. Also, to me, the conclusion of the parousia speech appears so powerful and effective that a longer presentation would only detract from it. In fact, all of these sections have been assigned to the ur-Mark solely for the purpose of alleviating the synoptic problem. Such an undertaking, which underestimates the uniqueness and intelligibility of our Mark is doomed to failure. The words of John the Baptist, the Temptation discourse, etc., may come from wherever they will. These sections are not

missing from Mark; they were never there in the first place. There is no compelling reason to postulate a shorter or longer ur-Mark as distinct from a canonical Mark. From this point of view the ur-Mark hypothesis simply collapses (*Die synoptische Frage*, 1899 p. 218).

Now we shall turn to Wernle.

Chapter IV

The Consummation

(Paul Wernle and Bernhard Weiss)

Paul Wernle

In 1899 Paul Wernle, a young unsalaried university lecturer, published his study *Die synoptische Frage.* In 1900 he became Professor of New Testament Studies at the University of Basel, and in 1901 Professor of Church History. He was considered the man who presented the clearest account of the two-source theory and who gave the "sayings collection" its definitive form. Of him Johannes Weiss wrote in his *Predigt vom Reiche Gottes* (1900²): "I must content myself with presuming the validity of the great fundamental finding—the two-source theory, as recently presented and confirmed by Paul Wernle in a convincing and comprehensive fashion" (p. 37).

And Heinrich Julius Holtzmann, who not only had given up his own ur-Mark hypothesis but had witnessed Wernle's rejection of it, nevertheless saw himself vindicated in his central conception of the correctness of the Marcan hypothesis. Three years prior to his death he wrote in his treatise "Die Markus-Kontroverse in ihrer heutigen Gestalt":

> No one who has really read the simultaneously-published books by Paul Wernle (*Die synoptische Frage*) and J. Hawkins (*Horae Synopticae*) can doubt any longer that the common root of the synoptic texts, the actual stock of our Gospels, is to be found in Mark (in: *Archiv für Religions-wissenschaft,* 1907 p. 18 ff.).

Paul Wernle himself stated his intentions in the preface of his work:

> The present investigation will bring nothing new or surprising to the solution of the synoptic question. Rather, it will closely scrutinize the many existing hypotheses by emphasizing the main issues and stressing the simple rather than the artificial or complicated.

Towards the end of his preface he stated: "If my book succeeds in putting aside the secondary and the uncertain and demonstrating that the main features of the synoptic question are solved, it will have achieved its purpose."

Here Wernle quite underrated his own project and was more modest than he needed to be. He did contribute something "new or surprising" to "the solution of the synoptic question" in two respects, the first of which was a new method. In his argumentation he cleverly began with the question of the most suitable starting point for an examination of the synoptic problem. Wernle opted for a research method which was different from that employed by C. H. Weisse and Holtzmann. They had started from the very beginning with the two-source theory, which they had tried to prove by the process of deduction. Wernle, however, adopted the inductive procedure. For this purpose, right at the very beginning he directed his reader's attention to the decisive question of method, as if he intended to solicit their participation in the search: "Which of the Gospels shall be the starting point? In terms of method, this question is not irrelevant. . . Is there a firm base from which we can proceed in a completely impartial manner?" (p. 2).

Wernle identified the prologue of Luke's Gospel as that starting point because it contains the only written statement by an Evangelist about his literary objective: "Therefore it belongs at the beginning of every inquiry into the synoptic problem" (p. 2).

Then Wernle invoked "three firm facts" which were clearly established by this prologue:

1) Luke did not write the earliest Gospel; rather, he had many predecessors.

2) These predecessors were not themselves eyewitnesses but had drawn from oral tradition.

3) Luke intended to surpass his predecessors in terms of completeness and chronological accuracy. (p. 2).

From this Wernle concluded: "Luke wrote as a man of the second or third generation. He drew, not directly from the oral tradition, but from written sources."

Wernle's practical application was as follows: "From all this it would seem most advisable to begin with the Gospel of Luke precisely because it is a relatively late work, and then to work backwards in search of his predecessors, who were his sources" (p. 2).

This sounded attractive and seemed to indicate willingness to proceed in "a completely impartial manner," which is what Wernle had promised to bring to his search for a "firm base." But then he posed the further question of what those sources of Luke actually were. Certainly the Evangelist himself had never said anything about this. Here Wernle's point becomes clear:

> Nevertheless, since the prologue makes it obvious that Luke used sources, it now becomes necessary to scrutinize Mark and Matthew for purposes of comparison. Are Mark or Matthew or both among the "many" which Luke had before him when he wrote his Gospel? (p. 3).

And then Wernle employed yet another seemingly insignificant but truly ingenious device: "In this we should take Mark first because comparison of his Gospel with Luke's is simpler and easier" (p. 3).

Who can read Wernle's methodical statement without recalling the similar ingenious stratagem that Wilke in his day had employed "for the sake of expediency" to take Mark first:

> Since Mark is always the one accompanied, so that one of the other two writers always adheres to the sequence he initiated, it seems most advantageous in surveying the material to put Mark first in a three-columned context (*Urevangelist*, p. 4).

For what Wernle asserts here is *objectively false.* There is nothing whatever to the proposition that it is easier to compare the Gospel of Mark with Luke than to compare Matthew with Luke. Both Matthew and Luke have a pre-history with nativity legend and genealogy and *evangelium infantiae,* as well as a post-history with resurrection stories and Christophanies. The Gospel of Mark includes neither. Hence an adequate comparison is possible only between Matthew and Luke. For Wernle it is certainly "simpler and easier" to take Mark first because he wants to prove that the Gospel of Mark was Luke's main source. He gives pride of place to Mark so as to demonstrate the extent to which he is "contained" in Luke. However, taking the Gospel of Luke as a starting point would result in quite another picture; then it would become evident how many parts of the third Gospel contain nothing whatever from Mark!

From this preconceived starting point Wernle then goes on to build his entire study on the basis of individual comparisons, first between Mark and Luke, then between Luke and Matthew, and finally between Mark and Matthew. Here the substantive errors which result from Wernle's methodology become apparent. He compares the Gospels in isolation from one another, Mark with Luke, etc., and from each individual comparison he immediately draws corresponding conclusions. But here it is a matter of the *synoptic* question! And it is possible to do justice to the synoptic problem only by treating it in a synoptic fashion from the very beginning; i.e., in a comprehensive consideration and in a comparison of all three with one another—but not in isolation. This is the only way to bring this problem closer to a solution, since it is not determined by the individual relationship of one Gospel to another, but by all of the relationships among all three. From the perspective of a single relationship only a distorted picture and an adulteration of the facts are possible. The question will be stated corrrectly only when it is posed on the basis of an overall synoptic view.

Now we shall briefly indicate the false conclusions that Wernle unavoidably arrived at as the result of his untenable starting point, viz. the comparison in isolation of two synoptic authors, in this case of Luke with Mark. His fundamental thesis was as follows: "If one author has adopted all the narratives of another, and in the same sequence, this is virtually conclusive proof that the latter was the source of the former" (p. 3).

There is certainly no need to waste words pointing out that the Gospel of Luke does *not* contain all the narratives of Mark. But Wernle knows how to fortify his position by carefully selecting certain passages from the very beginning while passing over the others in silence. He argues as follows: "What we have to consider are the following large sections of Luke where he is in accord with Mark: 3:1-6:19; 8:4-9:50; 18:15-24:10."

And now Wernle maintains with amazing audacity: *"Nearly all of Mark's narrative material is contained in these three segments of Luke"* (p. 4).

After this sentence which he himself emphasizes with italics, he writes:

The following pericopes are missing from these segments of Luke:

1.	Mk. 3:20-30	Jesus' apologia
2.	Mk. 4:26-34	Parables of the seed and the mustard seed
3.	Mk. 6:17-29	Episode of the death of John
4.	Mk. 6:45-8:25	Large gap containing: walking on the water, return from Gennesaret, the washing of hands, the Canaanite woman, the journey to the north, feeding of the four thousand, signs in the heavens, the leaven of the Pharisees, the blind man of Bethsaida
5.	Mk. 9:11-13	The discourse concerning Elijah

6.	Mk. 9:41-10:12	On causing offense, concerning salt, trip to Judea, Pharisees' question about divorce.
7.	Mk. 10:35-45	Jesus and the sons of Zebedee
8.	Mk. 11:11	First visit to the temple
9.	Mk. 11:12-15a 19-27a	Cursing of the fig tree and discourse about it
10.	Mk. 12:28-34	Question about the great commandment
11.	Mk. 14:3-9	Anointing in Bethany
12.	Mk. 15:1	Second sitting of the Sanhedrin

"Apart from these twelve exceptions," Wernle said, "all the passages of Mark are contained in Luke" (p. 4).

To maintain, in view of these twelve "exceptions" (one of which covers more than one and a half chapters) that "Nearly all of Mark's narrative material is contained in these three segments of Luke," is, to put it mildly, incorrect.

Let us now examine these pericopes of Mark that are not to be found in Luke from a *synoptic* point of view. Then we shall find that these Marcan pericopes which are missing from Luke fall into two groups:

a) the first group consists of passages that are also missing from Matthew; hence they represent special Marcan material.

b) the second group consists of passages that are fully present in Matthew. That means that in all these pericopes Mark moves parallel to Matthew!

Seen from this *synoptic* perspective, Wernle's arrangement becomes fundamentally modified. Now—*presented synoptically*—it looks this way:

1. Mk. 3:20-30
   a) 3:20-21   "His friends went out to seize him"   Unique to Mark
   b) 3:22-30   Jesus' Apologia   par Mt. 12:22-32
2. Mk. 4:26-34
   a) 4:26-29   Parable of the Seed   Unique to Mark
   b) 4:30-34   Parable of the Mustard Seed   par Mt. 13:31-35
3. Mk. 6:17-29   Episode of the death of John   par Mt. 14:3-12
4. Mk. 6:45-8:26   "Luke's great Marcan Gap"
   a) 6:45-7:30   Crossing over to and landing in Gennesaret, Laws of men

		and Commandments of God, The Canaanite Woman	par Mt. 14:22-15:28
b)	7:31-37	Healing of the deaf-mute	Unique to Mark
c)	8:1-21	Feeding of the four thousand, Demand for a sign, Discourse on the leaven of the Pharisees	par Mt. 15:32-16:12
d)	8:22-26	The Blind Man of Bethsaida	Unique to Mark
5.	Mk. 9:11-13	Discourse on Elijah	par Mt. 17:10-13
6.	Mk. 9:41-10:12		
a)	9:41	"Whoever gives you a cup of water to drink . . ."	par Mt. 10:42
b)	9:42-48	On causing offense	par Mt. 18:6-9
c)	9:49-50	Concerning salt	Unique to Mark
d)	10:1-12	Marriage and Divorce	par Mt. 19:1-10
7.	Mk. 10:35-45	Jesus and the sons of Zebedee	par Mt. 20:20-28
8.	Mk. 11:11	First visit to the temple	Unique to Mark
9.	Mk. 11:12-15a 19:27a	Cursing of the fig tree and discourse about it	par Mt. 21:18-22 (varied)
10.	Mk. 12:28-34	Question concerning the greatest commandment	par Mt. 22:34-40
11.	Mk. 14:3-9	Anointing in Bethany	par Mt. 26:6-13
12.	Mk. 15:1	Second sitting of the Sanhedrin	par Mt. 27:1-2

From this compilation, made from the *synoptic* perspective, it becomes apparent just how utterly false the results are when one attempts, with Wernle, to find a "solution" to the synoptic problem in the isolated juxtaposition of only two Gospels. And here it is already apparent just how right Wernle was when he gave his answer to the question about which of the Gospels should provide the starting point: "In terms of method this question is not irrelevant. . . ." It is an answer which could be taken in many ways.

We shall also demonstrate once more the erroneous effects of Wernle's incorrect methodology in the area of language. This will be accomplished by juxtaposing the wordings of Mark and Luke and then comparing them to Matthew's. In that way we shall obtain the whole synoptic image which alone offers the possibility of an evaluation of the true relationships among the three. Naturally, Wernle could not ignore the fact that quite frequently Luke's phrasing deviates from Mark's. In order to explain this he briefly asserts: "He (Luke) endeavored to translate them (the dominical sayings) into Greek, the language of his readers," and he adds: "Above all he changed the vocabulary" (p. 11).

In order to illustrate this, Wernle then introduces twenty-three instances in which Luke supposedly changed the phrasing of his alleged source Mark. We shall place the corresponding parallel words of *Matthew* alongside them, but we underline the fact that Wernle himself always compared only Mark and Luke. The overview gives the requisite whole synoptic picture:

MARK		LUKE		MATTHEW	
ἰσχύοντες	5:31	ὑγιαίνοντες	9:12	ἰσχύοντες	
ἐπιράπτει	5:36	ἐπιβάλλει	9:16	ἐπιβάλλει	
μόδιος	8:16	σκεῦος	5:15	μόδιος	
				Here Matthew has a dissimilar order	
χαλκόν	9:3	ἀργύριον	14:9	χαλκόν	
χοῦς	9:5	κονιορτός	10:14	κονιορτός	
ἀμήν	9:27	ἀληθῶς	16:28	ἀμήν	
μύλος ὀνικός	17:2	λίθος μυλικός	16:28	μύλος ὀνικός	
βέβληται	17:2	ἐπιράπτει	18:6	καταποντισθῇ	
				Here Matthew diverges from both	
ὑστερεῖ	18:22	λείπει	19:20	ὑστερῶ	
δός	18:22	διάδος	19:21	δός	
τρυμάλια τῆς ῥάφιδος	18:25	τρῆμα βελόνης	19:24	τρῆμα ῥάφιδος	
πατέρα ἤ μητέρα	18:29	γονείς	10:29	πατερα ἤ μητέρα	
βλέπετε	12.1	προσέχετε	16:5	προσέχετε	
ὑστέρησις	21:4	ὑστέρημα		without parallel: The widow's mite	
ἀκοὰς πολέμων	21:9	ἀναστασίας	24:6	ἀκοὰς πολέμων	
θροεῖσθε	21:9	πτοηθῆτε	24:6	θροεῖσθε	
προμεριμνᾶν	21:14	προμελετᾶν	24:19	μεριμνήσετε	
λαλεῖν	21:14	ἀπολογεῖσθαι	24:19	λαλεῖν	
θλίψις	21:23	ἀνάγκη	24:21	θλίψις	
ἐκφύειν τὰ φύλλα	21:30	προβάλλειν	24:32	τὰ φύλλα ἐκφύειν	
μέχρις οὗ	21:32	ἕως	24:34	ἕως	
ἐξαίφνης	21:34	αιφνιδιος		Matthew without parallel	

This *synoptic* compilation clearly shows that it is out of the question that Luke changed Mark's wording. The respective parallels in Matthew, insofar as they exist, show that in the majority of cases Mark corresponds in mode of expression to Matthew; in the remaining cases Matthew and Luke agree in their mode of expression against Mark. Here we get exactly the same image as that left by the pericopes which, according to Wernle, Luke supposedly passed over or omitted from the Gospel of Mark. *To the extent that Mark diverges from Luke in these examples, he converges with Matthew.* And this confirms again the fact that a solution to the synoptic problem is possible only on a synoptic basis.

Since Wernle attempted to work on an individual basis, he had no other choice than to look for "explanations" of these "missing" sections of Mark, which he considered "omissions," in terms suggested by the relationship between Mark and Luke, taken in isolation.

> Either Luke did not read them in his sources, in which case he did not have our Mark in front of him but merely a Gospel similar to Mark; or he read but intentionally omitted them. In that case there must be some signs that he read them, and reasons why he omitted them (p.4).

This search for "reasons why he omitted them" became one of Wernle's major preoccupations as he sought to demonstrate the priority of Mark and the posteriority of the other two synoptic authors, just as had been the case with Weisse and Holtzmann. We shall go into this question extensively in principle as well as in detail in the second part of this work, "Critical Analysis of Proofs of the Marcan Hypothesis," under the title "The Proof from Psychological Reflection." Here we shall limit ourselves to the "result" that is only to be expected from Wernle's line of reasoning:

> *Hence we arrive at the following result: Luke absorbed nearly all of Mark's narratives into his Gospel. Those that he omitted he nevertheless had read. As a rule he omitted them because of his dislike of duplication or because they lacked significance for his readers, but rarely because of dogmatic considerations.* Hence he had used the material as treated by Mark as a source. A reversal of the relationship is out of the question because the reasons for Mark's immense omissions could not be found (p. 6).

We would emphasize the last sentence, which Wernle does not italicize, in order to indicate how rashly and unhesitatingly he says of the omissions he attributes to Luke: "It is easy to name the reasons for omission" (p. 5). By contrast, how unwilling he is to contemplate the reverse possibility, declaring it "out of the question because the reasons for Mark's immense omissions could not be found." Moreover, this does not sound particularly convincing, in view of the fact that Wernle himself later states: "Mark's sole intention was to sketch briefly the life of Jesus in order to prove his divinity" (p. 211). (Exactly the same thing had been maintained by Henry Owen—"an abridgement"—and by Griesbach.)

Now, Wernle himself acknowledges that Mark's intention was to abbreviate. Would that not provide an adequate explanation for the omissions? But excluding the "reversal of the relationship" is certainly more opportune for his hypothesis; it permits Wernle to ignore altogether the necessity of examining the possibility. At all events it is difficult to reconcile with his initial assurance that he sought a "firm base" from which to "proceed in a completely impartial manner."

It is hardly surprising that Wernle comes to the same conclusion from comparing Mark with Matthew as he had from his comparison of Mark and Luke. But this time, in line with his principle that the starting-point of the investigation is "not irrelevant . . . in terms of method," he adopts an approach different from the one applied to the Gospel of Luke. He justifies this by saying that here there is no prologue mentioning predecessors that had been used as sources. Hence the first question must be "whether Matthew was an original work from the hand of the Apostle, or a later Gospel that had predecessors upon which it depended" (p. 109).

And then Wernle executes another of his ingenious stratagems by stating: "In the first case it will turn out on inspection to be a literary unity, and in the second a *compilation*. Once this question has been answered, we shall have arrived at the point where Luke's prologue leads us, with no need for further examination . . ." (p. 109).

Here one can already visualize where such an "examination" would lead. It is not difficult to prove and cannot be doubted that the Gospel of Matthew is not a "literary unity." Then Wernle has only to link this with the assertion that Mark has the character of a "literary unity"—which we also do not dispute. Then there remains only a small step to the thesis: since the Gospel of Luke is not unified and original, it follows that there is no other possibility than that the Gospel of Mark must be the source of Matthew, also. And with this Wernle believes that he has provided proof of Marcan priority over both the first and the third Gospel.

Apart from numerous factual errors, his deduction has only one small fundamental flaw. Uniformity and continuity of presentation by no means prove that a work is original, as will be explained in Chapter VII under the heading "Proof from Uniformity."

Wernle's argumentation regarding the relationship of Mark to Matthew forms an exact counterpart to his treatment of Mark and Luke. About this relationship he had stated grandly: "Almost all of Mark's narrative material is contained in these three segments of Luke," although Wernle had to admit twelve "exceptions," one of which is the "large gap" of nearly two chapters (Mk. 6:45-8:26). But by the time he had reached his "result" Wernle had as good as forgotten these "exceptions" as he wrote: "He had integrated it (the Gospel of Mark) *almost completely* into his presentation and had followed the sequence of Mark *almost without exception;* and had also adopted his text as his basis" (p. 40; author's italics).

He made a similar statement about the Gospel of Matthew: "All of Mark's narratives are contained in Matthew with the exception of *merely* eight (p. 124; author's italics).

Here, as in the case of Luke, one cannot help but notice Wernle's practiced disarming of facts which oppose the Marcan hypothesis. Comments like "with the exception of *merely* eight" and "almost *all* of the narrative material" or "almost completely" or "almost without exception" are tendentious, and designed to blur the actual situation. The only verdict that one can pronounce upon this kind of argument is that it casts doubt upon itself.

At issue, according to Wernle, are the following Marcan pericopes which are without parallel in the Gospel of Matthew:

1)	Mk. 1:12-28	Jesus in the synagogue at Capernaum
2)	1:35-38	Jesus' flight
3)	4:26-29	Parable of the seed
4)	7:32-37	Healing of the deaf-mute
5)	8:22-26	The blind man of Bethsaida
6)	9:38-40	The worker of miracles who did not follow Christ
7)	11:11	First visit to the temple
8)	12:41-44	The widow's mite

He followed this by putting forth his principle of analysis: "The question is, did Matthew know these eight stories, or did he leave them out intentionally; and, if so, why?" (p. 125).

Naturally, he decided in favor of knowing and intentional omission, exactly as in the case of Luke. In that case he had said: "It is easy to state reasons for the omissions"; here Wernle says: "The reasons for the omission of these stories are, as a rule, quite obvious" (p. 125). But Wernle could have spared himself this search for "reasons" if in both cases he had proceeded from a synoptic viewpoint and not indulged in individual comparisons. Then the following result would have come up:

1)   par Luke
2)   par Luke
3)   unique to Mark
4)   unique to Mark
5)   unique to Mark
6)   par Luke
7)   unique to Mark
8)   par Luke

A mere glance at the Gospel synopsis might have caused Wernle to reflect. One cannot get around the fact that four of these alleged "omissions" of Matthew must also be Luke's "omissions," since they are unique to Mark; nor the fact that Matthew's remaining "omissions" have parallels in Luke while, conversely, Luke's "omissions" have parallels in Matthew. In addition, Wernle could have spared himself this two-fold search for motives—or, as he put it, "reasons"—for omissions.

Along the way he gave further evidence of his own insecurity, as he asserts with reasons rather reminiscent of those offered by Wilke (see above, p. 34):

> In any case, it is easier to account for these mere eight omissions from Mark than to explain the absence in Mark of more than thirty longer and shorter passages in Matthew. To be sure, the proverb "seek and you shall find" holds true here, too. But one glance at Holsten's Procrustean bed shows vividly the kinds of sophistries and pedantries such a tendentious fantasy produces the moment it disdains to take simple things simply. Every attempt to derive Mark's small content from the larger one of Matthew, instead of deriving Matthew from Mark and other sources, turns into proof for the opposite in the hands of an impartial investigator (p. 126 f).

If we disregard for a moment the subjectivity of Wernle's diction, we are left with the substance of his argument, which reappears in the works of several representatives of the Marcan hypothesis: the emergence of a larger work from a smaller is more easily explained than the emergence of a smaller work from a larger one. In other words, enlargement is more likely to take place than abridgement. But this argument does not hold up. One is every bit as conceivable as the other; both can be realized and have been realized before, more than once. It is anything but logical to argue that adaptations of identical themes necessarily grow longer in direct proportion to their distance from the point of origin. Furthermore, it is interesting to observe how the same arguments reappear again and again through the centuries, even though they have long since been refuted. As early as 1782 Johann Benjamin Koppe had asserted: "Probabile est, brevius Evangelium tempore fuisse prius." ("It is probable that the shorter Gospel was chronologically prior.") And Griesbach had offered the well-aimed reply: "Ab auctoris consilio unice pendet, utrum iis, quae alii ante ipsum scripsere, addere aliquid an demere ab illis nonnulla satius sit" ("It depends solely on the intention of the author whether it is preferable to add to, or to subtract from, what others wrote before him.") (see above, p. 8).

Moreover, here again Wernle veils the true circumstances when he formulates the argument the following way: ". . . to derive the small content of Mark from the larger one of Matthew, instead of deriving Matthew from Mark and other sources." At issue is not the derivation of Mark solely from Matthew, but from Matthew *and* Luke. And one sees quite clearly which hypothesis is to be disregarded—Griesbach's. Wernle must have considered this thesis to be so dangerous—and with reason!—that he did not even mention it even though he knew very well that what was at stake was nothing less than the alternative: either Mark had been the basis for Matthew and Luke, or else Matthew and Luke had been the basis for Mark.

The utter untenability of Wernle's line of argument becomes especially evident in his second chapter, which he entitles "Arrangement" (of the material). Here is an example:

> The table shows that Mark's arrangement is the basis, in full, for Matthew's. Modification is in two points only:
>
> 1) Matthew incorporated material from other sources into the Marcan context whenever Mark offered a suitable situation or something on a similar subject.
>
> 2) In four cases Matthew rearranged things. Most of the miracles which are scattered about in Mark he pulled together in chapters 8 and 9 to form a cycle of miracles. Since the Sabbath sayings were more important as sayings than as miracles, he separated them from Mk. 2:3 and joined them with the attack on the Pharisees in chapter 12. The selection of the Apostles and their sending out he combined for simplicity's sake. Similarly, he later joined together the two temple visits as well as the two discourses about the fig tree.
>
> The consequences of these changes make themselves felt

immediately, to Matthew's detriment. Mark's portrayal of the first day is completely disrupted—so many other items are jammed in between the calling of Peter and Jesus' visit to his house that the continuity is torn apart. The discourses about the paralytic, the calling of Levi, and the question of fasting are wrongly incorporated into the miracle cycle—they simply do not belong under this rubric. And yet, they follow directly in Mk. 2. The consequence of anticipating the sending out and of joining it with the selection of the Apostles is the omission of the mission itself, of which nothing is said in the parallel Mk. 3 (p. 128 f.).

Thus far Wernle. The question occurs to us: if this rearrangement had such devastating consequences for the Gospel of Matthew, why did the Evangelist carry it out? It would really have been much simpler for him to maintain the arrangement which he allegedly found in Mark! But a treatment which "completely disrupted" the first day according to Mark, which "tore apart the continuity," which "wrongly" incorporated discourses which "simply do not belong under this rubric" and which caused the "omission of the mission itself"—such a procedure seems nothing less than absurd.

Wernle, too, is fundamentally of the same opinion—as far as Mark is concerned! For what he was prepared to concede to Matthew he was not prepared to grant Mark in equal measure; rather he indignantly rejected any possibility of the latter:

> The reverse, i.e., that Mark would have changed the arrangement, is inconceivable. What would have moved him to tear apart the cycle of miracles or to separate the selection of the Apostles from the sending out, when they were so beautifully combined! Moreover, the description of the first day could have been compiled from Matthew only by means of a cunning bit of artfulness. And what kind of blunderer would have wanted to supplant the Sermon on the Mount with the anecdote of the demoniac in the synagogue at Capernaum! Attempts to prove the opposite do not deserve serious consideration (p. 129).

Wernle's emotional involvement and lack of objectivity startle the reader. The very same thing that he now says is unthinkable for Mark, he has only just finished attributing to Matthew: ". . . completely disrupted, ... continuity torn apart . . . simply do not belong, . . . omission." And should one so much as raise the question whether Mark could have been the one who changed the arrangement Wernle exclaims: "What would have moved him, . . . to tear apart, . . . to separate when they were so beautifully combined?" Has Wernle completely forgotten that in the immediately preceding sentences he said: "The discourses about the paralytic, the calling of Levi, and the question of fasting are wrongly incorporated into the miracle cycle—they do not belong under this rubric"?

Again, the solution of the problem is a synoptic one, but Wernle does not perceive this because he does not think synoptically. For in the miracle reports, which Mark presents in a sequence different from Matthew's, he himself follows Luke's order. The same is true of the sending out and the selection of the Apostles. The decisive fact—which Wernle, as a result of thinking in isolated comparisons, cannot recognize—is that Mark, when he does not run parallel to the order of Matthew, follows Luke's sequence— except when he has special material to add. And again, one must say of Wernle's statements about only *two* of the Evangelists that of necessity they lead to a distortion of the fundamental synoptic relationship.

Wernle's illogical method of argumentation reaches its climax in the "conclusion" he draws from the comparison of Matthew's and Mark's "arrangement." "Conclusion: Matthew's arrangement is based entirely upon Mark's, *for which the rearrangements provide as much proof as do the passages which follow in like order"* (p. 130; author's italics).

The rules of logic which are generally accepted elsewhere permit only positive statements to be recognized as evidence, while negative statements count only as counter-evidence. However, if one recognizes the negative instance as positive proof, as Wernle does here, one has to make a *petitio principii:* the fact to be proved is accepted as proven already. Then it is certainly easy to argue!

Wernle's comparison of the "texts" in Mark and Matthew exhibits the same rational inconsistency. In several cases even Wernle himself cannot deny Matthew's priority. And that, after all, clearly contradicts his fundamental thesis. But here as well he knows how to extricate himself from these difficulties:

> Dominical sayings which appear to be (sic!) better preserved in Matthew's text should be taken first. Foremost of these is the parousia discourse with 24:20 and 29: "and not on the sabbath"[1] and "Immediately."[2] By omitting the first Mark has eliminated the Judeo-Christian mood of this apocalypse. By striking out the second he has moderated the longing for the parousia (p. 132).

And now Wernle himself poses the question: "But how is it possible that the younger Matthew retained these old features, if they were missing from his basic text?" (p. 132). One is astonished by the *deus ex machina* which Wernle

---

[1]μηδὲ σαββάτῳ.
[2]εὐθέως.

then sets in operation: "Here the answer is especially simple—Matthew also knew the apocalypse which is at the root of Mark 13" (p. 132).

Here, however, Wernle has to face two questions:

1) If the "younger" Matthew also knew the underlying apocalypse, but the "older" Mark did not, from which source did the latter draw his information?

2) How does Wernle know that Matthew was acquainted with the underlying apocalypse?

Now, we know where Wernle obtained his knowledge. Since at this point Matthew poseses priority, as Wernle himself cannot deny, while according to the hypothesis Mark is supposed to possess priority, Wernle was left with no choice but to "infer" a solution. Otherwise he would have had to abandon his Marcan hypothesis. Of this we can certainly say that "here the answer is especially simple."

Hence Wernle came to adopt another even further-reaching, equally fascinating "simple" solution:

> There is one axiom which is valid for this and similar cases: wherever a dominical saying is preserved more clearly, more simply, and in an older form in Matthew, there Matthew handed down the information better than Mark (p. 134).

Now this is certainly astonishing, if Mark was Matthew's source. After all, Wernle's entire effort is centered exclusively on establishing Marcan priority. But from the very beginning the advocates of the Marcan hypothesis have been inclined to accept "exceptions" without feeling the need to entertain doubts about the fundamental validity of their source theory. Rather, again and again they have searched for a way out—and found one. And when they have not quite been able to manage it, they have fled to the *Ultimum refugium* of the hypothesist who can see no solution, which is to ignore the facts and attack his opponent's intellectual standing. Wernle's disdainful remark, "What kind of blunderer would have wanted to supplant the Sermon on the Mount? . . . Attempts to prove the opposite do not deserve serious consideration" are on the same level as and painfully reminiscent of Wilke's dismissal of contradictions: "(One) might as well give such a dictum its due by ignoring it and continuing the investigation without further concern. Now we shall proceed."

It also created a certain fine irony, because Wernle's comment about the "blunderer" who "wanted to supplant the Sermon on the Mount" could be applied to Holtzmann's Mark, who left it out because he considered it "too long" (see above, p. 76).

Wernle then draws a conclusion from his comparison of Mark and Matthew that is exactly parallel to the conclusion he drew from the comparison of Mark and Luke (see above, p. 102):

> Matthew knew the Gospel of Mark, used it as a source, and even made it the basis of his historical narrative. He fitted almost all of the Gospel of Mark into his presentation, followed its sequence with very few exceptions, and also used its text as his foundation (p. 177).

Wernle's "conclusion" about Luke reads the same way on all the decisive points:

> Luke knew the Gospel of Mark, used it as a source, and even made it the basis of his historical narrative. He fitted almost all of the Gospel of Mark into his presentation, followed its sequence almost without exception, and also used its text as his foundation.

In view of the fact that Wernle portrays these two situations as essentially and textually identical, an objection must be raised. *If what Wernle says here is true, then Matthew and Luke would have had to produce two completely identical Gospels!* The content of both would have to be exactly the same, because he says the same thing of both Evangelists: He "made the Gospel of Mark . . . the basis of his historical narrative." Furthermore, both of them would have to have virtually the same order, that of Mark, because again Wernle uses almost the same words when he says of both that they usually followed Mark's sequence. In the third place, both texts would have to be identical with Mark's because Wernle says the same thing about both of them: he "also used its text as his foundation."

Now if what Wernle asserts really were true—if both Evangelists were led by exactly the same aspiration to take Mark as the basis of their historical narratives and follow his substance, order, and text,—then one can only oppose this with the same objection raised by Weisse against Wilke's "Sixth textual point," which said that Matthew had drawn his extra-Marcan material from Luke (see above, p. 40): "If Matthew had wanted to proceed in that way, why did he not just copy directly from Luke?" (see above, p. 43).

Wernle retorted that Luke as well as Matthew had the same intention—to revise Mark. In support of this Wernle presented, following his similar conclusions, reasons which were slightly modified in both cases, but which were virtually the same. For purposes of comparison we shall place them side by side:

LUKE	MATTHEW
The liberty which he permits himself is threefold:	The liberty which he permits himself is threefold:

1) He completely revised the text of Mark.

2) He commented on it, and improved it as he thought best.

3) He—very infrequently, to be sure—combined and fused the text with other sources. In doing so he proceeded in the manner of the man of a later period to whom authorial rights, to say nothing of inspired thought, do not exist, and who therefore has the right to accommodate tradition to the needs of his time (p. 40).

1) He combined and fused Mark's text with other sources, or else inserted sayings from other sources. This is the point on which Matthew differs most strongly from Luke.

2) He imposed numerous linguistic changes, improving the style of the Greek. To be sure, in doing so he showed greater consideration for the dominical sayings.

3) He commented on it, enlarged it, and improved it as he thought best, quite frequently motivated by scribal understanding of the Scriptures or by a more exalted faith. In individual cases more conservative than Luke, imbued with greater awe for Holy Scripture, he nevertheless proceeded on the whole in the manner of the man of a later period to whom authorial rights, to say nothing of inspired thought, do not exist, and who therefore has the right to accommodate tradition to the needs of his time (p. 177 f.).

Let us for the time being conclude our critical discussion of Wernle's first main source in his two-source theory, the Gospel of Mark, with the observation that he has *not* succeeded in substantiating the priority of Mark and the posteriority of Matthew and Luke. He has come no closer to this objective than Wilke, Weisse, and Holtzmann before him. Now we shall focus our attention on his sayings source.

Source "Q"

In the beginning we mentioned that in spite of Wernle's announcement that he would not "bring anything new or surprising to the solution of the synoptic question" he nevertheless did produce something new and surprising in two respects. The first was his new—"in terms of method not irrelevant"—starting point, the isolated, non-synoptic comparison of only two of the first three Gospels at a time.

The second is his renaming of the logia source. It is no exaggeration to identify this as the most momentous event in the history of research into the Marcan hypothesis. Its effects can still be felt today.

At first it appeared to be nothing more than a change of name and hence quite harmless. Having defined the character of the sayings collection more precisely as a "common source, consisting mostly (sic!) of discourses," Wernle continued: "The—hypothetical—source is to be designated by the letter Q" (p. 44).

This sounded harmless and insignificant enough. At least that was how it appeared at the beginning of Wernle's work. But by the end of his argument the effect has become considerably different:

> It is not unreasonable to suppose that from the moment of its genesis the sayings collection underwent continuous historical development until it was taken up into Matthew and Luke. As Jesus' legacy to the community, it belonged to every single individual, and everyone had the right to make improvements or additions. Probably only a very few equally long copies were in existence. Between the first written copy (Q) and the collection which Matthew (Q^{Mt}) and Luke (Q^{Lk}) found stood Q^1, Q^2, Q^3; for us the effort to differentiate between these three would be in vain. The Judaic form (Q^J) denotes a single stage on this path. This assumption alone provides an unforced diagnosis of what we find in our Gospels (p. 231).

It is clear that in Wernle's hands this re-naming of the *single* "sayings collection" leads to the emergence of no fewer than seven "Q" sources and that this formal change of name actually indicates a redefinition of the substance of the collection. The enormity of this expansion can best be realized if we replace the new designation "Q" with the former term "logia collection," which we shall abbreviate "log." Then, thanks to Wernle's transformation, the one and only documented logia collection becomes seven distinct sayings collections: Log, log^1, log^2, log^3, log^{Mt}, log^{Lk} and log^J.

It is evident that Wernle's unverifiable, hypothetically-postulated multiple source "Q" left open all hypothetical possibilities because of its unlimited potential for expansion. It contained seven allegedly detectable versions and also had supposedly been in a constant state of flux, and it even had a "history." At the same time it eliminated the calamities that confronted the Marcan hypothesis as it had been presented by Weisse and Holtzmann. In principle they had wanted to maintain the "consistent" logia source as their starting point, but found that in practice they could not sustain it, and, rather against their will, reached for the expedient of a sayings collection which consisted "mostly" or "primarily" or "in particular" of logia.

As soon as Wernle resorted to the expedient of renaming the source, this problem was eliminated. Then it was a matter of "Nomen est Omen." The name of the source was no longer "logia," but "Q." And this source no longer overstepped its bounds even though it contained narrative material. Now label and content were in harmony. Thus he could state without hesitation: "In every place where Matthew and Luke use similar wording, they used the text of the sayings collection" (p. 80). He continued to use this designation— for traditional reasons, as it were—but he meant "Q"!

Accordingly he then felt no further compunction about reincorporating the narrative material which Weisse, in his recantation, had removed from the logia document. Thus Wernle asserted without hesitation:

The following discourses unquestionably belong to it:

1) Words of John the Baptist. Mt. 3:7-12; Lk. 3:7-9, 16 f.

2) Temptation dialogue. Mt. 4:3-10; Lk. 4:3-12.

3) . . .

4) Centurion at Capernaum. Mt. 8:5-13; Lk. 7:2-10; 13:28-30.

5) . . .

6) Discourse concerning John the Baptist. Mt. 11:2-19; Lk. 7:18-35; 16:16. (p. 82).

Here one is reminded of the contortions that C. H. Weisse performed in order to declare the words of John the Baptist to be dominical sayings, and of how he endeavored to interpret symbolically the temptation story, and of how he twisted and turned in his attempts to portray the story of the centurion at Capernaum as a "parable although in the mode of a historical account" (see above, p. 54f.).

One is reminded further of how Weisse, in his self-correction, declared it "quite impossible to assign the first two sections that have been presented here to the sayings collection. To do so would be to transform the collection into an evangelical narrative quite similar in character to our canonical Gospels."

Wernle, having broadened the logia source to "Q", no longer had to be troubled by Weisse's scruples and doubts. At the same time it was a matter of indifference to him if the narrative part threatened to submerge the logia, as in the case of the pericope of the centurion at Capernaum, where the logion comes only at the very end (Mt. 7:11 f.); while in Luke it is missing altogether and can be found only in Luke's travel narrative (Lk. 13:28-30).

Here it is apparent just how much Wernle is dominated and imprisoned by his own hypothesis. There can be no doubt that the above-mentioned pericopes do not belong to a "sayings source." However, since they are not in the Gospel of Mark, they cannot properly be deduced from the "historical source Mark." Consequently Wernle has no other choice (short of disavowing the Marcan hypothesis) than to ascribe them to the sayings source, having already strongly rejected the possibility of an ur-Mark.

At this point Wernle, too, must face the fundamental problem. If stories like that of the centurion at Capernaum or others with an "introductory situation" may be counted as discourses, then there is no longer any fundamental distinction between "discourses" and "accounts." Then, as a consequence, the whole Gospel of Mark must also fall into the category of "discourses" and be ascribed to source "Q". This is true because in almost every story in the Gospel of Mark there is an "important series of sayings" by virtue of which alone, according to Wernle, the centurion's pericope must be assigned to the sayings collection. Therefore Wernle himself poses the following question:

> But did not the sayings collection contain other dominical sayings, for which Mark is now our source? The group of such sayings in Mk. 1:40-3:6, the words concerning true relatives, the parable of the sower, the sayings about the washing of hands, the parabolic miracle, the dominical sayings in 12:33-44, the words about the parousia in Mk. 13? (p. 225).

Wernle's answer to this tailor-made question is amazing, and extraordinarily sharp:

There are two decisive arguments against this hypothesis:

1) All the arguments offered in favor of the view that these sayings are based on Q are invalid. Absolutely nowhere is there any proof of Matthew and Luke having used another document besides Mark for these sayings. If they are in agreement in small details against Mark, or if individually they diverge from him, the reason always lies in the thoughts of the writers (How does Wernle know that?), who are not just copyists. One can manage quite adequately throughout with Mark as the only source.

2) The above-mentioned dominical sayings do not fit into the sayings collection because of their narrative, anecdotal character. These are not sequences of sayings, as are all the discourses in Q, but rather individual dominical sayings which form the nucleus of short stories having introductions, questions addressed to Jesus, and conclusions. For comparison one may refer to the discourses on righteousness, on confession, and John's discourse, etc. (p. 225).

What is really astonishing is the fact that in this connection Wernle gave this explanation about the pericope of the centurion: "The story of the centurion at Capernaum found a place in Q solely because of the important series of sayings at the end." And then he added explicitly: "The extent to which it is possible to get a clear picture of Q depends upon whether or not this distinction between discourses and anecdotes is observed" (p. 225).

Reading Wernle's answer, one is struck by the way he applies a double standard of measurement, and at the same time by the degree of error in his argument. If the dominical sayings in Mark "do not fit into the sayings collection because of their narrative and anecdotal character" then the pericope of the centurion does so even less—it has a distinctly "anecdotal character." And here we have to correct Wernle by applying his own hypothesis—or, more precisely, by pointing out his inconsistency. The purely narrative story of the centurion at Capernaum does not have its place in Q "solely because of the important series of sayings at the end" but *solely and exclusively because it is found in Matthew and Luke and has no parallel in Mark*. Thus, Wernle was once again caught by his own hypothesis and had no option but to allocate it to Q, even though the facts clearly spoke against doing so. For, having postulated a sayings collection containing dominical sayings, it was unjustified to assign to it only the dominical sayings in Matthew and Luke, while excluding those in Mark. Here, in fact, it must be either-or. But it is obvious why Wernle did not want to accept the fact that logically the Marcan logia must also be included in the logia collection. Wernle expressed this—transcribed into positive form—as follows: "one can manage quite adequately throughout with Mark as the only source" (p. 225).

By this he means: with the Marcan logia as well as with those of Matthew and Luke which have parallels in Mark. Thereby Wernle decidedly shifted the perspective. The question here is not whether Matthew and Luke had another source besides Mark, and whether in Mark's case, too, use of the sayings source should be assumed. That is to say, here we have to raise the same objections about Wernle's argument as we had to raise against Holtzmann—with the sole difference that in this context both give the concept "Mark" a different content: the former relates it to the canonical Mark and the latter to the fictitious (ur-) Mark.

Now, had Wernle assumed that Mark also drew his logia from Q, he would have found his hypothesis in serious difficulties. Therefore he raised an objection: "This would render completely incomprehensible the reasons why the later Evangelists Luke and Matthew did not simply follow Q, from which, after all, Mark had obtained all his sayings." (Naturally Wernle meant the subordinate clause in a purely ironic sense.)

In order to dispose of such an opinion once and for all, he attempted to impugn its representatives' intellectual respectability by adding: "This is the hypothesis of an epigone who thinks he can break the girders of the structure which supports him and use them to build a new structure in mid-air"(p. 210).

Here Wernle has fired his heavy artillery, and it has exploded in his face. Here once again the vulnerability of the two-source theory becomes obvious. It really makes sense only under the assumption that the one source was a historical source and the other a discourse source, and that Matthew and Luke drew upon the former for the historical part of the Gospels and upon the latter for logia material. But since it now turns out that this clear-cut distinction is only theoretical or hypothetical, this whole two-source system becomes questionable. It does not stand up in face of the fact that it is a matter of *mixed sources* in which the only difference between historical and logia elements is one of *emphasis*. The representatives of the Marcan hypothesis had done their part in bringing about this effect. They themselves had been the ones who, pressured by the problems besetting their hypothesis, had blended narrative elements into the *presumably pure logia source* and in so doing had corrupted the logia collection.

Now they were trapped by a source problem of their own making. In fact, it is not clear why the first and third Evangelists should have drawn part of their logia material from the Gospel of Mark and the rest of it (the sections which are not found in the Gospel of Mark) from the sayings source. Something similar may be said of the historical parts. Sometimes they are supposed to come from Mark, even when they include dominical sayings, while at other times it is assumed that they come from Q in the form of "outline narratives" which form "historical frames for the dominical sayings which they contain," even if they are as long as the framework of the centurion's pericope and John the Baptist's inquiry.

Here neither embellishment nor concealment could help. The reality had to be faced: either the two sources had to be distinctly separated into a historical source and a logia source, or the two-source theory would become a system of stop-gaps and evasions, thereby reducing itself *ad absurdum*. This says nothing of the impossible editorial procedures Matthew and Luke would have had to undertake to obtain their logia from Mark whenever he could supply them, obtaining the others from Q, but abandoning it again whenever Mark provided more logia.

Wernle himself sensed the deadly threat that was posed to the Marcan hypothesis by the view that Mark drew his logia from Q. Hence, he drew a graphic picture of the grave consequences:

This source hypothesis really makes sense only if two things are pre-supposed:

1) The Petrine tradition is false; if Mark drew all the above-mentioned dominical sayings from the (logia) document and not from Peter, then what other purpose did Peter serve?

2) The author of Q is also at the same time the originator of the sayings; for the assertion that Mark must have known all these words in written form invalidates the oral tradition; in other words, thought through to the end, this hypothesis reduces itself *ad absurdum*. Actually, to attempt to *prove* that Mark was dependent on Q amounts to nothing less than the denial that Mark had his information from Peter and that all these sayings were also handed on by word of mouth within the community (p. 210).

Here there can be no mistaking Wernle's reason for rejecting this "source hypothesis." His rejection contained the unstated admission: If this hypothesis is correct, then my own Marcan hypothesis must be false. . . .

But the Petrine origin of the Marcan account is insupportable in any case, as we shall demonstrate later (see Part II, "Critical Analysis of Proofs," Chapter XI, "Proof from Petrine Origin"). Moreover, if Mark obtained his knowledge of the historical material and the discourse components from Peter, then he needed to draw them neither from Q nor directly from the oral tradition. Rather, he could simply have obtained them from Matthew and Luke—as Owen and Griesbach had already perceived.

Wernle, however, persisted in maintaining that Mark had obtained his information from Peter and that he did not use the logia source. Expressing himself negatively, Wernle put it this way: "It cannot be proved that Mark used Q" (p. 211). On the other hand, Wernle believed that Mark was acquainted with the sayings source. We know from whom Wernle obtained this conviction: from Holtzmann (see above, p. 79ff.). The objection raised there about the unlikelihood that Mark "knew the logia source but did not make use of it" is tackled in a surprising way by Wernle. He flatly asserts without being able to adduce a shred of evidence,: "*At that time, every Christian learned the most important dominical sayings by heart when he entered the community*" (p. 221; author's italics).

Now perhaps one can understand that from the standpoint of his hypothesis Wernle held the view that: "The Gospel of Mark can be better understood if, during his time, a record of the most important dominical sayings already existed and was held in esteem by the community (p. 271). And yet, such an unfounded assertion as this one ought not to be admissible for—what was it that Weisse had said?—"if a hypothesis demands such acts of violence in order to be established, [it] cannot possibly have a sound foundation."

On the other hand, the renaming of the sayings source and especially the transformation of its content enabled Wernle to provide a satisfactory answer, from the point of view of the Marcan hypothesis, to the problem of the completely different usage of the logia source by Matthew and Luke. Time and again we have been particularly struck by this problem in the treatment of the Sermon on the Mount. Matthew presents it in a compact form—as a "continuum," to use Holtzmann's word—while Luke divides it up and gives parts of it different phrasing and meaning. This inexplicable incongruity caused considerable headaches for the champions of the two-source theory. How could such a discrepancy come about, if both Evangelists drew from the same source—*the* logia source? How was this astonishing phenomenon to be reconciled with its existence as a uniform, consistent source?

Wernle presented the solution to the problem (from the viewpoint of the Marcan hypothesis) when he asserted that there exists not *one* "Q" but several, and, moreover, that they "from the moment of their genesis underwent continuous historical development until they were taken up into Matthew and Luke." That seemed to lay to rest the doubts that had been expressed. But how could this be reconciled with Papias' simple note which mentioned only *one* logia collection?

Now, it was this very note of Papias upon which the representatives of the Marcan hypothesis depended. They sought in it evidence to substantiate the many modifications which Q allegedly exhibited. The Papias fragment contains not only the statement: "So then Matthew composed *ta logia* in the Hebrew language"[3], but it also continues: "and each interpreted it as he was able".[4]

The critical word in this phrase can only be rendered as "interpreted." However, the advocates of Marcan priority read the second part of the quotation as: "as each *translated* it as he was able."

---

[3]Ματθαῖος μὲν οὖν Εβραϊδι διαλέκτῳ τὰ λόγια συνετάξατο.

[4]ἡρμήνευσέν δ' αὐτὰ ὡς ἦν δυνατὸς ἕκαστος.

Now the Greek verb[5] can have two different meanings: 1. translate, and 2. interpret, as it is still used today in the theological discipline of hermeneutics.

If one now asks which of the two possible translations is correct in the present case, the only sensible decision must be in favor of "interpret." For if the reverse were true, one would have to wonder at the astounding linguistic abilities that must be assumed if "each" believed himself ready and able to translate such a work from a Semitic to an Indo-Germanic language. One wonders further at the peculiar method of translating presupposed here, if everyone translated "as he was able." Such a practice might be conceivable in verbal exchange in a foreign country, or in a conversation with a foreigner in which one has to make oneself understood under the pressure of a here and now situation, "as best one can"; that is, by murdering the language. But to assume the same of a collection of dominical sayings would be indefensible, since it formed the foundation of the Christian faith—which depends on the word-for-word accuracy of their reproduction.

Rather, the situation is this: either one is in full command of a foreign language, in which case one may be so bold as to transpose a work of the significance of the logia collection into one's own language or into a foreign tongue; or one is not in complete command and transfers this difficult, as well as highly responsible, task to an expert linguist—one who at the same time possesses the awareness that the translation of a fundamental document of the faith must be executed with painstaking accuracy; not casually, "as best one can."

Hence the only logical meaning that the Papias quotation can have is that of the second hermeneutical definition: interpret. It was understood in this sense by Herbert Marsh, Eichhorn's successor in pursuing the ur-Gospel hypothesis as well as by Schleiermacher in his essay *Über die Zeugnisse des Papias von unsern ersten beiden Evangelien* (1832).

In this connection it may also be fruitful to pose the question of for whom the Apostle Matthew could have prepared this compilation of dominical sayings in the "Hebrew language." For the Greeks? Obviously not, since they spoke neither Hebrew nor Aramaic. Consequently, the only remaining possibility is that he compiled and recorded it for his Judeo-Christian compatriots and fellow-believers. For what purpose? For the purpose of proselytizing among the *Jews*. And now, all at once the second part of Papias' quotation makes sense: "each interpreted it as he was able." This is nothing

---

[5]ἑρμηνεύειν.

other than what the preachers of the Gospel have done from the very beginning and are still doing today—interpreting the words of the Lord "as they are able."

But the followers of the Marcan hypothesis believed, by virtue of their interpretation "each translated it as he was able," that they had in their possession literary evidence for the various forms of "Q" embraced by Wernle. One may think of this what one will, but it cannot be disputed that the authors or redactors of the Gospels of Matthew and Luke could *not* have drawn their logia elements from the *same* source. That was also what had led Wernle to surmise—indeed, he had said nothing more than that—"that the sayings collection from the moment of its genesis underwent a continuous historical development until it was taken up into Matthew and Luke."

But as much as ever, there still remained an unsolved central problem for the two-source theory—Wernle's renaming and reinterpretation of the sayings source notwithstanding. For there still persisted, in the first part of Papias' quotation, the annoyingly unequivocal words "ta logia": Matthew collected the logia. But this could not be reconciled with the two-source theory. The logia concept was too narrow for the extra-Marcan material common to Matthew and Luke, which also contained narrative material. Weisse had simply assigned them to the sayings source—and then removed them again! Holtzmann and Wernle had taken them back again under the pretense that embellished logia were also logia. But the narrative frameworks, especially the more extended ones, still remained a stumbling block. They were more than mere surface blemishes; they could not be brought into accord with the Marcan hypothesis. Who would be its deliverer in its hour of distress?

Bernhard Weiss

It was Weiss who really "perfected" the two-source theory by virtue of his high scholarly and even higher official authority. Bernhard Weiss (1827-1918) was one of the most distinguished New Testament scholars of his time. In 1877 he became professor of New Testament studies at the University of Berlin, in addition to which he served as counsellor in the Ministry of Spiritual Affairs and as undersecretary with the title "Excellency." With all the personal and material weight of his unique position, he expounded and supported the view that one must "break" with the "prejudice" of presuming that the sayings collection consisted exclusively of "dominical sayings" (*Leben Jesu,* 1902[4] p. 32; *Die Quellen des Lukasevangeliums.* 1907 p. 193).

Then Bernhard Weiss returned to the sayings source the same *narrative material* which Christian Hermann Weisse had removed at the time of his recantation; Weiss explained that Weisse's retraction was founded on an erroneous evaluation of the true nature and character of the logia source:

> But this leads directly to the second point, where it will be necessary to go beyond the point of view of Weisse, who also still shared this prejudice. The very path that he indicated as leading to the discovery of those earliest sources obliges us to break with the prejudice that they consisted exclusively of dominical sayings. Not far down this path it becomes apparent that passages such as the words of John the Baptist, the three temptations in the desert, the healing of the centurion's son, and at least one case of the casting out of demons were also recorded in the logia source, since they are common to the first and third Evangelist. But once narrative passages are no longer excluded on principle, comparison of the first and second Gospels can determine which of the narratives which Mark has more freely and abundantly was contained in simpler form in the Q source. (*Leben Jesu,* p. 32).

Thus the narrative segments which had been taken out of the sayings source by C. H. Weisse were once more incorporated into it. According to Bernhard Weiss, Weisse's action was motivated by mere "prejudice," although in fact it was undoubtedly done after the fact, not before it. In doing this, Bernhard Weiss brought his predecessor new and undeserved glory. Because of Bernhard Weiss's almost unique authority, Weisse's rehabilitation appeared to have the effect of something like a Protestant decision *ex cathedra,* according to the principle "Rome has spoken, the question is settled." In any case, since that time the advocates of the two-source theory accepted as established scholarly knowledge the proposition that: "Source Q also contains narratives."

But even in source-criticism the law still holds that "As one sins, so shall he be punished." Once it was granted in principle that Q also contained narrative materials, their number and extent notably increased. Nor did there remain any real chance of applying a more rigorous standard. Thus very soon the original compass of the logia source was burst apart, and, as a result of the assignment of more and more new narratives, Q expanded into a kind of "Semi-Gospel," as it then came to be known:

> But since Q is a very hybrid entity, part narrative, part sayings collection; and since it remains most peculiar that the large number of the precious words of Jesus which Q contained—it is enough to mention just the Sermon on the Plain (Lk. 6:20-47; Mt. 5-7)—do not have even the slightest equivalent in Mark, we may permit ourselves to surmise, without too much audacity, that Q gradually grew from a series of sayings to be a *Semi-Gospel*, and that it was in this form that we came upon it in literary history (Jülicher and Fascher, *Einleitung* p. 347).

Now such a "Semi-Gospel" was something less than probable, especially since it lacked any kind of historical documentation. Nor could one speak of its actual existence, but only describe it as an inferred entity. Moreover, it really did appear to be nothing more than a "very hybrid" substance. In any case, it did not suffice to constitute a full Gospel because it did not include the decisive element of the Passion story. Therefore it was also called a "Gospel without a Passion."

No one was more sensitive to the burden that the dubious existence of this "Semi-Gospel" constituted for the two-source theory than Bernhard Weiss. It is almost painful to observe how he labored to impute a Passion story to the "Gospel without the Passion":

> This brings us to the main point which has so often been a stumbling block—once Q was assumed to have some kind of narrative. *If it did, then it seems impossible that Q did not contain a Passion story.* But the last events in Jerusalem could be presented only in a continuous narrative, and this Q did not want to give, but rather a collection of themes. But as far as the Passion story in particular is concerned, the Apostles knew nothing more than what was common knowledge. Therefore, such an account must have been absent from Q, since this source stemmed from the apostolic tradition. Nevertheless, here again it is apparent that Q was not a formless collection of material, since this source had a

formal conclusion as well as a pre-history. As has been shown (*loc. cit.*, p. 158), the only story set in Jerusalem which can be shown to have an earlier and simpler form in Matthew than in Mark is the story of the anointing. But it is obvious that this story, like the others, is included in Q not for its own sake but rather for the sake of the words in Mt. 26:12, which in comparison to Mark's most reflective version, exhibits a more nearly original form. But these words anticipate Jesus' burial as the conclusion of his earthly sojourn. Therefore, this story is intentionally placed with the familiar transitional formula of the last days of Jesus and *so, as it were, takes the place of the missing Passion story.* (*Quellen der synoptischen Überlieferung.* 1908 p.80; author's italics).

And so Bernhard Weiss had succeeded after all in making Q into a "Gospel with a Passion," even if it was only a substitute Passion. But what paradoxes he had to set in motion in order to be able to ascribe a Passion story to Q! Whatever has become of Papias' simple note that "Matthew collected the logia"? It has turned into a quasi-Gospel with a pseudo-Passion! If ever a source-hypothesis confuted itself, this is it. The only astonishing thing is how much its champions were able to say about this hypothetical source: what it wanted—what it did not want—what it could do—what it had to do. Now thanks to Q everything could be explained, because by virtue of its "stratified character," acquired gradually during research, it was capable of unlimited expansion. In other words, "Q" had reached the point at which it embraced everything which was necessary or would be necessary in order to confirm the two-source theory. Did it therefore really possess more than a merely hypothetical existence? English scholarship with its "common sense" more and more inclined toward the view expressed in the 1962 edition of the *Encyclopaedia Britannica*: "It is in any case wiser to regard 'Q' as a mere symbol, a designation for the non-Marcan material, which is common to Matthew and Luke" (1962 Vol. 10, p. 538, A. E. J. Rawlinson).

The opinion of German scholars has remained divided up to the present day. If one ascribes a real existence to Q, the question of whatever happened to Q is unavoidable, since there is no literary evidence for it. Given the great importance that has been ascribed to it, it could not simply have disappeared into an abyss, especially since it had had a "continuous historical development" and "an existence within the community."

The answer which was given—the only possible one—was not satisfactory: Q had been "absorbed into the Gospels," as Erich Klostermann puts it in his article "Evangelien, synoptische" in the second edition of *Die Religion in Geschichte und Gegenwart*: "The independent discourse collection had lost its importance after its assimilation by Matthew and Luke (where did Klostermann get this information?); there was not a trace of it left in the second century" (Vol. II col. 428).

Even so serious a scholar as Harnack held this opinion:

> We do not know how long the sayings collection existed. It was submerged in the Gospels of Matthew and Luke, and probably also in some of the apocryphal gospels. Mark alone could not have supplanted it; but the type of evangelical narration which he had created—which was dictated by the requirements of the catechetical apologetic—no longer left room for the separate existence of the sayings collection. It was deprived of its independence, in part by Luke, who fragmented it in the course of giving it historical form; in part by Matthew, who, while more conservative, was in a few places even more rigorous and tendentious (*Spruche und Reden Jesu,* 1907 p. 173).

But even the scholarly prestige of Harnack's towering personality is insufficient to convince us of his explanation for Q's disappearance. It is by no means certain that the "type of evangelical narration which [Mark] had created . . . no longer left room for the separate existence of the sayings collection." If one reasons according to the two-source theory, then Bernhard Weiss had been more consistent than Harnack when he observed that it is not enough simply to posit Mark's "knowledge" of Q. Therefore he ruled against Wernle: "Mark had also used Q." Ewald in his day had said the very same thing, and with as much firmness as Weisse (see above, p. 58ff.).

There was nothing arbitrary about Bernhard Weiss' decision; it was taken for well-considered reasons. He and his son Johannes Weiss (1863-1914), like his father a New Testament scholar and a partisan of the Marcan hypothesis, had recognized simultaneously and independently that in many instances the text of Mark is secondary compared to the text of the first and third Evangelists, especially Matthew; and not just with respect to logia, but also to narrative pericopes:

Bernhard Weiss:

> The phenomenon that the text (of the Gospel of Mark) is at times secondary in comparison with our Gospel of Matthew is not limited to discourse passages but is also to be found in narrative sections; and while Holtzmann tried to play down this fact as much as possible, Weizsäcker, by contrast, was obliged in large measure to concede it. (*Leben Jesu.* 1902 Vol. I p. 32).

Johannes Weiss:

> But in another respect, too, I am unable to meet the demands of the followers of the pure Marcan hypothesis. The triumphal joy with which the synoptic problem is regarded as solved in each and every respect I consider premature; the way in which contradictory phenomena are ignored or violently disposed of I regard as inadmissible; and the enthusiasm for the bare formula of the two-source theory, which regards simplicity as the seal of truth, I hold to be dilettantism. Unfortunately, there are all too many obscure points in the synoptic relationships which cannot be cleared up by the application of the Marcan hypothesis, but which again and again demand a supplementary hypothesis. There are pericopes in Matthew which cannot be comprehended as adaptations of the Marcan text. Thus I cannot agree that in the story of the paralytic, Matthew left out the most impressive and most popular feature—the stretcher-bearers climbing on the roof—in order to save paper or for want of interest in details; or that ingenious intuition enabled him to furnish the manifestly original version of the words Jesus spoke to the Canaanite woman. There are parts in Luke—the passion story for instance—which always give rise to the question of how he could have managed to "improve" Mark's text in such an original manner, so that it resulted in the more ancient and more historically valid version. But above all, there are numerous places where Matthew and Luke take the liberty of agreeing against Mark, although that is not permissible under the basic terms of the Marcan hypothesis (*Das älteste Evangelium.* 1903 p. 3).

Thus both astute scholars, Weiss father and son, are in agreement in diagnosing the symptoms of the illness afflicting the Marcan hypothesis, but they are not of one mind about how to cure it. Bernhard Weiss sees deliverance in "Q"; that is, he thinks he can explain all of the facts in the case with the aid of Q. It was precisely the secondary character of the Marcan Gospel which gave him the idea that Mark must have used Q. Then he reasoned as follows: He considered the Gospel of Mark as a principal source of Matthew and Luke. (He, like most men of his times, rejected the opposite opinion, the Griesbach hypothesis, for theological reasons [see below, Part III "The Ideological Background of the Marcan Hypothesis"].) But then the Marcan text appeared in numerous cases to have an unmistakably secondary nature compared to the first and third Evangelists. Thus Bernhard Weiss saw only the following possibility: Mark must have taken over not just logia but also narratives from the sayings source, specifically those of his Gospel which are of a secondary character.

Since in the cases which he presented the parallel versions of Matthew and Luke avowedly had priority, they must have used an earlier, "more nearly original" version of Q, while Mark, on the other hand, must have used a later, "secondary" one. Thus Bernhard Weiss added an additional Q—Q^{Mk}—(not explicitly, to be sure, but implicitly) to the modifications of Q suggested by Wernle, which Matthew and Luke supposedly used as their sources (Q^{Mt} and Q^{Lk}).

Seen from this vantage point, it becomes easier to understand, in a psychological sense, Bernhard Weiss's command to "break with the double prejudice that Q contained only discourse material and that Mark did not yet know Q" (*Die Quellen des Lukasevangeliums*. 1907 p. 193). But this resulted in an additional complication for the hypothesis, for on the one hand Matthew and Luke allegedly used two different versions of Q, but on the other hand they also used the Gospel of Mark as a model and source. However, Mark also used source Q, specifically in the modified form of Q^{Mk}, *before* the first and third Evangelists used their sources. Also according to Bernhard Weiss, Q^{Mk} underwent a "freer adaptation" at the hands of Mark. And B. Weiss felt further able to assert that "the first Evangelist quite often allowed himself to be influenced by the freer adaptation of the earliest source in the second Gospel" (*Leben Jesu* Vol. I p. 31).

Hence, according to B. Weiss, the sources of Matthew were: (1) Q^{Mt} and (2) the Gospel of Mark which had passed through the medium Q^{Mk}, whereby it had experienced a freer adaptation by Mark. Thus it came about that at times Matthew exhibits the primary text of his Q^{Mt}, at other times the secondary text of his Marcan source, and at still other times the tertiary text that has been "freely adapted." One can see that Bernhard Weiss has made the two-source theory even more complicated, but not exactly less problematical.

Now, if he thought that he could use Q to explain the secondary character of Mark, which otherwise contradicted his hypothesis, his son Johannes Weiss saw the solution of the problem in positing an ur-Mark—Wernle notwithstanding. In so doing he explicitly distanced himself from his father's point of view. Immediately following the above quotation that Luke and Matthew took "the liberty of being in accord against Mark," Johannes Weiss continued:

> The light-heartedness with which Wernle settles these matters is fortunately not common. In regard to these cases it is well known that a series of supplementary hypotheses have been constructed, like that of Simons, according to which Luke used Matthew as a

secondary text along with Mark. Another by *Bernhard Weiss* states that in the cases under consideration Matthew and Luke permitted the text of the discourse source, which had already been used by Mark, to shine through. And then there is the ur-Mark hypothesis, which, in the form given it by C. Weizsäcker, (in his *Untersuchungen zur evangelischen Geschichte*), seems convincing to me. It seems essential to me that we admit that our present-day Marcan text is not identical with the text of the old Gospel which was once read by Matthew and Luke. It must subsequently have undergone revision, probably during the collection and final redaction of the Gospels (*Das älteste Evangelium*. 1903 p. 3).

Chapter V

Conclusion: The Impasse of the Marcan Hypothesis

This controversy between Bernhard Weiss and Johannes Weiss stands as it were symptomatically at the end of the history of the Marcan hypothesis, at the point of its "consummation." They are two of the most distinguished representatives of this source theory, and no doubt the most sharp-witted and closely bound together, not only by the father-son relationship, but beyond that also by their mutual scholarly esteem and their similarity of aims in investigating the Gospels. It is almost tragic that they are unable to escape from their common awareness of the impasse of the Marcan hypothesis. Both sense that the two-source theory has maneuvered itself into a position that appears to have no exit, and both labor persistently, indeed almost desperately, to extricate it from this deadly threat. But they remain deeply divided on the decisive question of how to solve the central problem of the Marcan hypothesis. Each of them knows that the other's position is untenable, but neither of them sees that his own "solution" also cannot withstand critical analysis.

This is the situation at the terminus of the Marcan hypothesis. Here as at the beginning, the difficulties are exactly the same. And that means that they are permanent and immanent aspects of the two-source theory which run through its entire history, the only difference being that they are far more complicated at the end than in the beginning. What has remained constant and unchanged is the fact that the Marcan hypothesis has never satisfactorily accounted for all the facts because it could not; rather, "again and again it required a supplementary hypothesis" for one or the other of the two sources.

Just as in the beginning its problems were made explicit by Weisse's vacillation between enlarging the logia source, contrary to the hypothesis, and expanding the Marcan source, likewise contrary to the hypothesis; so now at its terminus they are mirrored in what is substantially the exact same controversy between Bernhard and Johannes Weiss.

This constant drifting between Scylla and Charybdis, the persistent attempt to escape from disaster on the one side, only to come in danger of falling victim to equally grave ruin on the other side, is the characteristic historical feature of the Marcan hypothesis.

Bernhard Weiss attempted to put an end to this inescapable situation, this interminable illness of the two-source theory, which C. H. Weisse had brought into the world with incurable birth-defects. Weiss cut the Gordian knot and declared it a "prejudice" to believe that the logia source contained only logia, a prejudice that must be "broken." Did he have any proof for this? Had he obtained some new scholarly insight? Not at all! It was only an arbitrary decree which he pronounced dictatorially, *ex cathedra*, in order to save the Marcan hypothesis at the moment of its "consummation."

What was it that Christian Gottlob Wilke had said at the moment of its foundation when he turned against Griesbach's hypothesis?

> The contrary claim that this is not true and that Mark compiled his text solely from elements of the parallel narratives is based on nothing more than a dictum which tolerates no criticism and holds itself to be above mere reasons and results. One might as well give such a dictum its due—by ignoring it and continuing the investigation without further concern. Now we shall proceed. (See above, pp. 45-46).

Nevertheless, in the controversy between Bernhard and Johannes Weiss concerning the solution of the problem inherent in the two-source theory, history has supported the father in his decision in favor of Q. The ur-Mark hypothesis, which his son advocated, has fallen into scholarly disrepute. But, in view of the state of their developing knowledge, it remained only a peripheral question. Both of them had already arrived in part at new and revolutionary scholarly insights which pointed to the future, and touched the very foundation of the Marcan hypothesis.

Johannes Weiss dedicated his work *Das älteste Evangelium* (1903) to his father on the fiftieth anniversary of his entrance into the academic profession. In the dedication he wrote:

> That I accept an ur-Mark, which he rejects, is insignificant in comparison with the great area of agreement between us that

many sections of the Marcan text are less original than the parallel texts in the other two Gospels (p. viii).

This insight stood in sharp contrast to the basic thesis of the founders, the new founders, and the consummators of the Marcan hypothesis: Wilke, Weisse, Holtzmann, and Wernle. Nevertheless, Weiss father and son did not yet dare to draw further conclusions from the results of their latest research. Was this caused by their belief that the traditional evidence for Marcan priority was so certain that it appeared indisputable to them? After all the two-source theory was considered by the entire scholarly world as—almost— "generally recognized."

Now we shall test the fundamental arguments for the priority of the second Gospel to see whether they are still able today to withstand renewed critical analysis.

Part II:

Critical Analysis of Proofs
of the Marcan Hypothesis

Chapter VI

The Proof From the Common Narrative Sequence

We have seen in the course of our examination so far that neither Wilke nor Weisse nor Holtzmann nor Wernle nor Bernhard Weiss was able to provide proof for the priority of the Gospel of Mark. Quite apart from this, one could now raise the question: Even if this is the case, are there not proofs, based on extensive research, that the Gospel of Mark was the source of the other two synoptic writers?

The most important and decisive argument presented for the Marcan hypothesis is the proof from a common thread of narration (Akoluthia); Karl Lachmann, in his treatise *De ordine narrationum in evangeliis synopticis* (1835), calls it "the proof from order."

The founder of the two-source theory, Christian Hermann Weisse, puts the main emphasis of his whole argumentation in favor of Marcan priority directly on this proof from order:

> Still different from the consideration of style and the representation of details, is that of the composition and arrangement of the whole. It is precisely this consideration which carries the ultimate, decisive weight in favor of our view on the mutual relationship of the synoptic gospels; just as it is this consideration that we will painstakingly pursue beyond the present introductory paragraph throughout the entire course of our historical presentation. (*Evangelische Geschichte*, Vol. I, p. 68).

Heinrich Julius Holtzmann, the "new founder of the Marcan hypothesis," champions the same viewpoint:

> Herein lies the essential strength of the Marcan hypothesis: here it never has been shaken, scarcely even attacked, let alone refuted. As if of their own accord, the passages of Matthew in particular transform themselves once more into a historical order which coincides with that of Mark as soon as they are freed from the subject order subsequently imposed upon them (*Einleitung N.T.* 1892³ p. 359).

And William Wrede declares in his famous work *Das Messiasgeheimnis in den Evangelien* (1901, 1913²):

> I agree completely with Holtzmann—and I may add, with Wernle, too—when he notes that the strength of the Marcan hypothesis lies specifically in the fact that the sequence of the narratives in Mark underlies the sequence in Matthew and Luke (p. 145).

What is to be made of this assertion of the common thread or sequence of narration, the "akoluthia"? Is there indeed such a sequence that is held "in common" by all three synoptic writers? The answer is that nowhere does the Gospel of Mark appear in the other two Gospels as an intact and continuous narrative; rather, it runs parallel to the others, always only temporarily and partially, in changing intervals and in quite different lengths. Sometimes it runs parallel to Matthew for a passage, sometimes to Luke, sometimes to both, occasionally to neither. Insofar as all three do not coincide, the parallelism of one of them to Mark ceases as soon as it begins with the other.

Now, instead of saying "Mark runs parallel to Matthew and Luke"—as long as this has not been incontestably proved—one can just as well say: "These two run parallel to Mark." Wilke, who together with C. H. Weisse is regarded as the founder of the Marcan hypothesis, says: "Mark is always the one accompanied" (see above, p. 31), and Weisse, Holtzmann and Wernle claim that Matthew and Luke always return to Mark's main thread of narration. *But this is precisely the question, whether Mark is the accompanied or the one who accompanies.* And when one returns to the other, he must have deviated from him beforehand. The question remains: Who from whom?

For there is not much to the "thread of narration, held in common by and running evenly through all three Gospels" (Weisse): Luke, in his so-called "lesser interpolation" (6:20-8:3), has a narrative block of one and a half chapters for which no equivalent whatever is to be found in Mark. But, worse still, in his extended "Lucan travel narrative" (9:51-18:14) an additional, this time extensive interruption appears in the "thread of narration, held in common by and running evenly through all three Gospels," one that extends for nine chapters, and for which there is in Mark likewise not the slightest equivalent! Griesbach had explained this as follows, "(ut Marcus) tertiam fere Evangelii Lucae partem intactam praetermitteret" [(that Mark) omits in toto nearly a third part of the Gospel of Luke] (*Commentatio* p. 366).

But it does not stop here. The Gospel of Mark, too, has an extended narrative block of almost two chapters (6:45-8:26) which has no parallel whatever in the Gospel of Luke! The existence of the so-called "Marcan gap in Luke" repeatedly so distressed advocates of the Marcan hypothesis that they took refuge in the *ultimum refugium* of all proponents of a floundering hypothesis; they argued that only a "defective copy" of Mark was available to Luke. Eduard Reuss (1804-1891), a supporter of the Marcan hypothesis, writes accordingly:

> Mark 6:45-8:26 did not appear in the book which Luke followed for the most part in one section of his work... *therefore all that we can do is pronounce his source a defective copy (Geschichte der Heiligen Schriften Neuen Testaments.* 1842, 1852? p. 174).

Even in our time no less a scholar than Bultmann followed him in this respect: "I shall not deal here with the question of whether Luke deliberately left out the section Mk 6:45-8:26 or whether he—as appears more likely to me—did not find it in his copy of Mark" (*Die Geschichte der synoptischen Tradition* 1957³, p. 387 footnote).

As a result it appears that one simply cannot ignore the fact that Luke and Mark have no common story line. Not only did B. H. Streeter come to this realization (*The Four Gospels.* 1924, 1930⁴, p. 167) but also Bultmann himself had to concede: "But in the joining of the sources he (Luke) proceeds differently from Matthew. *He does not take the structure of Mark as a basis"* (p. 347; author's italics).

Continuous divergences from Mark's narrative sequence also occur in the first half of the Gospel of Matthew (4:24-13:58). The earliest advocate of the Marcan hypothesis—before Wilke and Weisse—Gottlob Christian Stoor (*De fonte evangeliorum Matthaei et Lucae,* 1794) had already recognized this. In his second work *Uber den Zweck der evangelischen Geschichte und der Briefe des Johannes* he declares: "Only in the story of the resurrection and in the period of the life of Jesus described in Mark 1:21-6:13 and in Matthew chapters 5-13 do the two writers differ noticeably from one another" (1810², p. 294).

Precisely this deviation in the narrative sequence between Matthew and Luke provided *Lachmann* with the impetus for his work *De ordine narrationum in evangeliis synopticis.* He compared the same section out of Matthew and Mark (Mk 1:21-6:13; Mt 4:24-13:58) as had Storr; he divided the whole into chapters ("Capita"), and came to the conclusion: "intelleges: quae enim apud Marcum sunt tertium, quartum, septimum, ea Mattheo quartum, septimum, octavum; item Marci quintum, sextum, octavum, Matthaei tertium, quintum, sextum" [thus it appears that what in Mark comes third, fourth, and seventh in order, in Matthew comes fourth, seventh, and eighth; again Mark's fifth, sixth, and eighth are Matthew's third, fifth, and sixth] (*De ordine narrationum,* p. 576).

One can illustrate the diverging "Akoluthia" in Matthew and Mark still more clearly by starting out with a cohesive narrative passage by Matthew and juxtaposing the parallel reports of Mark, numbering the sequence on both sides:

1)	Leper	Mt 8:1-4	Mk 1:40-45	3)
2)	Centurion's pericope	8:5-13		
3)	Peter's mother-in-law	8:14-15	1:29-31	1)
4)	Evening healings	8:16-17	1:32-34	2)
5)	Rejected disciples	8:18-22		
6)	Stilling of the storm	8:23-27	4:35-41	7)
7)	Demoniac	8:28-9:1	5:1-20	8)
8)	Paralytic	9:2-8	2:1-12	4)
9)	Meal with the tax collectors	9:9-13	2:13-17	5)
10)	Question of fasting	9:14-15	2:18-20	6)
11)	Jairus's daughter	9:18-26	5:22-43	9)

The divergence becomes even clearer when one numbers the comparable passages in Mark's sequence and juxtaposes those of Matthew:

MARK	MATTHEW
1) Peter's mother-in-law	2)
2) Evening healings	3)
3) Leper	1)
4) Paralytic	6)
5) Meal with the tax collectors	7)
6) Question of fasting	8)
7) Stilling of the storm	4)
8) Demoniac	5)
9) Jairus's Daughter	9)

Missing in this arrangement of the sequence by Mark are the two Matthean pericopes about the centurion of Capernaum and about the rejected disciples, which in Matthew appear in second and in fifth place respectively, but have no equivalent in Mark.

In view of the evidence that has been produced of a strong discrepancy in the "Akoluthia" of all three synoptic Gospels, one asks: Just where is the "thread of narration held in common by and running evenly through all three Gospels?" And how, in view of such facts, can a coherent thread of narration be spoken of at all? For the truth is that there is no common thread of narration among the synoptic authors! Matthew has his story line, Luke has his story line, and Mark has his story line. But to declare the last as the "common" one is to give preference to the gospel of Mark that is not justified by the evidence. Ferdinand Christian Baur has spoken on this subject, as on so many others, the definitive word: "It is an *a priori* tenet."

A little reflection reveals the error made by the advocates of the Marcan hypothesis when they compare the three Gospels: They adduce for comparison from the Gospels of Matthew and Luke only those parts which have equivalent contents in the gospel of Mark, i.e., they start their comparison of the three Gospels only with the beginning of the Gospel of Mark. Thereby a key position is given to the latter from the very start. That, however, is an inadmissible anticipation of the result.

But even within the limitation set by the beginning and the end of the Gospel of Mark, one cannot speak even of any continuous common material in terms of content and theme: The Sermon on the Mount —with its partial equivalent, the Sermon on the Plain in Luke—as well as the centurion's pericope, John the Baptist's question, Jesus' sermon about John the Baptist, and the sermons of John the Baptist himself, all together constitute clear ruptures of the Marcan story line, quite apart from the fact that the extensive travel narrative of Luke cannot be fitted at all into a continuous thread of narration. In view of this Bruno Bauer correctly comments:

> For six chapters Jesus is active in Galilee; throughout nine chapters he travels to Jerusalem (*Synoptiker,* III p. 85).

Indeed, this characterizes exactly the enormous discrepancy in Akoluthia between Mark and Luke.

The grave, indeed the crucial mistake of the advocates of Marcan priority, lies in the fact that they also eliminate from the "comparative material" the contents of the other two synoptic Gospels which appear in the structural framework of Mark but not in the Gospel of Mark itself; they accomplish this by claiming from the very beginning—without being able to present proof for it—that this material was added by Matthew or Luke to the material and framework of Mark. Only on the basis of this unproven assumption can Holtzmann claim:

> But if one takes the sequence of the individual narrations by Mark and arranges the stories by Matthew in one sequence and those by Luke in another, one can prove step by step that each of the other two writers presupposes precisely this first sequence by Mark as the original. (*Einleitung N.T.*, 1855 p. 359).

Now, it is not really quite that simple. The only one who here assumes that the sequence of Mark is the original is Holtzmann. In doing so he commits an egregious classical *petitio principii*: the proposition that needs to be proven is already assumed proven and is used as evidence. Only in this way can he claim, as mentioned at the beginning (see above, p. 136):

> As if of their own accord, the passages of Matthew in particular transform themselves once more into a historical order which coincides with that of Mark as soon as they are freed from the subject order subsequently imposed upon them.

But here, too, one must again reply: Nothing whatever transforms itself into the order of Mark—it is Holtzmann who does it. For how does he know which is the "subject order subsequently imposed upon them" by Matthew and Luke from which the passages must be freed? Exactly that must be *proved* to begin with. Since Holtzmann is unable to do that and does not provide such proof, he postulates his assertion as proven even though the order of the material in Matthew and Luke is incongruent with that of Mark.

And how can this previous order really transform itself again into a "historical order which coincides with that of Mark"? Well, one has only to eliminate those parts of the Gospel of Matthew and Luke which have no equivalent in Mark and to regroup the remaining parts according to the order of Mark (who, it will be recalled, sometimes parallels Matthew, sometimes Luke); then, of course, these parts transform themselves into a historical order which coincides with the one by Mark—but not "as if of their own accord!"

Bornkamm has asserted in the *RGG*[3]: "If Mark were not available to us, he could be reconstructed in his main features from the other two [Evangelists]." (Vol. II p. 755). For the scholar who could accomplish this without knowledge of the Gospel of Mark one would have to erect a monument more lasting than bronze. Such reconstruction is possible only if one postulates knowledge of the Gospel of Mark. If one does not do that, another Gospel, even in its "main features," could indeed be constructed only on the basis of the common material of the first and third Evangelists. Then the reconstruction would yield the following, not contained in Mark: a prehistory, an *evangelium infantiae*, a genealogy, a post-history, the resurrection appearances as well as a Sermon on the Mount, and the entire remaining parallel material common to Matthew and Luke. However, from the actual content of Mark it would have only those pericopes which he has in common with *both* of the other synoptic authors, but not those in which he runs parallel only to *one* of the two. For how should the restorer know, without knowledge of the Gospel of Mark, that it has the report of the beheading of John the Baptist in common only with Matthew, and the pericope of the strange exorcist only with Luke? Or viewed the other way around: that this Lucan pericope has a parallel in Mark, but that the raising of the widow's son does not? The same is true of the widow's mite. On the other hand, the parable of the talents, which is contained in both Matthew and Luke without having an equivalent in Mark, would at all events have to be included in that Marcan Gospel which is reconstructed from the other two Gospels.

Hence the whole argument that the Gospel of Mark as a common narrative line in Matthew and Luke— so that these two are constructed "as if of their own accord" after the Marcan order—rests on a preconceived opinion and is not secured or supported by reality. The truth is that *there is neither a continuous actual nor even a merely reconstructible common narrative line. What then is there? There are only shifting parallels between Mark on the one hand and Matthew and Luke on the other—sometimes with one, sometimes with the other.*

Now the remarkable, distinctive, and hence decisive fact here is one that may be derived logically: With the exception of those passages where all three authors are periodically in agreement or where Mark gives his own special material (as, for example, the two miracles of healing the deaf-mute and the blind man of Bethsaida), Matthew and Luke alternate in running parallel to the Gospel of Mark; that is to say, at the same moment that the parallelism of one of these two Evangelists to Mark ceases, the parallelism of the other one to Mark begins. Mark is therefore always—well, what? The *"accompanied,"* as Wilke claimed, or is he the one *accompanying?* In the first instance the initiative thereto would lie with Matthew and Luke—in the second instance, however, with Mark. In the first case Mark would possess priority, in the second posteriority. The "accompanied" Mark would have provided the basis for Matthew and Luke; the accompanying Mark, however, would have used these two as sources.

Let us suppose that Mark were indeed the accompanied, as advocates of Marcan priority claim. How then could the alternating accompaniment of

Matthew and Luke be explained? According to the unanimous opinion of supporters of the Marcan hypothesis, both had the Gospel of Mark in front of them and used it as a model, independently and without knowledge of each other. How, then, does this rhythmical change in the "accompaniment" of Mark come about? Can it be explained at all?

It is completely inexplicable—unless through a transcendental contact. What a mysterious understanding would have had to exist between the two for Luke to have known exactly when Matthew stopped accompanying Mark; that he then should have jumped in, at that same moment and without being told, in order to assume the accompaniment in place of Matthew, until after some time he stopped again, to be replaced by Matthew. This would have had to go on, back and forth, throughout the entire Gospel of Mark, from the beginning to the end. What magical events could have caused this repeated exchange of roles, and in uneven sequence and length at that? What utterly enigmatic understanding would have prompted the first and third Evangelists to sense, without knowledge of each other, when the other departed from the narrative sequence of Mark, and what uncanny parapsychological contact could, from time to time, have sent out the magical impetus for them once more to take their turns accompanying Mark? This whole conception is—well, let us just say: scarcely believable.

Hence, only the other possibility remains—and it is the only one that has any sense and meaning—that Mark revised the Gospels of Matthew and Luke, using them as his basis and choosing freely between them. In so doing he followed sometimes the narrative sequence of one and sometimes that of the other, or—whenever they coincided—both at the same time.

Christian Hermann Weisse, in his "Akoluthia proof," has given a central function to this occasional congruence of all three synoptic authors in matters of narrative sequence and theme, actually placing it at the center of his argumentation. Since then (1856) "Weisse's canon" has been considered the main support of the Marcan hypothesis. It states:

> Even within those parts held in common by all three synoptic authors, *the agreement of the other two is always mediated by Mark.* That is to say, in these sections the other two coincide with each other only insofar as they also coincide with Mark, and this relates to the order of the whole as well as to the detailed choice of wording. But whenever they deviate from Mark, they also always diverge from each other (except for a few insignificant omissions where the concurrence may be considered accidental) (*Evangelienfrage,* p. 72f; author's italics).

For the moment we shall pass over the fact that Weisse's canon obviously leaves questions open, forcing him to appeal to the insignificance of the exceptions and to chance circumstance. Instead, let us limit ourselves to the factual content of his canon, his main principle. It states: Matthew and Luke concur with one another always only insofar as they at the same time agree with Mark; therefore, says Weisse, their concurrence is "always mediated by Mark."

Here, Christian Hermann Weisse makes a serious error in logic. For if all three synoptic authors concur with one another, it does not necessarily follow that the concurrence of the other two is "always mediated by Mark." This is readily shown by the simple fact that one could just as well reverse the conclusion: Mark concurs with Matthew and Luke only as long as these two agree with each other; but whenever they do not agree with each other, Mark concurs with neither. Consequently, the concurrence of Mark with these two is always mediated solely by the agreement of these two with each other.

One of the few who have recognized this fundamental error in logic is B. C. Butler, the "Abbot of Downside," in his book *The Originality of St. Matthew: A Critique of the Two-Document-Hypothesis,* (1951): "The argument conceals a schoolboyish error of elementary reasoning at the very base of the Two-Document-Hypothesis" (p. 63). The objection is wholly justified. Butler, in an amusing example taken from the book by E. A. Abbott, *The Fourfold Gospel* (sect. 1 p. 2) shows just how wrong Weisse's argumentation is:

> Matthew and Luke are in the position of two schoolboys, Primus and Tertius, seated on the same form, between whom sits another, Secundus (Mark). All three are writing (we will suppose) a narrative of the same event . . . Primus and Tertius copy largely from Secundus. Occasionally the two copy the same words; then we have agreement of three writers. At other times Primus (Matthew) copies what Tertius (Luke) does not . . . . But Primus and Tertius cannot look over each other's shoulders, and hence agreement of them 'against' Secundus is only by accident. *As the same results (exactly) will follow, if Secundus copied from Primus (or Tertius) and was himself copied by Tertius (or Primus),* we must hope that Abbott, who was headmaster of a famous school, is not illustrating from real life (p. 66).

In order to illustrate the full dimension and significance of Weisse's fallacy, one which had such extremely momentous consequences for the entire further development of the Marcan hypothesis, it is useful to display in purely theoretical terms the logical possibilities resulting from Weisse's premise. Already Butler had recognized that "We are left with three possible 'relations' of the problem of the 'triple tradition' and none of them is more probable than the other, on the evidence so far presented" (p. 66). But even that has not been thought through completely. In the following we set out all of the theoretical possibilities by contrast with Butler's scheme of the "possible relations:"

Butler:

1. Matthew
    |
    Mark
    |
    Luke

2. Mark
    ╱   ╲
Matthew   Luke

3. Luke
    |
    Mark
    |
    Matthew

Actual possibilities:

I. *Without source:*

Matthew, Mark and Luke arrived at agreement without mediation, and thus independently and without knowledge of one another.

II. *Utilization of a preevangelical source:*

1) All three use the same preevangelical source.

2) Two use the same preevangelical source (=Q); the third uses both other Gospels:

a) Mt and Lk use Q,
    Mk uses Mt and Lk,

b) Mt and Mk use Q,
    Lk uses Mt and Mk,

c) Mk and Lk use Q,
    Mt uses Mk and Lk.

3) Two use the same preevangelical source; the third uses only one of the other two Gospels:

a) Mt and Mk use Q,
    Lk uses either Mt or Mk,

b) Mt and Lk use Q,
    Mk uses either Mt or Lk,

c) Mk and Lk use Q,
    Mt uses either Mk or Lk.

4) One Evangelist uses a preevangelical source; the other two use this Gospel:

   a) Mt uses Q,
      Mk and Lk use Mt,

   b) Mk uses Q,
      Mt and Lk use Mk,

   c) Lk uses Q,
      Mt and Mk use Lk.

5) One Evangelist uses Q; the second uses the first; the third uses the second:

   a) Mt uses Q,
      aa) Mk uses Mt, Lk uses Mk,
      ab) Lk uses Mt, Mk uses Lk,

   b) Mk uses Q,
      ba) Mt uses Mk, Lk uses Mt,
      bb) Lk uses Mk, Mt uses Lk,

   c) Lk uses Q,
      ca) Mt uses Lk, Mk uses Mt,
      cb) Mk uses Lk, Mt uses Mk.

6) The permutations and combinations can be multiplied in a manifold manner when one Gospel is independent of Q and the other two are independent of each other but dependent on Q and/or the first Gospel. And when the number of pre-evangelical sources is increased the possible permutations and combinations can become astronomical.

III. *Internal utilization of the Evangelists without a preevangelical source:*

  1) One Gospel is original; the other two use this Gospel:

    a) Mt is original,
       Mk and Lk use Mt,

    b) Mk is original,
       Mt and Lk use Mk,

    c) Lk is original,
       Mt and Mk use Lk.

  2) One Gospel is original; the second Evangelist uses the first; the third uses the second:

    a) Mt is original,
       aa) Mk uses Mt, Lk uses Mk,
       ab) Lk uses Mt, Mk uses Lk,

    b) Mk is original,
      ba) Mt uses Mk, Lk uses Mt,
      bb) Lk uses Mk, Mt uses Lk,
    c) Lk is original,
      ca) Mt uses Lk, Mk uses Mt,
      cb) Mk uses Lk, Mt uses Mk.

3) One Gospel is original; the second Evangelist uses the first; the third uses the first and the second:

    a) Mt is original,
      aa) Mk uses Mt, Lk uses Mt and Mk,
      ab) Lk uses Mt, Mk uses Mt and Lk,
    b) Mk is original,
      ba) Mt uses Mk, Lk uses Mk and Mt,
      bb) Lk uses Mk, Mt uses Mk and Lk,
    c) Lk is original,
      ca) Mt uses Lk, Mk uses Lk and Mt,
      cb) Mk uses Lk, Mt uses Lk and Mk,

4) Two Gospels are original and have reached concurrence independently of each other; the third Evangelist uses the two others:

    a) Mt and Mk concur originally,
      Lk uses Mt and Mk,
    b) Mt and Lk concur originally,
      Mk uses Mt and Lk,
    c) Mk and Lk concur originally,
      Mt uses Mk and Lk.

5) Two Gospels are original and have reached concurrence independently of each other; the third Evangelist uses one of the two.

    a) Mt and Mk concur originally,
      aa) Lk uses Mt,
      ab) Lk uses Mk,
    b) Mt and Lk concur originally,
      ba) Mk uses Mt,
      bb) Mk uses Lk,
    c) Mk and Lk concur originally,
      ca) Mt uses Mk,
      cb) Mt uses Lk.

Out of all of these possibilities Christian Hermann Weisse considers only possibility III 1 b as given: Mark is the original; Matthew and Luke use Mark. The unfortunate thing about this is the fact that out of all of these theoretically feasible possibilities he declares this one to be logically compelling and with that considers the Marcan hypothesis as proved. Worse yet, scholars have—with few exceptions—accepted this fundamental fallacy. What was it that Holtzmann said? "Herein lies the essential strength of the Marcan hypothesis: here it never has been shaken, . . . let alone refuted" (see above p. 136).

On this subject of the "Akoluthia" proof there remains yet another fundamental mistake in historical research to be clarified and corrected, one that has misled scholars ever since Christian Hermann Weisse conceived the Marcan hypothesis. It will be recalled that Weisse, in establishing the two-source theory, had laid claim (without justification) to the authority of Schleiermacher in order to support his contention that Luke, too, must have used the logia collection of Matthew mentioned by Papias. He had stated that "the famous theologian" himself undoubtedly would have abandoned his contrary opinion and "after closer examination" would have conceded that which he had always denied, "that Luke, too, must have used this collection, directly or indirectly" (*Evangelische Geschichte,* Vol. I, p. 84). Having taken unfair advantage of the prestige of Schleiermacher with respect to Luke's use of the logia collection, Weisse then did the same thing to Lachmann in order to enlist the latter's learned authority in favor of Marcan priority.

As mentioned above, Lachmann, in his treatise *De ordine narrationum in evangeliis synopticis,* made the narrative sequence in the first three Gospels the sole subject of his investigation: "I wish to consider nothing but the order." In this way he reached the conclusion that the deviation in sequence is not as great as it appears to most observers. It is greatest when one compares all three to one another, or Luke to Matthew; it is least when one places Mark parallel to each of the other two separately—"but the diversity of the order of the Gospel stories is not as great as it seems to many, it is greatest when you compare either all these writers together or Luke with Matthew; it is least if you compare Mark with both" (p. 574).

Lachmann then tried to carry this out in detail, that is, as shown above, first by using Matthew as the example in the comparable passages Mk 1:21-6:13; Mt 4:24-13:58. After he pointed out the divergences, Lachmann sought an explanation for them and found it in the thesis championed by Schleiermacher in his work *Über die Zeugnisse des Papias,* i.e., that the logia collection of Matthew mentioned by Papias constituted the core of the first Gospel; according to Lachmann, narrative material from other sources had been added later on to this collection.

In the same way, Lachmann then examined the divergences in order between Luke and Mark ("There is a certain surprising discrepancy of words and things"). He attributed the divergences partly to a possible special source of Luke, and partly to exceptional considerations which might have motivated Luke to deviate.

And then Lachmann asked what conclusions are to be drawn from the deviations of Matthew and Luke from the narrative sequence of Mark in spite of the high degree of agreement they otherwise display. His answer is of decisive significance in regard to the Marcan hypothesis: "If having regard to this close agreement it is clear that the other (Gospels) did not have the pattern of Mark available for their imitation, what remains but to say that the common order, which they all found available before they wrote, was the order established and confirmed by a kind of evangelical tradition and authority?"

That is to say: "If it is *obvious* that they (Matthew and Luke)—in spite of this extremely high degree of agreement—nevertheless *did not have a copy of Mark which they imitated, as a basis,* what other assumption, indeed, is left, than that *this Akoluthia, followed by all (three) as if it had been prescribed to them, had already been authoritatively and definitively determined by the evangelical tradition before their own literary activity?"*

We conclude from this that *Lachmann clearly rules out the contention that Matthew and Luke used the Gospel of Mark; rather, he assumes a preevangelical order of the narrative sequence determined authoritatively by tradition.*

For the moment Lachmann chooses not to examine the issue of whether it was transmitted by oral tradition, in order not to digress from the main subject: "Whether this order was apparent to the evangelists in a written form or acquired by some kind of custom of teaching or hearing, I do not now intend to pursue further, lest I digress from my main task" (p. 582).

It is sufficient, Lachmann continues, if one recognizes that evangelical history cannot be investigated on the basis of the testimony of three Evangelists any more reliably than it can be if a single and, moreover, unknown author were called as a witness. To him it is not nearly as important to determine who the first author of that narrative sequence was as much as it is to recognize the nature and disposition of the sequence itself. According to Lachmann, nobody should believe that this entire "body of gospel history" came into the world all at once in a single delivery "as if by a single birth"— with individual parts complete. Rather, various indications point to the theory that at first some smaller "story units" were formed, originating, presumably, from different authors and later tied together by a common bond. Lachmann holds that such "little units of gospel history" were used by our Evangelists. He believes that he is able to demonstrate rather precisely how many there were and what their content was. He identifies altogether six such "small units"—not five as most authors state. This implies that Lachmann's concept of "small units" represents nothing other than a modified Latin equivalent of Schleiermacher's "Diegesen"—smaller preevangelical narrative units.

According to Lachmann, the first five of these six "small units of gospel history" are contained in purest form, relatively speaking, in the Gospel of Mark. And yet, Mark at times had an inferior source or else deliberately omitted smaller parts; but on the other hand, he also had a certain special source. Thus the account of the two healing miracles in Mark (7:32-37 as well as 8:22-26) is not taken from the narrative context of one of the "corpuscula." According to Lachmann, Mark generally seems to have omitted little, if one disregards the fact that his Gospel ends unfinished with 16:8, minus the sixth "small unit" which includes Luke's travel narrative.

Matthew and Luke, however, deviated from each other by adding and omitting material; at times they undertook "traiectiones," i.e., textual transpositions from the proper place to another narrative context. The parable of the talents, which Matthew places in the sermon on the Last Judgment but which Luke has Jesus pronounce while he was in Jericho with Zacchaeus, is transmitted in such radically divergent forms that it could not have originated from a common tradition. Rather, it must have been rendered by both Evangelists using different authors as sources. It is also noteworthy that Luke calls Jesus "Kyrios" here (19:8), but does so only in places in which he diverges from the common tradition.

So much for Lachmann. We must conclude that one simply cannot appeal to Lachmann for proof of the Marcan hypothesis and still less for any substantiation of it through proof from order. Nowhere, not even with one single word, does he contend that Mark constituted the basis for Matthew and Luke; on the contrary, he explicitly eliminates this possibility ("it it is obvious that they [Matthew and Luke]—in spite of this extremely high degree of agreement—nevertheless did not have a copy of Mark which they imitated, as a basis"). Similarly, he does not make even the slightest claim that the narrative sequence of the first and third Evangelists is determined by the Gospel of Mark. Rather, he assumes a preevangelical stage in which the Akoluthia was determined authoritatively on the basis of the tradition—not only for Matthew and Luke but also for Mark, i.e., before the beginning of their own literary activity. In view of that, Lachmann states, the original narrative sequence is contained in its purest form, relatively speaking, in the Gospel of Mark—he does not say that the two are identical.

Seen from this point of view, the Gospel of Mark gains a quite different importance for Lachmann from that it had up until then. And this is Lachmann's real purpose in his treatise: "Praeterea harmoniarum, quas hodie synopses dicere malunt, conditores, quibus ordinis et consecutionis diversitas maxime adferre solet incommoda, in negotio suo faciendo ne Marci auctoritatem nimis contemnere velint, fortasse non inutiliter commonuero." This may be translated: "Moreover, I hope to admonish, and not in vain, the authors of the synopses—as one prefers to call these nowadays instead of harmonies—by no means to underestimate the importance of the Gospel of Mark in their work, in which major deviations from the narrative sequence present them with so many problems."

It is not difficult to recognize who it is that Lachmann has in mind here: Griesbach, and if one wants to go back still further to the very beginning of Gospel research, Augustine, who had declared, in his treatise "De consensu evangelistarum": "Mark seems to have followed him (Matthew) in his very footsteps and as his abbreviator" (Vol. 1, p. 2).

Thus, what can be said about Lachmann's treatise "De ordine narrationum in evangeliis synopticis" in support of the Marcan hypothesis is that he warns against an underestimation of Mark in Gospel research. But what one cannot claim under any circumstances is that he founded the Marcan hypothesis on the basis of the Akoluthia proof.

Only three years after Lachmann's treatise, Christian Hermann Weisse published his *Evangelische Geschichte* (1838) and right away laid claim to the authority of the former in support of his two-source theory, just as he had done with Schleiermacher. At the same time he twisted the results of the research of these two predecessors for his own purposes. At first he rendered Lachmann's fundamental thoughts essentially correctly and then took the liberty of thinking for him, rather like a teacher who, earnestly setting the course for a student who stands several steps away from mature proficiency, combines fatherly admonition with a "device to win approval": "Nevertheless the sagacious philologist, who has successfully advanced the explanation extracted from these presuppositions, will not fail to recognize that he cannot feel confident that he stands firmly on the ground which he has reached or is about to reach as long as he does not dare to demolish those bridges which have led him to his present position" (*Evangelische Geschichte* Vol. I, p. 40).

Lachmann thought it beneath his dignity to react to such scholarly pretension and the unsolicited lecture—for who, indeed, was Christian Hermann Weisse compared to the great Lachmann?

In his second treatise on the question of the Gospels, Weisse once more claimed Lachmann's authority for his purposes and in doing so went considerably further than before. He could afford to do so: Lachmann had died in the meantime. At the same time Weisse augmented Lachmann's scholarly significance considerably—indeed, he himself gained most from it, since he obviously understood matters even better than Lachmann did. We will quote the entire passage since, as we will demonstrate, Weisse's falsification of Lachmann had a far-reaching and disastrous effect:

> Taking his lead directly from Schleiermacher's discovery, . . . Lachmann—in a Latin treatise written in 1835—was the first to follow a course which had to lead to a second discovery if pursued without prejudice and with calm circumspection. This treatise bears splendid witness to this famous scholar's critical acuteness and temperate, cool-headed caution, qualities repeatedly proved in several fields of philology and, as is well known, in the realm of the New Testament. And yet, so far it has found no recognition among present-day theologians with but one exception [C. H. Weisse himself]. Starting with the question which arises so naturally from this standpoint, i.e., in which manner the apostolic collection of sayings was used by the authors of the canonical Gospels —*Lachmann became aware of a narrative thread, running evenly through all three synoptic Gospels,* one which occurs plainly in Mark while it is interrupted in the first and third Gospels by interjected narrative passages. Since the content of these sections always consists essentially only of speeches and didactic maxims of the Lord, and since, according to Lachmann's own observation, details are also changed several times in a manner which almost invariably can be explained quite satisfactorily by taking into consideration the parts which are adopted and inserted from the collection of sayings, the presumption which followed quite naturally soon thereafter [thanks to C. H. Weisse] would have suggested itself from the very beginning. And yet, Lachmann, with his usual caution, did not venture to draw the conclusion that our Mark really was available to the authors of both other Gospels and was used by them as their structural foundation, to which each in his own peculiar way added the words of the sayings collection and, beyond that, still other narrative passages obtained from various sources. (*Evangelienfrage*, p. 81 f).

Weisse's entire statement constitutes sloppy scholarship and inadmissible logic. What is more, it misrepresents Lachmann's thoughts. We have already seen above how Weisse appealed to Schleiermacher's authority in the same, indeed in an even worse, manner, and how he then foisted his own opinion upon the latter as well. He does exactly the same thing here. For when Weisse writes: "Lachmann became aware of a narrative thread, running evenly through all three synoptical Gospels," one asks in astonishment where Lachmann says this. This is the first falsification of Lachmann by Weisse.

The second is even worse: Weisse claims that Lachmann had become aware of the "narrative thread running evenly through all three synoptic Gospels, . . . starting with the question which arises so naturally from this standpoint, i.e., in which manner the apostolic collection of sayings was used by the authors of the canonical Gospels." Now, nothing of the sort can be found in Lachmann. One can see how Weisse already imputes to him the standpoint of his two-source theory. By no means does Lachmann raise the question of "the manner in which the apostolic collection of sayings was used by the authors of the canonical Gospels"; rather, he identifies himself expressly with the viewpoint of Schleiermacher that Matthew's logia collection, as mentioned by Papias, constitutes the core of the Gospel of Matthew, into which narrative material from other sources was later woven in.

And now comes yet a third falsification: In regard to the narrative thread, Weisse goes on to say that it "occurs plainly in Mark while it is interrupted in the first and third Gospels by interjected narrative passages," and he continues: "Since the content of these parts always consists essentially only of speeches and didactic maxims of the Lord . . . ." Now, a "narrative thread" which is "interrupted by interjected narrative passages" which in turn consist "essentially only of speeches and didactic maxims of the Lord" is a unique occurrence in itself. But be that as it may, it is palpably obvious that Weisse reverses Schleiermacher's thesis—a thesis with which Lachmann had identified himself—and turns it into its exact opposite, and that he imputes it to Lachmann as the latter's scholarly opinion. While Schleiermacher had explained: "To the logia collection, contained only in the Gospel of Matthew in the form of the Sermon on the Mount, narrative materials have been subsequently added." Lachmann, acording to Weisse, is supposed to have determined, while searching for the manner in which the logia collection had been incorporated into the other Gospels, that all three synoptic authors have a continuous common narrative thread which is preserved by Mark in its pure form; into this narrative thread Matthew and Luke are supposed to have interpolated "sections" that "always consist essentially only of speeches and maxims of the Lord."

And now the complete two-source theory has emerged! And who is its spiritual father, distinguished by highest scholarly authority? Apparently Lachmann—with considerable "prompting" from Christian Hermann

Weisse! This is the "Lachmann fallacy," as the English scholar B. C. Butler (*Two-Document Hypothesis,* p. 63) calls it.

Weisse's falsification of Lachmann has produced far-reaching effects that still have influence today. After Weisse had claimed Lachmann for the Marcan hypothesis on the basis of the proof from a common narrative sequence, Holtzmann, too, referred to it, and so did Albert Schweitzer (*L. J. Forsch,* p. 90.). And in 1905 Julius Wellhausen bewailed the fact that Lachmann's influence on the Marcan hypothesis was still frequently overlooked:

> One can understand that Strauss in his time influenced a broader public than Lachmann with his Latin and his dry circumspection; but it is astonishing that the latter is ignored even today as the *real founder of the Marcan hypothesis (Einleitung in die drei ersten Evangelien,* p. 43; author's italics).

Twenty-six years later the weight of Lachmann's argument in support of the Marcan hypothesis and above all the "Akoluthia" proof had grown still more impressively. In Jülicher and Fascher's *Einleitung* of 1931, we read:

> Our first thesis runs thus: Mark was a main source for Matthew as well as for Luke. *As early as 1835, Lachmann demonstrated one of the main proofs for this: the "ordo narrationum evangelicarum." This proof alone would be quite sufficient:* the sequence in Mark is the original, not only because it is the most basic and because Matthew as well as Luke present, in comparison, an unnatural, often affected arrangement, but above all because Matthew and Luke essentially adhere to this sequence from the beginning to the end. The only exception is that they interpolate major parts—but in different places, like Mt 5-7 and Lk 6:20-8:3; 9:51-18:14—and that now and then they undertake transpositions according to their own particular inclinations (p. 331, author's italics).

Would it not have been a greater service to scholarship if Jülicher and Fascher themselves had checked Lachmann's "main proof," supposedly "sufficient by itself" to substantiate the Marcan hypothesis, against Lachmann's original text?

Again we let twenty-seven years pass and look into the latest edition of the *RGG* (1958) on the subject of Lachmann's share in the founding of the Marcan hypothesis:

> The solution to the problem of the synoptic sources that has been advocated most commonly in research till today—that Mark is the oldest Gospel—was put forward convincingly and

independently of each other by C. Lachmann (!) in 1835, Chr. G. Wilke in 1838 and Chr. H. Weisse in 1838." (Vol. I, 754, Bornkamm).

It is apparent, then, that the alleged substantiation of the Marcan hypothesis through Lachmann's proof from order is comparable to Lessing's famous snowball which grows bigger the longer it is rolled. The point of departure lies with Christian Hermann Weisse. The *peccatum originale* rests entirely with him.

Our conclusion, short and to the point, is that the Akoluthia proof for priority does not hold water.

Chapter VII

Proof From Uniformity

The proof from uniformity is based on the proof from order. The contention that Mark is the oldest and first Gospel and thus takes priority over Matthew and Luke does not depend solely on the "common narrative sequence." On the contrary, it is derived from the fact that the Gospel of Mark is uniform and consistent. Christian Hermann Weisse himself declared that the Gospel of Mark is

> conceived on the basis of a living, total perception of the subject, from a complete, immediate image that had been left on the mind and soul. Alone among the Gospels it evokes a similar complete impression of its contents simply by being read, while the other Gospels must be studied for some time before such an image emerges (*Evangelische Geschichte,* Vol. I, p. 67f).

This interpretation gains even greater prominence in the works of Heinrich Julius Holtzmann. He declared in his *Synoptische Evangelien* that one cannot speak of Matthean priority because

> Mark proves himself to be the bearer of an original and unitary complex within the synoptical tradition, since he alone puts the individual elements in a convincing sequence, and since the divergences in the other two Gospels can be explained only as divergences from him (p. 56).

Holtzmann, in his *Einleitung in das Neue Testament* (1885), develops this further:

Even the narrative subject in this second Gospel appears before our eyes in its simplest primary forms. For, indeed, the great turning-points and epochs of Jesus' life and work in Galilee can be traced clearly only through Mark. In this regard Mark alone provides a continuous, *unified* portrayal of historical developments. He alone preserves the common thread of all the synoptic accounts in the natural sequence of its individual nodal points. Only the Gospel of Mark shows steady progress toward the final unfolding of the messianic banner (p. 347).

In this connection, Holtzmann emphasizes that in the Gospel of Matthew "the original sequence of the individual narratives is completely broken up... so that it is impossible to gain an impression of the continuity and development of evangelical history by using the first Gospel alone as one's guide" (p. 347).

It is clear that Holtzmann immediately interprets the facts temporally and evaluates them causally. As he sees it, Mark alone *still* provides a continuous, unified portrayal of the historical developments, and Mark *still* preserves the common thread in the natural sequence of its individual nodal points. Only here is steady progress toward the final "unfolding of the messianic banner" *still* noticeable.

There can be no mistake about the fact that Holtzmann infers the priority of the Marcan Gospel from the uniformity of the narrative presentation. Almost all advocates of the Marcan hypothesis make this move: Wilke, Weisse, Holtzmann, Wernle, and Bernhard Weiss; until Wrede finally declares: "And does it not have its seal in the internal consistency of the whole?" (*Messiasgeheimnis*, p. 7).

Now it is an indisputable fact that the only Gospel that exhibits an unbroken narrative continuity is the Gospel of Mark. It forms a perfect whole. This holds true not only in matters of composition and content, but also in matters of style. It shows continuous literary unity and uniformity. Long before Holtzmann, Henry Owen had observed: "The order indeed is his own, and is very close and well connected" (*Observations*, p. 50 f.).

When one juxtaposes the other two synoptic Gospels against Mark, they could scarcely be more different. Compared to Mark they appear to lack unity; one can even say that they are poorly composed. A major block of discourse material is inserted into the middle of Matthew's historical narrative. In Luke the genealogy is interpolated inorganically between the baptism and the temptation, interrupting the previous train of thought. The "Lucan travel narrative" appears chronologically and topographically so disorganized that in the end one does not know where one actually is; Bruno

Bauer, as one will remember, said of this: "For six chapters Jesus is active in Galilee; for nine chapters he is traveling to Jerusalem." And the stylistic differences, as, for example, between Luke's introductory dedication and the diction of this first chapter, are so great that one can hardly assume that both are from the same author. Matthew and Luke, therefore, are not uniform in terms of composition. They bring together elements of completely different character with regard to both form and content.

Hence the assertion that the Gospel of Mark possesses the most unified and consistent presentation of all the synoptic Gospels is quite pertinent and deserves special emphasis. The only question is whether the conclusions drawn from it are correct.

Imagine a situation in which there are three authors whose work deals with the same subject. Two are thematically and stylistically so different that their individual parts stand far apart. They possess neither a consistent narrative thread nor a continuous and systematic train of thought. The work of the third, however, has everything that the other two lack. Is that proof that the third one has priority, that he is the first, the earliest, the most nearly original of the three authors? Can one conclude that something was written at an earlier point in time on the basis of uniform composition and uniform diction?

Now, consistent composition and uniform literary presentation are by no means proof of temporal proximity to the experienced object; nor are they proof for the priority of a work as opposed to other thematically similar works which diverge from it in terms of composition as well as of diction. Rather, they are exclusively a measure of the abilities of an author, and merely permit us to reach a conclusion about his literary skill—not about the time of his writing.

Moreover, if one wants to draw inferences from the comparison of a rough and a polished version about their temporal relationship, the polished version, according to Bengel's canon "Proclivi scriptioni praestat ardua" (Apparatus criticus ad N. T. in : *Gnomon*, XXXIV), is usually to be regarded as the final one. As early as 1843 Albert Schwegler had established a rule concerning the historical sequence of the three synoptics: "The less complete, less organized, more chronicle-like a narrative is, the closer to the sources and the more nearly original it must be" (Review of Wilke's *Urevangelist* in: *Tübinger Theologische Jahrbücher*, ed. E. Zeller, 1843, Vol. II, p. 213).

There can be no doubt that the less perfect and less organized accounts among the synoptic Gospels are those of Matthew and Luke. If they are supposed to have come later in time, as the advocates of Marcan priority claim, their two authors would have had to accomplish the feat of transforming the well-composed, well-organized, consistent, "polished" account of Mark into one that is disorganized, disjointed, poorly composed, and, in short, "rough." They would have had to tear the Gospel of Mark apart, dividing it up and inorganically inserting parts of speeches and other narrative material, thereby confusing Mark's Akoluthia.

The proof from uniformity reduces itself *ad absurdum*.

Chapter VIII

Proof From Originality

Throughout the entire history of the Marcan hypothesis one main argument appears as a *Leitmotiv*; an argument that is repeated by all the advocates of this hypothesis: the Gospel of Mark unavoidably gives the *impression of originality*.

We shall first trace this view back to its beginnings and show to what extent it helped to establish the Marcan hypothesis. The first to use this argument was Christian Hermann Weisse:

> It will be agreed that, stylistically, Mark Hebraizes more than the other Evangelists . . . But one could extend this remark even further so that it could—correctly and keenly framed—exhaust perhaps all that could be said for the probability that Mark was used by the others and the improbability of the opposite. The Hebraisms of our Evangelist are, so to speak, a consequence, or more correctly, an essential impulse belonging to his more general and decisive stylistic characteristic which speaks most eloquently for his own independence and originality. On the one hand one can attribute this characteristic to awkwardness and clumsiness; one can say that it arose from unfamiliarity with written expression, partly in general, partly in its application to this specific subject, which Mark had not yet pursued in a similar fashion.
>
> But on the other hand this same characteristic gives the

impression of fresh naturalness and appealing liveliness which
distinguishes Mark's account most palpably from all the other
Evangelical accounts. We believe that it would be justifiable to
call the Gospel of Mark—in spite of those formal defects—the
best written of all historical books of the New Testament as far as
the essential, spiritual characteristics of style are concerned
(*Evangelische Geschichte,* Vol. I p. 67f.).

It seems that C. H. Weisse's balancing act has succeeded in "harmonizing"
mutually contradictory stylistic principles. On the one hand he declares Mark
is the most awkward of the Evangelists, and in that way tries to prove his
priority over Matthew and Luke. On the other hand he deduces, from the
same material and from the very same primitiveness just ascribed to Mark,
the "impression of fresh naturalness and appealing liveliness"; and without
hesitation he declares the Gospel of Mark, "in spite of those formal defects,"
to be the "best written of all the historical books of the New Testament"—in
any case he "believes it would be justifiable" to say so.

It is not difficult to perceive how Weisse arrives at these absurdities and
contradictions in his argumentation. On the one hand he is aware that
according to the above mentioned canon of Bengel ("*Proclivi scriptioni
praestat ardua*") the stylistically rough version deserves preference over the
polished version because awkwardness of style represents an earlier stage of
written expression than does stylistic elegance. On the other hand he could
not help recognizing that the Gospel of Mark displays greater literary ability
than the first and third Gospels in its consistency and uniformity of
presentation, but most of all in its greater vividness and transparency of
description. Only C. H. Weisse would have tried to bring these two conflicting
principles into harmony!

The classic champion of the subjective evaluation of Mark is Heinrich
Ewald. He, too, seeks to substantiate the priority of Mark with stylistic
analysis (using himself the latest styles in orthography and punctuation):

One must concede that the whole presentation, as well as the
narrative content peculiar to this work, reach back to absolute
originality and a comparatively early date. The presentation has a
fresh liveliness and fullness of picturesque detail, and yet, in spite
of its overflowing richness, it has a tight compactness, uniformity,
and greater calmness. Hence the attentive observer easily notices
that only someone who bore the material in himself with the
clearest perception and the most primordial certainty could have
sketched such a portrayal. The contents of our present Gospels of
Matthew and Luke no longer bear this sweet smell of a fresh

flower, bursting with the pure life of the subject (*Jahrbücher*, 1849, p. 204).

Here it is then, the famous quotation which in time to come would return again and again as an argument for the priority of the Gospel of Mark: "this sweet smell of a fresh flower, bursting with the pure life of the subject" and the "fresh liveliness and fullness of picturesque detail."

The "fullness of picturesque detail" in Mark has never been seriously disputed in research and remains incontestable. Indeed, Griesbach said precisely the same thing with his view that Mark "expresses paraphrastically and explains more clearly and distinctly." And Herbert Marsh expressed himself similarly when he noted that Mark "frequently offers a paraphrastic translation" as well as some smaller supplements "in describing special circumstances." But it did not occur to either scholar to see in Mark's detailed depiction and his fine qualities as a narrator indications of originality and proof of priority.

But that is exactly Ewald's intention. He states explicitly that Matthew and Luke "*no longer*" bear this sweet smell of a fresh flower, bursting with the pure life of the subject. Here he obviously wants to say—according to his general view on the chronological relationship between the three synoptic authors—that Matthew and Luke are posterior because they had not written from the concrete, bountiful experiences of the first author but from the reflective standpoint of the second and third-hand authors, already "sicklied o'er with the pale cast of thought."

Now, Ewald obviously perceives, along with Weisse, that Mark's narrative skill, which he praised so highly for its "fresh liveliness and fullness of picturesque detail and . . . overflowing richness" does not square with the principle expressed in Bengel's canon and cannot really be reconciled with it. Therefore he now makes the same mistake as Weisse by attributing to Mark, too, the characteristics of a rough style. He does not accomplish this with Weisse's transparent artifice of first turning Mark into a novice writer and next granting him masterly abilities. Rather, Ewald makes his point in another context in a single stroke:

> This much is evident: Mark's narration is absolutely original and coheres perfectly with the entire structure and distribution of narrative material in the Gospel; moreover, its cumbersomeness and somewhat awkward form are unmistakable signs of originality (*Drei Evangelien* p. 258).

Clearly, this is essentially the same double standard of evaluation as that used by Weisse. First it is the "sweet smell of a fresh flower," then the "cumbersomeness and somewhat awkward form" are "unmistakable signs of originality." And both points serve the same line of reasoning, that of establishing the priority of the Gospel of Mark. But such alternating arguments amount to internal inconsistency.

Once again Holtzmann follows C. H. Weisse unhesitatingly:

> The impression of cumbersomeness and awkwardness is to a great extent based on those Hebraisms in style and in language, an impression which comes from reading Mark, in contrast to Matthew and Luke, but which also attests quite certainly to the originality of the second Evangelist (*Synopt. Evangelien*, p. 289).

And on the other hand:

> This truly epic style of emphasizing details and leaving the general context in the background . . . result of a direct, exhilarating coloring of the presentation . . . this picturesque impression . . . a historical narrative in whose vivid and substantive characteristics the most original recollection of the disciples manifests itself (p. 447 f.).

Bernhard Weiss, too, sees the vividness of Mark as the full proof of his originality: "Indeed, there is a great gulf between any process of compilation and abbreviation and the peculiar character of language and presentation in the Gospel of Mark, with its lively freshness and painting of details . . ." (*Markus-und Lukasevangelium* in: *Meyers Kommentar*. 1876[6] p. 6).

And likewise in Weiss's commentary on Matthew (1883[7]):

> The distinctive nature of the Gospel of Mark . . . and especially the original impression of immediate liveliness and picturesque vividness of narration and description speak eloquently in favor of the assumption that Mark is the earliest among the synoptic writers (p. 32).

Adolf Jülicher's reasoning follows the same line of thought:

> Mark is characterized by a lively narration that strives for vividness and full depiction of scenes . . . In some passages Mark's pleonastic, vigorous expression sounds like an intentional exaggeration of the all too monotonous and unemotional diction of his co-referents—Griesbach and Baur could refer to such occurrences when they placed Mark after Matthew and Luke— but actually his naive freshness displays the opposite of the epigonic reflectivity of those distorters (Jülicher/Fascher *Einleitung*. 1894. 1931[7] p. 305 f.).

"Those distorters" are Matthew and Luke.

Nor is Hermann von Soden absent from this chorus: "The local color is brilliantly fresh and yet appears in no way affected . . . Situations and expressions are original in a way that could not be contrived. Everything breathes the smell of Palestine's earth" (*Die wichtigsten Fragen im Leben Jesu* 1904 p. 37f.).

But the most forceful arguments concerning stylistic subjectivity made in favor of Marcan priority are those of Paul Wernle:

> Of all the Gospels Mark is the only one which narrates with total vividness . . . . Every comparison with parallel passages [in the other two Gospels] sheds new light on his freshness and liveliness. . . . An eyewitness would not have been able to describe it differently in written form . . . . How scanty, mangled, and distorted the parallel narratives in Matthew and Luke appear beside it! This continues throughout the entire Gospel. As a rule, one can spot the first fresh narrator by the passages that are omitted by the other Evangelists. He narrates as he heard it from eyewitnesses, with enormous enthusiasm, using all of his imagination, placing himself in Jesus' soul as well as in the hearts of Jesus' listeners, impetuously, high-spiritedly, without tiring. Frequently he forgets a small note which he then appends; these are the passages which Matthew and Luke anticipated and rearranged. But further explanations are superfluous here, since the unreflectiveness, impulsiveness, forcefulness, and roughness of this narrator cannot be described in words. If ever a narrative gave the impression of having originated in the stories of eyewitnesses, it is Mark's. The brief passage about the youth in Jesus' entourage who fled at night from Gethsemane when he was seized by his shirt has all along given rise to the supposition that Mark here speaks of himself. It is the likeliest of all presumptions, even though it cannot be proved. The other Gospels have omitted this episode since it was meaningful only to the one who was present (*Synoptische Frage*, p. 204f.).

Can there really be a more subjective argumentation than this? Now, Wernle knows how to blunt this objection by impugning the intellectual standing of any who might dissent:

> It is always a sign of irremediably inadequate historical understanding if one chooses to see in the detailed style of Mark the finished composition, and in the brief style of Matthew its basis. Even the epithet 'legendary' to describe Mark's presentation says little or nothing. One tells stories in the same way Mark

narrates them. Matthew's stories were never told (p. 158).

Even thirty years later we find similarly immaterial arguments in Jülicher and Fascher: "The fact that Matthew and Luke obtain half of what they write exclusively from Mark is denied only by those who cannot or will not correctly envisage the working methods of these Evangelists" (*Einleitung* p. 335).

That means in plain language: whoever has a different conception than we about Marcan priority is either incompetent or willful.

This subjective "proof from originality" appears even in the standard scholarly work of Protestant theology. In the first edition of the *RGG* we read:

> Thirdly, proof of the priority of Mark can be adduced from the details of its presentation and language. The Gospel of Mark has a quite uniform style . . . . Furthermore, at all times Mark proves himself to be the simple, awkward narrator and chronicler of the people, one who recites his stories without worrying about artistic rules—for the most part with the joy of a first reporter. None of the observations is comparable with the assumption that the Gospel of Mark is a painstaking compilation of older sources. On the other hand, there are distinct signs everywhere that both other Evangelists polished and revised the Marcan text . . . . They have eliminated the pleonasms in Mark's narrative style, as is natural for second-hand writers (Vol. II p. 704 Bousset).

In the second edition of the *RGG* we read:

> The *linguistic style* of the material reveals Mark as the common basis . . . his whole presentation is kept in a lively, simple, popular narrative tone, without literary pretensions, comfortably pleonastic, with less periodization and many popular phrases . . . Here, too, the general impression is not that Mark repeats what he obtained from Matthew and Luke, but rather the opposite, that these two work on a Marcan foundation (Vol. II, p. 424 Klostermann).

The last edition of the *RGG* refrains from offering its own version of the proof of the Marcan hypothesis; it simply points to the "proof that Mark is the earliest Gospel . . . , put forward independently by Lachmann, Chr. G. Wilke and Chr. H. Weisse." (Vol. II, p. 754 Bornkamm).

What can we say of these characteristic examples, which are selected from a multitude of similar ones? These are not the casual comments of secondary or peripheral minds but the official views of the founders or leading advocates of the Marcan hypothesis. Their main argument for Marcan priority has become a principal argument for the Marcan hypothesis in general, and for more than a century it has been brought up again and again in order to consolidate the hypothesis. Taken together, these examples represent nothing other than more or less modified variations of the same basic theme: "the radiance of a fresh flower, bursting with the pure life of the subject," "the fresh liveliness and fullness of picturesque detail"—they all point to "pure originality."

The error of the conclusion is obvious. There is simply no law in literary or in intellectual history that vividness of presentation is a measure of the sequence in which literary accounts originated. But in every case the advocates of the Marcan hypothesis act as if such a law exists: the first one narrates most vividly; then creative power diminishes in proportion to the square of the distance to the experience until we come to Jülicher's assertion about the "epigonic reflectivity of those distorters." But David Friedrich Strauss had already pointedly demonstrated the error of inferring proximity to experience from vividness of presentation: "Even if we concede that no one who does not always narrate vividly could be an eyewitness, it does not follow that everyone who narrates vividly is an eyewitness" (*Leben Jesu*[3], p. 745).

One can illustrate the point with examples from secular literature. Goethe's "Heidenröslein" bears, to use Ewald's words, "the sweet smell of a flower," and yet it is not a folk song but an art song which takes the diction of the folk song as its stylistic model—thereby surpassing the folk song. A similar observation may be made of Uhland's song "Ich hatt' einen Kameraden" and of Hauff's "Morgenrot, Morgenrot, leuchtest mir zum frühen Tod?" All three poems represent copies of the folk song, but how many folk songs are there which could measure up to them? And how many people really know that "Morgenrot" and Ich hatt'einen Kameraden" are art songs? They are widely held to be folk songs because they bear the "sweet smell of a fresh flower, bursting with the pure life of the subject!"

Now one could object that the comparison is unfair, inasmuch as the *Tertium comparationis* is not the relationship to a literary genre but to experience; the "sweet smell of a fresh flower" derives from the fact that this poem was for Goethe the expression of first love. Now this may well have been true, but where is the relationship to experience in "Morgenrot" and in the song about a good comrade? Neither Hauff nor Uhland had ever experienced situations remotely similar to those he depicted—neither of them was ever in a war, nor even a soldier.

It is therefore an error to suppose that the only author who can narrate vividly is one who has experienced things at first hand or knows them from close spatial or temporal proximity. The best depicter of battles in German literature is Gustav Frenssen. His descriptions of the battle of Gravelotte in "Jörn Uhl" and of the naval battle in the Skagerak in "Brüder" are just as unsurpassed as his rendering of local color and of the atmosphere of the Herero rebellion in "Peter Moors Fahrt nach Südwest." And Frenssen, like Hauff and Uhland, was never either in a war or even a soldier.

There are other examples on the same order as these. One could refer to Schiller's "Wilhelm Tell." Its three lyrical introductory songs of the fisherman, the shepherd, and the hunter are rightfully regarded as the best prologues in classical drama. They positively "burst with the pure life of the subject" and breathe the "sweet smell of a fresh flower." Hence one should be able to say, following Ewald, that "the attentive observer easily notices that only someone who bore the material in himself with the clearest perception and the most primordial certainty could have sketched such a portrayal."

However, anyone concluding this would commit an error. Schiller had neither seen this landscape himself nor had he ever been in Switzerland. Hence the only conclusion to be drawn from the vividness and liveliness of narration is that the ability to create matters much more than does the personal experience of the author. Vividness of narrative presentation is not a question of temporal proximity to the experienced object but is exclusively a matter of literary skill.

Hence it follows from all this that the conclusions drawn from Mark's concrete presentation by the advocates of the Marcan hypothesis are strictly subjective in nature. But as such they are not debatable. Where would it end if we were to base all our source-critical perceptions on "impressions"? An objective basis for these assertions and similar ones, i.e., that Mark "recites his stories without worrying about artistic rules, for the most part with the joy of a first reporter" has not been and cannot be established.

Here we must ask: what really motivates the advocates of the Marcan hypothesis to draw conclusions about originality of a document from the vividness of presentation, and thereby to grant the Gospel of Mark such a position of priority? It can be understood only in the light of the history of ideas. We must go back to an eminent literary event of that time which attracted a great deal of attention and met with widespread approval— Friedrich August Wolf's *Prolegomena ad Homerum* (1795). In it Wolf had championed the view that Homer's epics are not the work of a single poet, of one great poetic personality, but rather that they consist solely of individual songs which emerged out of the depths of the common people and were passed on orally by rhapsodists. It was a later age which first cast them in written form and united them in an epic poem.

This notion was embraced by Herder and applied to the Gospels. Just a year after Wolf's *Prolegomena,* he labelled the Evangelists "evangelical rhapsodists" in his work *Vom Erloser der Menschen'*(1796; Vol. 16, p. 1276) but he added, as if frightened by his own boldness: "If I may be allowed to use this name." Herder borrowed this rhapsodist principle from Wolf and saw it embodied above all in the Gospel of Mark. For him the latter became thereby the literary equal of Homeric poetry transposed into the Christian realm; and hence Herder called it a "Sacred Epic."

One must view this occurrence against the background of the general mentality of that time, for only in that way does it become fully understandable. For two and a half decades the literary world of the German-speaking countries was kept in suspense by a modern "Sacred Epic" whose genesis it witnessed and which it could follow at intervals of several years at a time *in statu nascendi*: Klopstock's *Messias*—written in hexameters like the Homeric epics. In 1748 the first three songs were published in the *Bremer Beiträgen*; by 1755 ten songs had been finished, and by 1773 all twenty. Their author was considered by his contemporaries to be "Germany's greatest poet," as the words on his gravestone in Ottensen have described him since 1803.

Was it then so strange if now another poet, who was at the same time a theologian, also viewed the Gospels from a literary perspective, regarded one of them as a "Sacred Epic," and dared to call it that?

On the basis of this rhapsodist theory, applied now to religious matters, Herder attributed to Mark the grand characteristics of a "living rhapsodist":

> No Gospel has so few literary qualities and so much of the lively sound of someone telling a story as this one. . . . This Gospel is meant to be read aloud; he knits together words and shortens discourses for heart and ear. It is even more characteristic for an *Evangelist, i.e., for a living rhapsodist* of this story, to omit whatever is inappropriate to his audience. . . . It was the Evangelist's obligation to narrate and recite for his entourage. . . . In short, *the Gospel of Mark is written from living stories in common language for public reading.*

Of Matthew and Luke, on the other hand, Herder says: *"They do not speak, but write. The stylus changes the tone"* (p. 1279).

Herder's "rhapsodic" assessment and characterization of the Gospel of Mark has been eminently portentous for historical research. The "lively sound of someone telling a story" that he attributed to Mark returns again and again for one hundred and thirty years, throughout the whole argumentation in favor of Marcan priority—until this very day.

And yet, Herder had not said a single word about Mark being the first Gospel or the source for Matthew and Luke. Nothing was further from his mind than to initiate a Marcan hypothesis. Rather, he had assigned a significant function to the Gospel of Mark in the framework of his rhapsodist theory. If one proceeds from the theory that the Evangelists could possibly personify Christian rhapsodists of some kind then, of course, Mark had to come closest to this conception because of his narrative talent, as Herder at once intuitively apprehended.

C. H. Weisse and his followers relied on Herder's authority and accepted his conclusion as scholarly, even though it could have only relative validity within the classical-romantic conception of Homer. Detaching this conclusion from its historical context, they made it the cornerstone of their Marcan hypothesis, and then averred for more than a century, in ever-changing variations: "Mark is the original and possesses priority over Matthew and Luke." Proof: "the lively sound of the narrator," and "sweet smell of a fresh flower," the "fresh liveliness and fullness of picturesque detail," "bursting with the pure life of the subject. . . ."

We summarize our conclusion: neither Christian Hermann Weisse nor Ewald nor Holtzmann nor Bernhard Weiss nor Wernle nor any of the other advocates of the Marcan hypothesis succeeded in proving the priority of the Gospel of Mark with the help of stylistic characteristics.

Chapter IX

Proof From Language

According to a long-standing traditional view, all source theories pass their crucial test only when they have been substantiated linguistically. Systematic research on the linguistic nature of the Gospels was begun for the first time by a country clergyman in Saxe-Altenburg, Gotthelf Gersdorf, in his work: *Beispiele zur Sprach-Charakteristik der Schriftsteller des Neuen Testaments, eine Sammlung meist neuer Bemerkungen* Part I, 1816. The second part was never published.

Gersdorf had submitted his investigations beforehand and in all modesty to the great Griesbach, who instantly recognized their value and gave them high praise. Today Gersdorf is forgotten and is not mentioned in any of the three editions of the *RGG*, even though his research had epoch-making effects. It is from him that we get two statements which have influenced textual analysis and which even Holtzmann mentions: "It is the small details which enable us to differentiate more exactly the authors of the New Testament" (p. 13) as well as:

> Higher Criticism is the most useless thing in the world if it is not governed above all by a careful study of the nature of language. Without such study it makes little difference whether a work heretofore considered authentic is declared spurious, or an inauthentic one genuine (p. 15).

Holtzmann then took up this thought: "But our specific assertions about the synoptic relationship can really stand up only if they prove themselves to be substantiated by an exact philological examination" (*Synopt. Evangelien,* p. 274).

And then he anticipated the results of his investigations, following the example of Weisse, who also liked to forestall objections.

> Therefore, as a test of our particular conclusions, we list here the following investigations into linguistic usage, which will demonstrate:
>
> 1) That all three synoptic Gospels are based upon source A, and that Matthew and Luke are based additionally upon source L, with each source representing a particular language-speaking area.
>
> 2) But that, moreover, every individual Evangelist has his own style which runs uniformly through narratives as well as discourses. Both kinds of passages have been similarly revised; indeed, Matthew and Luke, who combine the two principal sources, exhibit the most literary activity even in regard to the discourses.
>
> 3) These considerations do away with the older opinion that the synoptic authors are mere copyists of an ur-Gospel; rather, they are authors who use their own language independently. No one directly reproduces source A or L.
>
> 4) The Griesbach Hypothesis in particular is hereby proved false, since otherwise the epitomizer would always and persistently have had to detect and omit the literary peculiarities of Matthew and Luke down to the minutest detail (p. 274 f.).

Thus far Holtzmann's anticipated "conclusion." Now for his "proof." He bases his entire linguistic argumentation on the two fictitious sources A and L and claims that all three synoptic Gospels represent nothing other than variations of these two alleged original documents. Specifically, he maintains that all three synoptic authors represent modifications of A, while simultaneously Matthew and Luke did the same with L as well.

This of course naturally assumes that these two original sources really existed. But they did not! Holtzmann was unable to provide proof

> 1) that there really was an ur-Mark,
>
> 2) that there really was a source L in the form in which he construes it,
>
> 3) that these sources were used by the synoptic authors.

The two ur-sources which he posits do not exist in reality. Rather, they represent nothing but purely hypothetical, fictitious subsidiary constructions without real substance. Therefore all of the "linguistic conclusions" which Holtzmann deduced from these sources must necessarily be regarded as false.

Certainly one can determine the linguistic character of the Gospels only by basing it on the *actual sources* available to us, i.e., the canonical Gospels, as Gersdorf did. But it is quite impossible to deduce the linguistic character of the *Gospels*, which do indeed exist and are always available to us, from imaginary "original documents" thought up by Holtzmann.

But Holtzmann does exactly that:

> At all events, from the facts that have been described, the following becomes evident: all the synoptic authors (including Mark) demonstrate through their usage of language that they refer to a certain text beyond the one used only by Matthew and Luke which they sometimes follow literally and from which they deviate at other times when rendering its mode of expression (p. 278).

No, they do not demonstrate that! For this alleged "certain text beyond the one used only by Matthew and Luke" does not exist at all but has only been proposed theoretically by Holtzmann. In that sense it proved to be a truly rich source for the Marcan hypothesis. Consequently Holtzmann can say that the synoptic authors follow this text "sometimes literally"—i.e., at any point at which they concur with the text of Holtzmann's imaginary "source"; while they deviate from it "at other times when rendering its mode of expression" inasmuch as their text does not agree with his fictitious source.

Now this relationship does not present a problem as long as the texts of all three synoptic authors agree verbatim. Then, of course, they represent the text of source A. But in the opposite case, when all three differ, it becomes difficult; for Holtzmann must then decide in each case under consideration which of the three synoptic authors represents the text of A—or at least comes closest to it, where Holtzmann has chosen his own solution somewhere in between.

That, of course, opens the gate wide, if not to arbitrariness, then surely to subjective judgment; and allows Holtzmann at any given time to arrive at conclusions that are fully in accord with his hypothesis. It empowers him to associate the text of A sometimes with Mark (as is usually the case), sometimes with Matthew, and sometimes with Luke; just as he transfers to source A Luke's short version of the Sermon on the Mount, which Mark later "omits" from the ur-Mark because it "was too long" for him.

But how then can Holtzmann speak of uniform linguistic usage of source A and L? The result of all this in every case is nothing more than Holtzmann's clever hypothetical linguistic usage of two likewise invented, imaginary "sources" *without any valid proof whatsoever.*

The *circulus vitiosus* is endless: The asserted existence of A and L is supposed to demonstrate their "linguistic character," and the "linguistic character" of A and L is supposed to prove their existence.

Chapter X

Proof From Doublets

Since the time of Christian Hermann Weisse, the proof from doublets has constituted the main support of the two-source theory. Weisse referred to the fact that quite a number of passages in the Gospels display variants. He called them "doublets." Eighteen years later he still took pride in having coined this expression:

> I had in mind that phenomenon which I—not inadequately, I believe—termed doublets of evangelical apophthegms: the repeated occurrence of one and the same significant saying in different passages of one and the same Gospel (*Evangelienfrage*, p. 146).

Seventy years later Wilhelm Bussmann invariably—and also with pride—wrote "Dupletten" (*Synoptische Studien*, 1925-31) by deriving from the Latin "duplex" what Weisse had related to the French "double." No doubt that, too, is due to "German thoroughness."

Now the occurrence of variants in the Gospels is generally considered to be a sign that a tradition has become indeterminate and unsure. Of course it can also be attributed to the fact that the respective Evangelists had found these variants in two different sources. Finally, it can be traced back even further by assuming that both variants were already present in the same source. Determining which is the real cause in a particular case is difficult, and invariably requires special investigation.

Weisse assumed that the occurrence of variants in Matthew and Luke proved that one passage was taken from the Gospel of Mark and the other from the logia document:

> Especially in the first Gospel it is possible to identify an entire series, so to speak, of doublets of individual sayings of the Lord. That is specifically true in cases where one doublet belongs to that narrative sequence which this Gospel has in common with Mark while the other doublet proves to have originated from that other main source whose name the Gospel bears (*Evangelische Geschichte*, Vol. I p. 82).

By this Weisse means the "Genuine Matthew" = logia document.

He lists the following doublets (we quote here from his second work, the *Evangelienfrage*, because there the compilation is arranged more clearly):

a.) *Common doublets of the Gospels of Matthew and Luke*

1)	Mt 16:27	par Mk 8:38	par Lk 9:26
	10:32 f.		12:8 f.
2)	13:12	4:25	8:18
	25:29		19:26
3)	16:1	8:11 f.	(11:16)
	12:38 ff.		11:29
4)	24:9-14	13:9-13	21:12-19
	10:17-22		12:11 f.
5)	24:26 f.	13:24-27	17:23 f.
	24:29-31		21:25-28

b.) *Doublets of the Gospel of Matthew*

1)	Mt 15:19 f.	par Mk 7:21 ff.	par Lk 6:45
	12:34bf.		
2)	18:5	7:37 f.	9:48
	10:40		(10:16)
3)	5:29 f.		
	18:8 f.	9:43-48	
4)	19:3-9	10:2-12	
	5:32		16:18

5)	21:21	11:23
	17:20	
6)	24:24	13:35
	25:13	

c.) Doublets of the Gospel of Luke

1)	Lk. 8:16 f.	par Mk. 4:21 f.	par Mt. 5: 25
	11:33		
	12:2		10:26 f.
2)	9:3-5	6:8-11	
	10:4 ff.		
3)	20:46 f.	12:38-40	20:45 ff.
	11:43		

Weisse, of course, owes us proof that one variant stems from Mark and the other from the logia document. Here, too, there is no mistaking the *petitio principii:* the two-source theory is supposed to prove that the variants which Weisse calls "doublets," stem from (a) Mark, and (b) the logia document, both of which were their sources. The doublets are also supposed to demonstrate the validity of the two-source theory.

Moreover, there are two clear refutations of Weisse's proof from doublets. The first is that *the Gospel of Mark also contains doublets.* But that invalidates Weisse's whole hypothesis. Therefore we shall examine the literal formulation of his proof from doublets once more by quoting from his *Evangelienfrage,* where it is expressed in clearest terms:

> Since we encounter this phenomenon in an imposing series of explicit, at times very odd examples in the first and third Gospels, *but not in Mark,* they are best suited to illustrate the true state of affairs even to someone who does not possess detailed comparative knowledge of the texts of the three Gospels. *For these doublets can be explained only if one accepts the assumption that the authors of those Gospels,* in all the cases where both or one of them reports a saying of the Lord in two different contexts, *actually found such a saying in two forms; once in Mark, the other time in a second source that was either used by them collectively or by only one of them.* This assumption explains the doublets most simply and naturally, while any other theory would have to

attribute them to unexplained, willful arbitrariness on the part of
the Evangelists (*Evangelienfrage,* p. 146 f.).

Let us disregard the characteristic traits of his argumentation in this
decisive passage; i.e., that his own theory explains everything "most simply
and naturally" whereas "any other theory would have to attribute [it] to
unexplained, willful arbitrariness on the part of the Evangelists." What
remains is Weisse's explicit assertion that there are *no* doublets in Mark.
Now, in fact, the Gospel of Mark contains several of them. How does he deal
with this fact? He himself quotes two examples in his second essay on the
Gospels: "The first example is very simple," he explains. In any case his
treatment of the difficulty is, indeed, quite "simple":

> It is the *repetition* of the saying Mk 9:1 (Mt 16:28; Lk 9:27) in Mk
> 13:30 (Mt 24:34; Lk 21:32) against a different background and in a
> different context; a *repetition which,* even attributed to Christ
> Himself (as indeed it is attributed to Him in all three narratives,
> running completely parallel to one another in both passages)
> *cannot be regarded as in any way unusual* (Evangelienfrage, p.
> 152; author's italics).

Weisse does not trace this doublet in Mark back to the logia document, as
he does in the cases concerning Matthew and Luke. Rather, he simply
characterizes it as a "repetition." As little as one can contest such a possibility,
one is struck by the fact that Weisse proceeds in this fashion only where the
Marcan doublet is concerned, while treating those in Matthew and Luke as
proof of his two-source theory.

Weisse has more difficulties with the second Marcan doublet (9:35 and
10:43 f.). Using his own peculiar tactics of argumentation, he admits at first
that things appear to speak against him, only to affirm immediately thereafter
that a closer examination eliminates all doubts:

> On the other hand it could appear as if the repetitions by Mark
> must either testify against the validity of our explanation of the
> other doublets, or force us to assume that Mark also used two
> sources. Yet one has only to examine the narrative sections in
> question a little more closely. Then one realizes that in Mark the
> dual occurrence of such a repetition, which in both cases appears
> to be easily explainable (*there is not a third one like it in this whole
> Gospel*), is indeed quite compatible with the originality of this
> author, an originality which cannot be denied here with respect to
> any of the remaining details of the two narratives
> (*Evangelienfrage,* p.153; author's italics).

Weisse's explicit assurance that "there is not a third one like it in this whole Gospel" indicates that he is not comfortable with his "explanation" of this Marcan doublet—and rightfully so. For he gives us the choice of only two possibilities: repetition or confusion.

> The two narratives report obviously different, although similar events. The saying is equally appropriate in both, whether the Lord really made the statement on both occasions, or whether *the narrator added it in one case as the result of confusion on his part* (p. 153; author's italics).

Neither theory is convincing. Moreover, Weisse has overlooked something here, since this doublet has a still further variant in Mk 10:31. Hence we have a triplet here. What a pity that Weisse did not notice it. *This* explanation would have been something to look forward to.

And yet this hardly exhausts all the doublets in Mark. First of all, the double report in Matthew and Mark of the miracle of the feeding (once of four thousand, the other time of five thousand) clearly represents a variant—in Weisse's terms a "doublet." How could Weisse miss that? In any case, it would not have served his purpose, since *logia* variants were the only ones that he could use to substantiate his two-source theory.

Furthermore, the parable of the growing seed, which is to be found only in Mark, must be regarded as a fragmentary variant of the parable of the sower. Smaller variants of Mark may be found in the following passages:

Mk 3:8b, 10; 6:54-56	Healing of the sick.
3:14; 3:16	Double investiture of the twelve Apostles.
5:3; 5:4	Double reference to the chaining of the demoniac.
5:2; 5:3; 5:6	Triple reference: "he lived among the tombs."
11:18a; 12:12a; 14:1b	"and they sought a way to destroy him."
13:5 f.; 13:21 f.	"Take heed that no one leads you astray. Many will come in my name....."
14:18; 14:20	"...one of you will betray me, one who is eating with me."
15:23; 15:31 f.	The two mockings.

With two exceptions, these doublets contain no logia, but are historical variants. Weisse's proof from doublets, which was designed to substantiate this very logia theory, is hereby doubly refuted.

In addition to this, there is a whole series of variants that are found in only one of the Evangelists. They, too, oppose Weisse's logia theory, since his doublet theory should establish proof that both Matthew and Luke used *two* sources. Hence Weisse has no choice but to explain in every single case why the other Evangelist did not also present the doublet.

Now, there is one doublet among them that is to be found in Matthew alone, and which has a textual equivalent in neither Mark nor Luke. But according to the hypothesis there must be such an equivalent. The passage in question is Mt 15:24, from the pericope of the Canaanite woman, where Jesus says: "I was sent only to the lost sheep of the house of Israel." A variant of this is to be found in the discourse on the mission of the twelve, Mt 10:5 and 6: "go nowhere among the Gentiles, and enter no town of the Samaritans, but go rather to the lost sheep of the house of Israel."

How does Weisse face this clear contradiction of his proof from doublets?

> Hence we have here, to be sure, the exceptional case of a doublet which cannot be explained by the dual nature of the source documents. Rather, in view of the peculiar character of this saying, it is derived in all likelihood from an apocryphal source (*Evangelienfrage*, p. 155).

This reference to an indeterminable "apocryphal source" certainly represents an argumentation with whose help one can clear away virtually all of the difficulties which stand in the way of one's own hypothesis. Weisse's argumentation does not fare much better where the other variants found only in Matthew or in Luke are concerned. Weisse prefaces his acknowledgement of their omission by the other Evangelists with a general explanation—or, more precisely, an apology:

> In addition to the mutual doublets cited here, there exists a still larger number of them which occur only in one of the two Evangelists [Matthew and Luke] *while the other of them has perceived the similarity of the apophthegms and has avoided their repetition.* He may have done so by shortening the corresponding passage in Mark or omitting or changing the corresponding word in the sayings collection; or, as also happens, *he may have thought it appropriate to fuse the expressions of both in his own characteristic way* (p. 154; author's italics).

The only reply that one can make to this is: how strange that, in these cases which contradict Weisse's proof from doublets, one Evangelist has "perceived the similarity . . . and avoided their repetition"—but not in the other cases!

In individual cases, of course, Weisse's reasoning is frequently even more foolish than it appears here in this general summary. Moreover, once again his method is strictly one of psychologizing, allowing *him* to think for the Evangelist; i.e., in favor of the Marcan hypothesis. Hence he says of the variant Mt 5:29f.; Mt 18:8 par Mk 9:43-48 ("And if your hand causes you to sin, cut it off."):

> Luke, who found the saying in both sources, has nevertheless not only failed to copy it from the sayings collection but also has omitted it from the passage in his Gospel that runs parallel to Mark (17:1 f.), *no doubt because he took offense at its paradoxical quality* (p. 155; author's italics).

This, of course, is another one of the inadmissible presumptions about motivation which Weisse allows himself. The apodictic "no doubt" does not exactly make the matter less doubtful. The same holds true for his explanation of the Matthean variant concerning divorce (Mt 5:32; 19:3-9 par Mk 10:2-12):

> Luke omitted it because, having incorporated the saying in Lk 16:18 from the sayings collection, *he wanted to avoid what seemed to him superfluous repetition, while the author of the first Gospel* assimilated this saying into an earlier context (Mt 5:32) *and was not bothered by the repetition* (p. 155; author's italics).

Holtzmann's Proof from Doublets

This proof from doublets, put forward by the founder of the two-source theory, was adopted by that theory's new founder. Holtzmann identified himself with it completely. He declared: "Among Weisse's most sensitive discoveries is his having first drawn attention to certain phenomena which he called 'doublets,' from which he drew inferences about the origins of the synoptic Gospels" (*Synopt. Evangellen*, p. 254 f.).

We shall limit ourselves mainly to the modifications which Holtzmann made in the proof from doublets, and examine the question of whether they offer any new considerations which could weigh in favor of the two-source theory.

Holtzmann defines doublets as "sayings which appear twice in the same Gospel and which testify irrefutably to the dual nature of the sources out of which the Gospel was composed."

At the same time he gives a remarkable explanation: "The regularity of these observations speaks sufficiently against the *weak excuse* of past and present harmonists, *according to which Jesus must have said all these sayings twice"* (p. 256).

But simultaneously Holtzmann concedes: "Now in essence the possibility of such repetitions by all means must be admitted."

And then he cites the two cases which Weisse had already been forced to regard as Marcan doublets. And one discovers to one's astonishment that all at once Holtzmann, too, sees the matter differently; for here, just as with Weisse, where Mark is concerned we suddenly find "genuine repetitions." And now, suddenly there is no mention of a "weak excuse" anymore, "according to which Jesus must have said all these sayings twice." Instead we read: "The less the form in both passages demonstrates any kind of far-fetched attempt at conformity, the less complex the situation is" (p. 256).

It is obvious that the spirit of C. H. Weisse lives on in Holtzmann.

Then his own source theory gets him into an even more difficult situation than Weisse's. Weisse of course, in his first work, *Evangelische Geschichte*, tried to establish proof from doublets without reference to an ur-Mark=source A. Rather, he had confined himself to reasoning on the basis of the canonical Mark. But Holtzmann starts immediately with A, the ur-Mark, which, according to the hypothesis, contains an extended Gospel of Mark (expanded, that is, by that Gospel's parallels to Matthew and Luke).

Consequently his ur-Mark now contains even more doublets than Weisse's simpler Mark. Hence Holtzmann necessarily must admit still further Marcan variants which, according to him, come from A:

    a) Lk 6:38 = Mt 7:2 = Mk 4:24

    b) Lk 6:44,45 = Mt 12:34,35

    c) Mk 7:21,22 = Mt 15:19,20

But Holtzmann has an answer for this just as C. H. Weisse did; he likewise declares them to be real repetitions, although he expresses himself somewhat more diplomatically: ". . . and hence the same evaluation will apply to this doublet as to the other two" (p. 257).

To be sure, it is painfully reminiscent of Weisse's above-mentioned excuse and assurance ("But there is not a third one like it in this whole Gospel,") when Holtzmann adds: "But these are the only doublets in A" (p. 257).

Now, since Holtzmann had transferred the Lucan Sermon on the Mount to A, i.e., to the ur-Mark, and since at the same time he had made the Matthean Sermon on the Mount into a mixture of A, L, and "other sources" and called it a "compilation," he could not simply assign quotations from the latter to L. Rather, he felt obliged to undertake fairly difficult transactions. In doing so he naturally had to distance himself from Weisse's argumentation:

> On the other hand, Matthew contains doublets which are to be distinguished from these passages, and which Weisse does not rightly judge. In them, Matthew has anticipated passages from A for reasons of literary composition and then encountered them again in their proper context, and incorporated them once more (p. 258).

He offered the following examples of doublets from Matthew's Sermon on the Mount:

a) Mt 5:29,30; 18:8,9 = Mk 9:43,47 ("logia on offenses")

b) Mt 5:32; 19:9 = Mk 10:10f. ("logia concerning adultery").

At this point Holtzmann became the prisoner of his own theory. As a result of his vivisection of the Matthean Sermon on the Mount and its over-structured reconstruction, he could no longer employ these texts as arguments in favor of his proof from doublets, since Matthew had "anticipated passages from A for reasons of literary composition."

Something similar is true of Mt 10:40,42 (conclusion of the missionary discourse: "He who receives you receives me . . ."): 18:5 (=Mk 9:37,41), since Holtzmann, following his two-source theory, had declared Matthew's version of the missionary discourse to be a combination of A (the sending out of the twelve) and L (the sending out of the seventy). Hence these passages, too, could not be used as evidence for the proof from doublets.

Finally, the same must be said of the last text of this kind, Mt 17:20; 21:21=Mk 11:23 (faith that moves mountains). Holtzmann had characterized Mt 17:20 as "an amalgam of A and L, but one in which Matthew, who had become familiar with the form of A, Mk 11:23, put the mountain in the place of the fig tree" (p. 194). After having asserted without any proof that Matthew had again anticipated a passage from A, Holtzmann could no longer appropriately refer to it as proof for Mark's dependence on two sources.

The conclusion is short and simple: Holtzmann's proof from doublets offers nothing new that would be likely to convince us of the validity of the two-source theory. On the contrary, he had damaged its position with his "anticipations from A."

Wernle's Proof from Doublets

It is essentially the same one which we already know from our considerations of Weisse and Holtzmann—with a few "improvements." Wernle states his fundamental opinion without reservation: "The doublets have served as the main argument for the two-source theory" (*Synopt. Frage,* p. 209).

Then, more pragmatically:

> the large number of doublets in Matthew demonstrates that it is not a first work but a work dependent on sources. The larger part of it can best be explained, as is the case with Luke, as a combination of Mark and the sayings collection (p. 111).

But this "main argument for the two-source theory" runs up against the fact that Mark also contains doublets. What was to be done about them? They had been defused by Weisse and Holtzmann, who had presented them as "real repetitions". And Wernle proceeds in the same manner. But while those two had always offered excuses with noticeably bad scholarly conscience ("cannot be regarded as containing anything unusual"; "but there is not a third one like it in this whole Gospel"; "but these are the only doublets in A"), Wernle has fewer scruples. He portrays the repetitions as necessary:

> Of course Mark does not completely lack doublets. The most conspicuous is 9:35 = 10:43 (variant of the saying: "If any one would be first, he must be last of all.") Evidently these are the same dominical sayings in different form. But both times they are necessary. They had to be included in the dispute for precedence among the disciples, and they could not be left out of the discourse about rewards (p. 214).

Wernle also knows what to do about the second Marcan doublet he cites. He distinguishes two different senses and attempts to present them as two intentional modifications:

> Twice Jesus takes a child in his arms (9:36 and 10:16)[1]; but in the first case he does so in order to show the value and nobility of the little ones to his disciples; in the latter, to show the priority of children in the Kingdom of God (p. 214).

There are, however, still other doublets in the Gospel of Mark, as well as in Matthew and Luke, which do not consist of logia; such as the double feeding

---

[1] ἐναγκαλισάμενος.

miracle already mentioned above. Such *narrative* variants must have constituted proof *against* the two-source theory even according to Wernle's presupposed definition of the concept of doublets. How does Wernle regard this matter? It certainly causes him no embarrassment:

> The originality of the Marcan text is guaranteed by the Matthean parallel to such an extent that the omission by Luke is of no consequence. But how, then, is the doublet to be explained? There are two possibilities. One is that a single story was told so differently—especially with such different numerical data—that a later hearer concluded that it happened twice; much as when, in Gospel harmonies, the centurion at Capernaum and the royal official are told as two stories. The assumption that one version stems from written and the other one from oral tradition does not make it any easier, of course. The other possibility is that the story, i.e., its basic events, happened twice; Jesus' belief in providence twice triumphed overwhelmingly over the despondency of the disciples. The presumption that, in the story of Jesus, the words "Those who above all seek the Kingdom of God shall inherit the earth" were fulfilled more than once   this is the meaning of these narratives—is perhaps not so absurd . . . .
> One cannot see how the assumption of written sources would be of any help here (p. 214 f.).

Here it would seem that Wernle has not exactly rendered a great service to the doublet theory. For his first objection, that because of variations within the oral tradition "a later hearer concluded that it happened twice," is a foregone conclusion which is equally valid for all other variants that found a place in the Gospel as assumed repetition of events.

In the second place, Wernle (like Weisse and Holtzmann before him) inferred from the logia doublets that their dual historical transmission is *proof* that they originated in two sources, which they considered to be (a) Mark, and (b) the logia document. But here, where what we are concerned with is first a *narrative* variant and then a *Marcan* doublet, Wernle simply declares: "One cannot see how the assumption of written sources would be of any help here."

Of course, he is quite right; for this narrative variant in Mark represents a clear refutation of the proof from doublets, which, according to Wernle, has "served as the main argument for the two-source theory." The two "sources" for the doublets cannot be applied here. Neither can one of them be Mark—for indeed he himself is involved—nor can the other one be the sayings collection; for here we are not dealing with a logion but with a historical narrative report: Hence for Wernle—and similarly for C. H. Weisse and Holtzmann—this self-induced impasse of their two-source theory should properly have led to only one result—admission that the proof from doublets does not stand the test.

It rests on a transparently erroneous evaluation of their evidence. For what are doublets essentially? Nothing other than variants of tradition and therefore an expression of fluctuations in the tradition. They must not only be regarded as such but also *evaluated* as such. It is the fundamental error of the advocates of Marçan priority that they are incapable of seeing the matter in the right perspective. They do not realize that doublets, just like all other variants, do not occupy a special position within the framework of the vast variational possibilities offered by historical tradition. But they bestow upon them precisely such a position by branding them as "doublets," one part of which can only originate from Mark, the other only from the sayings source. By doing this, however, they inadmissibly narrow down (in contradiction to the real facts) the almost boundless scope of the historical tradition.

Moreover, here again we find the same *petitio principii* that accompanies most other "proofs" of the Marcan hypothesis. The proof from doublets is supposed to demonstrate the validity of the two-source theory, and the validity of the two-source theory is a presupposition on which the proof from doublets is based, with the result that half the doublets must be viewed as stemming from Mark and the other half from the logia document.

Apart from that, the proof from doublets has been reduced *ad absurdum* in the course of the internal historical development of the two-source theory. The proof from doublets really made sense only when it was based on the "consistent" two-source theory as it was founded by C. H. Weisse and developed further by Holtzmann and Wernle; i.e., that there are two different sources which can be clearly distinguished from each other: a purely historical source and a pure sayings source. This was the hypothetical prerequisite for Weisse's doublet—"aperçu." But now that it had become clear that this led nowhere—Q must have contained narratives too, and Mark must also have used Q—the proof from doublets collapsed because it had become superfluous. From this viewpoint we can at last see, at least psychologically, why the three main advocates of the proof from doublets were so insistent that Matthew and Luke must have taken the logia, which also appeared in the Gospel of Mark, from the *latter* and *not from Q*. For Mark, they said, obtained them from *Peter*.

We shall now turn to their proof of Petrine origin.

Chapter XI

Proof From Petrine Origin

The pioneers of the Marcan hypothesis have always taken great pains to establish proof for the Petrine origin of the second Gospel, and subsequently have tried to defend it tooth and nail. From the first, the two founders of the hypothesis, Wilke and Weisse, made this proof the cornerstone of their source theory. Mark's report was supposed to have had its origin directly in the eyewitness testimony of Peter, who passed on everything he had seen and heard directly to Mark. Peter, the most prominent disciple of Jesus, who himself called Peter the "rock"—what a rock he was at the same time for the Marcan hypothesis! The authenticity of the second Gospel as a *historical* source for the life of Jesus depends on him. Therefore they fought relentlessly for the primacy of the Gospel of Mark. For if that primacy was not established beyond any doubt, then the cornerstone of the Marcan hypothesis actually became questionable, too—i.e., that the second Gospel was the main source of the first and third Evangelists.

C. H. Weisse, and after him the rest of the advocates of Marcan priority, had already tried to establish stylistic proof   through proof from originality as well as proof from uniformity—that the Marcan Gospel is to be traced back to Peter's eyewitness testimony, transmitted through the medium of Mark. Then he tried to furnish historical proof for it, too. To accomplish this he went back, as he had done in the case of Matthew, to the Papias note in Eusebius (*hist. eccl.* III, 39) concerning Mark:

> This too the presbyter said: Mark, who was the translator of
> Peter, wrote down carefully from his memory—but not in correct

sequence—what the Lord had proclaimed or what deeds he had performed; for he had neither heard the Lord nor followed Him, but later, as stated, he had followed Peter. The latter shaped his lectures as circumstances required, but not as one who prepares a compilation of the words of the Lord. Therefore Mark did not do anything wrong when he wrote down some things as he remembered them; for he took care to omit nothing from what he had heard and to misrepresent no part of it.

Καὶ τοῦθ' ὁ πρεσβύτερος ἔλεγεν· Μάρκος μὲν ἑρμηνευτὴς Πέτρου γενόμενος, ὅσα ἐμνημόνευσεν, ἀκριβῶς, ἔγραψεν. οὐ μέντοι τάξει τὰ ὑπὸ τοῦ κυρίου ἢ λεχθέντα ἢ πραχθέντα, οὔτε γὰρ ἤκουσεν τοῦ κυρίου οὔτε παρηκολούθησεν αὐτῷ, ὕστερον δέ, ὡς ἔφην, Πέτρῳ· ὃς πρὸς τὰς χρείας ἐποεῖτο τὰς διδασκαλίας, ἀλλ ' οὐχ ὥσπερ σύνταξιν τῶν κυριακῶν ποιούμενος λογίων, ὥστε οὐδὲν ἥμαρτεν Μάρκος οὕτως ἔνια γράψας ὡς ἀπεμνημόνευσεν. ἑνὸς γὰρ ἐποιήσατο πρόνοιαν, τοῦ μηδὲν ὧν ἤκουσεν παραλιπεῖν ἢ ψεύσασθαί τι ἐν αὐτοῖς (Papias Fragment, p. 39).

Weisse then claims that Mark's written record of the words and deeds of Jesus are nothing other than our canonical Gospel of Mark. However Papias did not say anything about that. Also, against this conjecture stood the opinion of a distinguished scholarly authority: Schleiermacher, in his work "Uber die Zeugnisse des Papias von unsern beiden ersten Evangelien," had stated quite clearly:

> But whether this scripture is our present Gospel of Mark is, in my opinion at least, highly questionable; and if the question must be answered in the negative, then a second question arises about the relationship between our Gospel and that other document (p. 384)

Two pages later Schleiermacher summarized his result:

> What then was this text of Mark which Papias describes to us? It is equally unlikely that this should be our Gospel of Mark as that the other one should be our Gospel of Matthew, but rather a collection of individual events from the life of Christ, words and deeds rendered exactly as Peter had interspersed them into his lectures. They are neither connected to a continuous whole nor even to certain sections, without regard for whether it followed a temporal or material order, but written down as these features individually came to mind (p. 368).

Similarly Schleiermacher regarded it as "the least likely thing in the world" that "Mark should have written such a text as our Gospel if he—as is most likely—still wrote as Peter's translator, and hence was, as it were, hard pressed to find even time for that."

Christian Hermann Weisse replied to this: "We, for our part, feel obliged to turn these remarks about probability and improbability completely around" (*Evangelische Geschichte,* Vol. I p. 42). He claimed that it is altogether improbable that Mark wrote down Peter's report during the latter's lifetime; and expressed this opinion again in the affected manner so characteristic of him:

> Precisely here, one would have to assume that Mark made his observations carefully and calculatingly, with an eye toward eventual publication; and to imagine Mark as someone constantly on the alert, just as Las Cases and O'Meara watched Napoleon on St. Helena or as Falk and Eckermann observed Goethe (Vol. I p. 42).

Hence Weisse stood by his view that the text by a Mark mentioned by Papias is identical to our canonical Gospel of Mark. Allegedly, it was written after the death of Peter by his translator and travelling companion, Mark, who wrote as best he could from what he recalled of what the Apostle had communicated about the words and deeds of the Lord. However, as is the nature of such matters, these recollections were not written down exactly in correct sequence, "since he had not heard Peter narrate them in order, but had himself to imagine such an order as well as he was able, without the assistance of his master" (Vol. I p. 43).

Then Weisse had to provide proof that Mark's informant—specifically Mark the Evangelist—was the Apostle Peter. If what Weisse maintained were true, one would have every right to expect that the figure of Peter would not only take a central position in the Gospel of Mark, but also, beyond that, would stand out considerably more than in the other Gospels. *This, however, is not the case—on the contrary.* The following important passages which refer to Peter in the two parallel texts have no equivalent in Mark:

Mt 14:28-31:   Simon walks on the water, sinks and is rescued by Jesus: "O man of little faith, why do you doubt?"

16:17-20   Simon's beatitude; the bestowal of the name Peter; the granting of the keys.

17:14-27:   The questioning of Simon by the tax collectors as to whether Jesus paid the half-shekel tax; Jesus' charge to Peter; the shekel in the fish's mouth.

18:21,22:   Peter's question about how often one should grant forgiveness.

Lk 5:3-10:   Peter's miraculous catch of fish. "Depart from me, for I am a sinful man."—"Henceforth you will be catching men."

22:31-32:   "Simon, Simon, behold, Satan demanded to have you, that he might sift you like wheat, but I have prayed for you that your faith shall not fail; and when you have turned again, strengthen your brethren."

22:8   In order to prepare the Passover feast, Jesus sends out Peter and John (Mark: "two of his disciples").

All of these passages refer to Peter, and emphasize his name to such an extent that one could make a case for their derivation directly from Peter—if they were found in the Gospel of Mark. But, as it is, they speak *against* Weisse's thesis and underline the fact that his assertions about the Petrine origin of the Gospel of Mark are unfounded.

But Weisse refused to be impressed by this hard fact and once more knew just what to do about it:

Especially in a not insignificant sequence of passages in the first Gospel, but also a few times in Luke, remarks and other anecdotes of Peter are told of which Mark has nothing to say; *in respect of the passages, therefore, we can assume only that the authors of those Gospels obtained them from other sources* (Vol. I, p. 62; author's italics).

Weisse's contention that this is the only assumption to be made contains the unstated presumption that the Marcan hypothesis is correct. But the assumption that it is *not* correct was in any case still a possibility.

But this doubt evidently occurred to Weisse himself, for he immediately set about stilling it:

This assumption [that Matthew and Luke obtained material about Peter that is not in Mark from "other sources"] itself contains nothing that contradicts our fundamental belief. That is especially true if one considers that the same greater detail or greater liveliness of the Petrine narratives, which had the effect of bringing into existence the first and only cohesive written presentation of Jesus' life story, could indeed also have given rise to many other anecdotes associated with his person, some of nay even have contained legendary features (Vol. I, p.

But this was not sufficient. Weisse had still more to say about these alleged "other sources" from which Matthew and Luke are suddenly supposed to have obtained material, just as they had from the Gospel of Mark and the logia:

These (the cited passages) in both synoptic Gospels are by no means all derived from sources of equal rank with Mark; rather, it is likely that they were obtained from a tradition bordering partially on the realm of the apocryphal (Vol. I p. 63).

One sees that Weisse always manages to get by somehow. But how strange that elsewhere we cannot find out anything about these extra-Marcan sources "bordering on the realm of the apocryphal." It is clearly a tendentious fantasy designed to promote his hypothesis.

Weisse then tried another way of demonstrating the existence of "signs that historical tradition originated with Peter; if not in every single point, then surely now and then in meaningful, prominent passages" (Vol. I p. 59). He regards the first one as being the summoning of Simon and his brother Andrew to become disciples of Jesus (Mk 1:16-20). But the summons of the two sons of Zebedee occurs in the same narrative context. Hence the primacy of Peter cannot be deduced from this passage.

Weisse sees a second point at which Mark brings Peter into special prominence in the passage Mk 1:36, following the healing of Peter's mother-in-law, when Mark designates the disciples and companions of Jesus as "Simon and those who were with him"—[1]. "A strange expression," Weisse says, "which he (Mark) would hardly have used if he, for personal reasons, had not been accustomed to think of Peter first where he had to mention the disciples" (Vol. I p. 60). Weisse adds here:

> We consider it superfluous to call special attention to every single one of the other passages in this Gospel and the corresponding passages in the other two Gospels where Peter appears more prominently than the rest of the disciples. It is manifest, and certainly cannot be denied by anyone, that these passages are frequent and important enough in order to prove—provided *our* general line of questioning is accepted—what needs to be proved; this is especially convincing in view of the fact that they are opposed by few or no passages from which one could draw similar conclusions about another way the Gospels could have originated (Vol. I p. 60).

Now, the formulation "Peter and those who were with him" could be of significance only if it were Mark's own expression and if he used it frequently. But we also find a precisely corresponding formulation in Luke, following this narrative, in his special material about Peter's catch of fish (5:9).

---

[1]Σίμων καὶ οἱ μετ' αὐτοῦ.

Moreover Weisse has interpreted the facts too quickly here. It follows from the situation that Jesus entered the house of Peter and withdrew from the crowd in the dawn of the early morning; and that he went into seclusion to pray. Because the crowd was looking for him and Jesus could not be found, the disciples went in search of Jesus, led by Peter, in whose house, of course, he stayed. To deduce from this that Peter is mentioned prominently is not justified, since it follows naturally from the situation that Peter should place himself at the head of the searching disciples and take up their leadership. Nor is there any other single citation in Mark that supports Weisse's assertion that Mark, "for personal reasons, had been accustomed to think of Peter first where he had to mention the disciples."

Therefore it is with no justification whatever that Weisse declares: "We consider it superfluous to call special attention to every single one of the other passages in this Gospel and the corresponding passages in the other two Gospels where Peter appears more prominently than the rest of the disciples." That Peter is the most mentioned disciple *in all three synoptic Gospels* is not at issue; it is merely a question of establishing proof that he occupies a singular position in *Mark* by contrast with the other two Gospels. *But it is precisely this proof that cannot be presented.* If a second passage of the kind just discussed could be found in Mark, Weisse certainly would not have neglected to mention it in order to provide further proof for his assertion.

Instead of providing direct proof for the primacy of Peter, he then attempted to furnish it with indirect proof from Matthew and Luke. The manner in which he accomplished this is once again typical of Weisse's style of argumentation, and at the same time permits us to reach a conclusion about its ability to convince:

> On the other hand some of the passages in Matthew and Luke deserve and require special consideration; in them Peter is introduced by name without any explicit precedent in Mark. Among them are two that are of such a nature that they provide, in the most surprising and compelling way imaginable, double proof for the dependence of those two Gospels on Mark and for the authenticity of the latter. The first of these passages is contained in the discussion which Jesus holds before the Pharisees and with his disciples concerning purification rites. Here a question, which in Mark is asked by the disciples in general, is attributed explicitly to Peter (Mt 15:15cf. Mk 7:17). At first glance this seems to stand in sharp contradiction to the assumption that the Gospel of Mark is derived more directly from Peter's narratives than is the Gospel of Matthew. But closer examination reveals the explanation of this

peculiar circumstance. The author of the first Gospel had inserted into a narrative borrowed from Mark some words derived from another source and likewise occasioned by a question of the disciples. (Footnote: v. 12-14. That he really inserted these words and that it was not perhaps a case of Mark having omitted them is made evident by the fact that they most strikingly interrupt the continuity between v. 11 and v. 15). As he returned to the Marcan narrative, *he felt the need* to distinguish the new question of the disciples from the earlier one, since it cannot be posed with the former in an uninterrupted sequence of discourse. Assuming, then, that Mark, whose Gospel Matthew had before him, had heard this question as well as the whole discourse from Peter, and that Peter had probably reported his own words first, we can conclude that he put the question directly into Peter's mouth (Vol. II p. 63; author's italics).

One can see what horrendous falsifications the psychological method of argumentation can lead to. The simple facts present in Mt 15;15 par Mk 7:17 are the following: in Mark we read: "his disciples asked him about the parable," in Matthew, on the other hand: "But Peter said to him, explain the parable to us."

Weisse, with the help of his psychologizing method of argumentation, wants to furnish proof that Matthew has derived "Peter" from Mark even though we read there, clearly and unequivocally: "his disciples asked him."

Now Mark, in contrast to Matthew, has a clear, cohesive sequence of thoughts and narration in 7:14- 23 (Jesus teaches: "there is nothing outside a man which by going into him can defile him, but the things which come out of a man are what defile him." After this is the disciples' request for an explanation of the words). In Matthew, on the other hand, the teaching of Jesus and the request for an explanation are interrupted by a displaced passage that belongs in an entirely different context (The disciples tell Jesus: "Do you know that the Pharisees were offended when they heard this saying?" Jesus answers: "They are blind guides.")

From this interruption in Matthew's continuity Weisse draws the conclusion: "That he really inserted these words, and that it was not perhaps a case of Mark having omitted them, is made evident by the fact that they most strikingly interrupt the continuity . . ." Such a conclusion is simply absurd. Who, after finding such a clear, cohesive narrative as Matthew must have found in Mark (according to Weisse), could have been motivated to insert several words which do not belong there, and which "most strikingly interrupt the continuity"? On the other hand, Mark had every reason, in conformity with his tendency to revise, to omit the words which interrupted the narrative continuity.

Then Weisse asserts further: "As he (Matthew) returned to the Marcan narrative"—why indeed did he deviate from it?— "he felt the need ..." Now, just what that need on Matthew's part could have been—if indeed he had been using Mark's narrative as his basis—Weisse cannot know any more than anyone else. Rather, he gives his historical imagination rein and seeks to underpin his unproven assertion of the Petrine origin of the Marcan Gospel with an alleged knowledge of the Evangelist's thought processes. Hence he permits himself to think for Matthew, and then claims that the latter

    1) had the Gospel of Mark before him,

    2) knew that Mark heard the entire discourse from Peter,

    3) assumed "that Peter probably reported his own words first" and

    4) "put the question directly into Peter's mouth."

The question remains: what about Mark? Why in this case does he not say a single word about *Peter*, who, after all, was his authority and his oral source, according to Weisse's hypothesis?!

Weisse presents yet another comparable case from Luke which follows very similar lines:

> Similarly, Luke in the narrative of the woman with a flow of blood (Lk 8:45 par Mk 5:31). Here, too, one can clearly see what it was that may have persuaded the author of the third Gospel to transfer an answer explicitly to Peter which in Mark is given by the disciples. He found this answer as he read it in his predecessor to be insufficiently clear if it was not motivated by the prefacing remark that, in response to Jesus' question: "Who touched my garments?" all of them denied knowing anything about it; whereupon one of them replied: "You see the crowd pressing around you, and yet you say 'Who touched me?' " Here he deemed it necessary to name this one disciple in order to distinguish him from the rest of the disciples who only answered negatively. Now, *since the answer had been reported by Mark, this one disciple consequently must have been Peter; but in order not to deviate too far from his predecessor, Luke still adds "and those who were with him"* (Vol. I p. 61 f.; author's italics).

Here the full measure of Christian Hermann Weisse's inconsistency becomes apparent again. For if—as Weisse wants us to believe—Luke regarded the answer found by Mark as "insufficiently clear," how strange it is that Mark himself evidently found it "sufficiently clear." But Luke "deemed it necessary"—according to Weisse—"to name this one disciple," and hence he then wrote "Peter." But at this point Weisse equivocates in such a way as to reduce his own argumentation *ad absurdum*: "but in order not to deviate too far from his predecessor, Luke still adds 'and those who were with him.' "

Now if Luke felt the need "not to deviate too far from his predecessor" then it is certainly not comprehensible why he did not keep the latter's formulation "the disciples" instead of giving it half a correction, which essentially is none at all. For Peter does not speak as an individual but simultaneously with "those who were with him"—the disciples as a whole.

These examples should suffice to show just how shaky the foundation of Weisse's "proof" from Petrine origin is. Matthew says here explicitly: "Peter," and Mark just as explicitly: "the disciples." But Weisse—on the basis of the knowledge he claims to have about the Evangelists' thought-processes—adduces "psychological proof" that Matthew derived his "Peter" from the Marcan "the disciples." And on what does he build his case? On the assertion that the Marcan narrative is founded directly on the eyewitness testimony of Peter. But precisely that has yet to be proved!

On a foundation that is no less shaky than the proof from Petrine origin that was established by the founder of the Marcan hypothesis stands the proof of its consummator, Paul Wernle. He devotes a special passage of twelve pages to this question. His basic thesis states: "*Mark is in essence the Petrine Gospel*" (*Synopt. Frage*, p. 208).

He also attempts to verify this fundamental statement in a methodologically dexterous manner. He thinks it advisable not to take the point of departure—as in Matthew—from tradition, "so that our view will not be distorted by it," but to ask first: "What does Mark himself have to say to us?"

Of course one could reply that everything depends on how one interprets what Mark tells us. This is immediately apparent in Wernle's case. He states: "Of all the Evangelists, Mark alone has a clear, understandable structure" (p. 195). Wernle demonstrates this as follows, declaring that, in view of the arrangement of the Gospel of Mark, three points deserve special emphasis:

1) The gradual progress from the large, public sermon before the people, to instruction in a small circle, to teaching.
2) The clear recollection of the particulars of belief in Christ.
3) *The leading position of Peter* (p. 196 f.).

Wernle underlines all three of these points. After the last word "Peter," there stands in small type, and in parentheses: "(and the sons of Zebedee)."

Wernle then seeks to elucidate the leading position of Peter through a survey which can show it "best":

> The first day: the calling of Simon, of his brother Andrew, and of the sons of Zebedee. Jesus heals Simon's mother-in-law. Simon and those who are with him seek Jesus. Gathering and parting: during the calling of the Twelve, Jesus confers upon Simon the name Peter, upon the sons of Zebedee the name "sons of thunder." Revelation of the secret: Peter acknowledges Jesus as Messiah. During the transfiguration he is an eyewitness along with the sons of Zebedee. Peraea; wealth and reward: Peter says to Jesus: "Lo, we have left everything and followed you." Then follows the demand of the sons of Zebedee.
>
> The future: Peter, the sons of Zebedee and Andrew alone learn of the prophecy.
>
> The passion narrative: Peter most vehemently states his loyalty. In Gethsemane he and the sons of Zebedee are the most intimate disciples but the reproach falls on Simon: Are you asleep? Peter alone follows Jesus and denies him.
>
> Resurrection: Peter especially is promised the vision of Jesus (p. 197).

Concerning Wernle's references to the leading position of Peter in the Marcan Gospel, and in connection with the analysis of Weisse's argumentation, the following needs to be pointed out: the role of Peter in both other synoptic Gospels is in no way less prominent than in Mark; on the contrary, in Matthew he stands out even more. What does Wernle have to say about this fact? His point of view is instructive:

> What Matthew presents that goes beyond (the Gospel of Mark) serves merely to highlight Mark's faithfulness to his teacher: the legend of Jesus' walking on the water; Jesus' discussion with Peter about temple taxes which ends in a legend; the exaggerated comment to Peter about his being the foundation of the church of Christ, a comment that far surpasses historical recollection. The fact that Mark does *not* have these three passages hardly speaks less for the significance of the Petrine tradition than do the passages (that are) transmitted by him (p. 198).

A curious way of reasoning. According to Wernle, what Mark writes about Peter speaks for the significance of his Petrine tradition. What he does *not* write speaks for it just the same, in one case even more ("serves merely to highlight Mark's faithfulness to his teacher"), the other time not much less ("hardly speaks less for the significance of the Petrine tradition than the passages that are transmitted by him").

In this way Wernle devalues the additional passages in Matthew, one as much as the other. The unique recognition accorded to Peter as distinct from all the rest of the disciples—the benediction at Caesarea Philippi—is explained away as the "exaggerated comment to Peter about his being the foundation of the church of Christ, a comment that far surpasses historical recollection," just as Jesus'discussion with Peter about temple taxes is pushed aside because it "ends in a legend." As if that were the quintessence of the story!

All this shows a manner of argumentation that is far removed from objectivity. The same attitude confronts us in the treatment of the same cases in the chapter "Matthew and Mark." There Wernle says of the episode of Peter walking on the water: "Certainly the Evangelist himself [thought of this] in a symbolic sense" (p. 166). But that is not at all "certain." Rather, it is an unfounded assertion serving Wernle's cause of maintaining the primacy of the Petrine tradition of *Mark*; for he adds:

> Matthew has several such episodes involving Peter that Mark lacks. But just a glance at their legendary character shows that *their absence in Mark is only an argument for the Petrine origin of his tradition.* Peter quite certainly had not related such anecdotes to Mark, much less experienced them (p. 166; author's italics).

Now, Wernle must know what Peter told Mark and what he did not tell, "much less experienced." But this argumentation turns upon itself; for, indeed, it is simply misleading to evaluate as *counter-evidence* such special recognition of Peter as the bestowal of the keys, the benediction, and his attempt to meet Jesus on the water. This would have made sense only if a passage directed *against* Peter, perhaps Mt 16:23 "Get benind me, Satan!"[2] were missing from Mark and present only in Matthew. But that is not the case; it is also present in Mark (8:33).

Wernle italicizes the title of the whole section "The Leading Position of Peter." In the same way he emphasizes:

> At all important points from the beginning to the end of the narrative, he is the leading person in the circle of disciples. He is the first-called, the first to acknowledge Jesus as Messiah, and the first to behold His glory. This is true in spite of the denial by that very disciple who followed Him longest, the first who was to be honored by His appearance after His death (p. 197).

---

[2] ὕπαγε ὀπίσω μου, σατανᾶ.

In this connection we will not pursue the fact that the expression "Get behind me, Satan!" does not exactly lead to the conclusion that Peter was "from the beginning to the end of the narrative the leading person in the circle of disciples"; rather, these words contain a definite banishment from Jesus' following. However, it is essential to show that Wernle unmistakably uses two sets of standards depending on whether the material is in Mark or Matthew. It is not the case that, in the Gospel of Mark, Peter is "the first who was to be honored by His appearance after His death." It is written in Mk 16:7, clearly and unequivocally: "But go, tell his disciples and Peter that he is going before you to Galilee; there you will see him, as he has told you."[3]

To attempt to deduce from this "an enormous emphasis on the priority of Peter" would be unfounded. At most one could draw from the fact that Peter is named *after* the disciples, a quite different conclusion, i.e., that the expression "Get behind me" must have resulted in temporary banishment from the circle of disciples and therefore in demotion to a position behind the other disciples. If it is supposed to signify, as Wernle wants us to believe, an "enormous emphasis on the priority of Peter," then Peter should at least have been named first and Mk 16:7 should have read: "tell Peter and Jesus' other disciples . . . ."[4]

Contrast this with Wernle's evaluation of what is really "an enormous emphasis on the priority of Peter" in *Matthew* (16:17). Because this *benedictio Petri* is found in Matthew, Wernle characterizes it as "the exaggerated comment to Peter, . . . a comment that far surpasses historical recollection." But if anyone exaggerates here, it is Wernle when he says that Peter is "in spite of the denial . . . that very disciple who followed Him longest." In Mk 14:53f. we read: "And they led Jesus to the high priest; . . . and Peter had followed Him from a distance[5]—right into the courtyard of the high priest"[6].

Wernle then gave this prominence as evidence that Peter enthusiastically followed Christ longer than any of the other disciples. But its substance is not at all an acknowledgement by Peter of Jesus and a steadfast intercession in His behalf, but a triple denial of his discipleship. Hence to declare Peter "that disciple who followed Him the longest" is to misrepresent the facts. This "following" is a betrayal. Of the other disciples nothing similar is reported.

---

[3] εἴπατε τοῖς μαθηταῖς αὐτοῦ καὶ τῷ Πέτρῳ ὅτι Προάγει ὑμᾶς εἰς τὴν Γαλιλαίαν ἐκεῖ αὐτὸν ὄψεσθε, καθὼς εἶπεν ὑμῖν.

[4] εἴπατε τῷ Πέτρῳ καὶ τοῖς ἄλλοις μαθηταῖς αὐτοῦ.

[5] μακρόθεν.

[6] ἕως εἰς τὴν αὐλὴν τοῦ ἀρχιερέως.

Beyond that, Wernle then seeks to establish yet another indirect proof for the Petrine origin of the Gospel of Mark. He makes the audacious assertion: "Rather, the Gospel of Mark is the most valuable source for Peter's theology" (p. 200). He tries to demonstrate this as follows:

> What we know for certain about Peter (aside from what we know from Mark) is limited to the information given by Paul in the Epistle to the Galatians and to general reflections. Galatians 2 makes it possible for us to distinguish exactly the standpoint of Peter from that of James. Peter sees himself as an apostle of circumcision, adhering to the prerogative of Israel but at the same time taking delight in Paul's great success among the Gentiles. The belief in Jesus as Messiah, not fear of the Law, is at the center of his piety. When he came to Antioch, he made no effort to observe purity regulations, but rather ate together with born Gentiles as well as with fellow-believers without any hesitation whatsoever. But his freedom from the Law was of an immediate kind that came from the heart; it did not rest on a break with the Law, on the recognition of its abrogation. Therefore James' admonition could intimidate him at once and move him to retreat in fear. Since he had always acknowledged the Law theoretically as the highest order, he could free himself of it in a practical sense only in fits and starts, and in single instances. And as highly as he thought of Christ's death and resurrection according to 1 Cor 11 and 15, he never found himself in opposition to the Law because of his belief.
>
> All this is easier to understand as soon as we consider that Peter—like Jesus—had been a layman, albeit not a pharisaical one. As such he could attempt to reconcile things which appeared to the theologian Paul as mutually exclusive opposites. And as such, even in matters of the Law, he held to ideas of simplicity and morality that spoke to him as if they were the only things God wanted. That also explains his exceptional freedom and independence alongside his faithful regard for the authority of the Law. The *Gospel of Mark shows us precisely that* (p. 201; author's italics).

In view of this one must ask: where does the Gospel of Mark show us "precisely that"? Of all that Wernle has had to say here about Peter's theology, the only thing that one finds in the Marcan Gospel is "the belief in Jesus as Messiah." But is this belief not to be found in all three synoptic Gospels in the same way? Everything else that Wernle wants to attribute here to the Marcan Gospel as its significant characteristics reflects nothing other than a tendentious over-interpretation that seeks to provide indirect proof for the Petrine origin of the Gospel of Mark. But it is obvious that such "proof" does not possess the power to convince.

Wernle himself does not seem to be so certain of his contentions, for later he comes around and declares:

> Now it would be wrong therefore to want to claim all of the views in the Gospel of Mark for Peter and to trace them back to him. In the first place, it is always the Evangelist himself who speaks. But in my opinion not a line in his work speaks against the predominant influence of Peter (p. 209).

Now, there is a considerable difference between the assertions that "In my opinion not a line in his work speaks against the predominant influence of Peter" and that "On the contrary the Gospel of Mark is the most valuable source for Peter's theology." And who would deny that in the same way one can say of the Matthean and Lucan Gospels that "not a line speaks against the predominant influence of Peter"?

Finally Wernle reduces himself *ad absurdum* with his proof from Petrine origin. He falls back on the "proof from originality" in order to corroborate his contention that Peter must have been Mark's informant. As already mentioned above in our refutation of his "proof," he reaches the "conclusion": "He (Mark) narrates as he heard it from eyewitnesses" and "If ever a narrative gave the impression of having its origin in the report of an eyewitness, it is that of Mark" (p. 204 f.).

Then Wernle feels obliged to bring up a problem that stands in opposition to the assumption of eyewitness testimony, the question of miracles—only, of course, in order to invalidate it: "But the miracles? Can a Gospel which reports so many miracles of Jesus from the first until the last day be based on the accounts of an eyewitness, of Peter?" (p. 205).

At this point Wernle makes a fundamental concession with regard to the "originality" of the Marcan narratives:

> First of all, two preliminary considerations: The point in question is what was related and believed, not what happened. These two questions, while closely related, are not to be confused. Secondly, the Evangelist and his informant are not identical, either; it is always a rather long way from Peter's oral statements to the written record set down after his death by his companion. One must always keep these two preliminary considerations in mind when examining individual passages (p. 205).

It is amazing to see how critically Wernle thinks for a change. Of course it would have been better had he always observed and taken to heart his own admonition in the first place. Only one page earlier he states: "An eyewitness could not have described it any differently" and: "As a rule one recognizes the first, fresh narrator by the passages omitted by the other Evangelists. He narrates the way he has heard it from eyewitnesses," and also "If ever a narrative gave the impression of having its origin in the report of an eyewitness, it is that of Mark" (p. 204).

But now we read suddenly: "It is always a rather long way from Peter's oral statements to the written record set down after his death by his companion."

Now, to be sure, Wernle says that "one must always keep [this] in mind when examining individual passages." In other words, from case to case one must always argue in such a way as to serve the needs of the hypothesis. For if it appears that Wernle takes a fundamentally critical attitude toward the miracle question, this is true only insofar as this question might impair his argument for the Petrine origin of the Gospel of Mark. Elsewhere, he completely upholds the idea of miracles as such and believes that he can convince those who think otherwise by casting aspersions on their intelligence or their good will:

> Nowadays it may be said that many things that were earlier paraded as historical criticism resulted from dogmatic narrow-mindedness and prejudice. Regardless of how everyone may interpret and explain the miracle for himself, it is certain that the story of Jesus was full of miracles, that in this person and in this time the limits of the possible, of reality, extended immeasurably further than our narrow minds care to draw them (p. 205).

Yet evidently Wernle relates his contention "that in this person and in this time the limits of the possible, of reality, extended immeasurably further than our narrow minds care to draw them," only to the Gospel of Mark but not to Matthew. Rather, he takes this viewpoint: "What Matthew presents that goes beyond the Gospel of Mark serves merely to highlight Mark's faithfulness to his teacher" (p. 198).

But then Wernle makes a slight tactical retreat; unexpectedly he declares, all of a sudden: "We certainly do not maintain that Mark took all his information from Peter" (p. 206).

Of course, earlier the message was different, and later the old version reappeared: "Mark is essentially the Gospel of Peter" (p. 208).

To be sure, Wernle still owes us proof for this statement.

It remains to be added that there is another important reason why the conception of the Petrine origin of the Gospel of Mark cannot be upheld. The agreement in the wording of the logia and in general of all rhetorical parts between Mark on the one hand and Matthew and Luke on the other is so striking that the contention that the former took them from the oral Petrine tradition while the latter derived them from the written sayings source is insupportable. The laws of oral transmission in history—as a result of its changing character, the broadness of its distribution, "the fate of all oral tradition"—are so fundamentally different from those of the written tradition that it appears impossible that a continuous verbal similarity could result from both forms of tradition. Continuous verbal agreement therefore leads to no other conclusion than that which assumes the use of a written source.

Chapter XII

The Proof From Psychological Reflection

This is the proof which the founders of the Marcan hypothesis use the most and talk about the least, for the simple reason that it is the most subjective, problematic and questionable of all the proofs. It represents a truly troublesome, thorny path on which obstacle after obstacle is piled up for the advocates of Marcan priority and one *crux interpretum* after another confronts them.

In the beginning of our presentation we stated that the scholar who wants to prove the Marcan hypothesis finds himself in a position which is not exactly enviable, for he has to carry what is frankly a gigantic burden of proof. Recalling once more the enumeration of problems (see above, pp. 9-22) which the pioneers of the Marcan hypothesis were obliged to solve, one may have difficulty deciding whether to admire them for their courage or to warn them: "Give up all hope, you who enter here."

Griesbach had had it easier when he interpreted the 180 cases of extra material in Mark as additions by Mark to the texts of Matthew and Luke (in line with his inclination, "to express paraphrastically and more clearly and distinctly"); and when by turn he explained the extra-Marcan material in the first and third Gospels as Mark's omissions from their texts. He treated all other divergences according to the same principle.

But now an almost insuperable Sisyphean task lay ahead of the advocates of Marcan priority who wanted to prove the opposite in all these cases. After all, what methodological possibility was available to them here? Only one—to try to make it psychologically believable that, in all of these almost innumerable cases, Matthew and Luke had been the ones who altered the material, either simultaneously or one at a time, whether in the form of omissions, additions, or changes in Mark's text.

Wernle puts it in the language of the supporters of Marcan priority:

> Either Luke did not read them in his sources, in which case he did not have our Mark in front of him . . . . Or he read but *intentionally omitted them.* In that case there must be evidence indicating that he read them, *and reasons why he omitted them* (*Synopt. Frage,* p. 4; author's italics).

Here with Wernle this psychologizing method of providing proof reaches it apogee. He it is who explicitly elevates this method of argumentation to the status of a principle : "Almost always, we are able to recognize the author himself, together with his reflections and motives" (p. 37).

Of Luke's use of the Gospel of Mark he claims: "Here too one can say that he transforms his basic text by constant reflection, but without a fixed intention" (p.36).

Similarly: "We have seen that Luke followed his source text with constant reflection" (p. 58).

And he adds: "The very same thing will be proved true of Matthew."

In the following sentence one realizes why he reached this opinion and result prematurely: "No wonder when these reflections often enough coincided" (p. 58), i.e., those of Matthew and Luke.

Proceeding in this manner, Wernle saved himself "often enough" the trouble of accounting for double motivation.

"Coming up with reasons" then became one of the main tasks of the advocates of Marcan priority in their detailed examinations of the Gospels; their quest was for reasons why Matthew and Luke should have left anything out of or added anything to the Gospel of Mark.

But where would they find them, since not a single word is said about them in the Gospels? And what do we really know in an objective sense about the Evangelists' motives and mental deliberations which moved and motivated them while they were conceiving their work? We must truthfully admit that we know nothing about it.

Could one infer them from the Gospels? This is precisely the point where the hazard or, better put, the danger lies—that one might psychologize in favor of the hypothesis. For depending on which source theory one starts with, the investigation will turn out to have widely varying results. Hence one could essentially "prove" every source theory with the help of this psychologizing method of argumentation. That had been the case earlier with respect to the written ur-gospel; Eichhorn and Herbert Marsh had also found ways of undergirding their hypothesis by attributing to the Evangelists "reasons" which were in conformity with it, i.e., suited to render consistent the inconsistencies of their source theory.

And even Griesbach was not free from this, even though the more favorable nature of his hypothesis gave him less occasion for it. For example, he explained Mark's omission of chapters 1 and 2 of Matthew and Luke by arguing that Mark wanted to confine himself solely to the kerygmatic activities of Jesus: "Omittuntur haec capita integra, quia Marcus res a Christo, tanquam doctore publico, gestas enarrare tantum voluit" (*Commentatio*, p. 371).

Similarly, he explained Mark's omission of the Sermon on the Mount by contending that Mark, who wanted to write a shorter work, found it too verbose and, besides that, too full of things which spoke primarily to the needs of those who heard the Sermon:

> Mark, having followed Matthew up to 4:21, forsakes Matthew and passes over to Luke since he had decided to omit Christ's Sermon on the Mount, which follows at this point in Matthew; for, as he meant to write a short book, it seemed to him too verbose, and besides, it comprises many things which specially pertained only to those persons who heard Christ speaking on the mountain (p. 371, n. 17).

There is a certain nice irony in the fact that Holtzmann later took over Griesbach's reasoning verbatim: "The Sermon on the Mount in particular was too long for him" (see above, p. 76).

Hence one cannot especially reproach the Marcan hypothesis for likewise making use of the proof from psychological reflection, for both sides have sinned in this respect. But the devil lies hidden here, as everywhere, in the detail—or, to be exact, "in matters great and small." For in this respect the pioneers of the Marcan theory are prisoners of their own hypothesis, and there is no escape for them. It was their task, and no one else's, to prove, or at least render credible the reasons why both Matthew and Luke

1) in 180 cases left out the extra material that is found in the Gospel of Mark,

2) in 35 cases added exactly the same word to the text of Mark,

3) in a further 35 cases replaced the text of Mark with the same alternate wording,

4) in 22 cases undertook the same small modification of the very same word which they and Mark both use.

What other possibility did they have but to think reflectively "from the viewpoint of the Evangelists"? As Wernle had asserted: "almost always, we are able to recognize the author himself, together with his reflections and motives."

But here we encounter a mistake regarding the speaker, for in reality it is not the reflections of the Evangelists which we can recognize, but those of their interpreters. They take the liberty of thinking for them, and they let the Evangelists reflect in such a way as they must have reflected, or could have reflected if the Marcan hypothesis were valid—and hence, in a sense, in full conformity with it. As long as this kind of inquiry limits itself to conjecture and is presented as such, it may be tolerable. But as soon as it is proclaimed with apodictic certainty as presumed knowledge about the Evangelists' motivations, it oversteps the limits of what is permissible, and remains unproven in any objective sense.

Thus the difficulty for the advocates of the Marcan hypothesis lay in the fact that their argumentation was all-pervading, merciless and unyielding. They found themselves in an embarrassing situation—one which no one could help them out of. They had to deal with all three Gospels with their endless textual additions and omissions on one side or the other, to search endlessly for "reasons" for them, and to explain, explain, explain . . . . Hardly an enviable position! No wonder that they often found themselves at a loss, and at the end of their psychology. Thus Wernle cries out resignedly, indeed, almost desperately: "Not everything can be explained" (p. 61). And: "We cannot expect always to be able to recognize the author's motives" (p. 156). Earlier, to be sure, he had sounded more confident: "Almost always we are able to recognize the author himself together with his reflections and motives" (p. 37). And Wernle is not the only one landing in the *ultimum refugium* of interpreters at the end of their rope—"simple coincidence": "Much remains simply coincidental" (p. 61).

Even before Wernle, C. H. Weisse had found himself in a similar situation. In the case of the "sending out of the twelve," Mark (6:7) had referred to the sending out of the disciples in pairs with the Hebraism "two two."[1] This note is missing in both Matthew and Luke. Here, indeed, even Weisse knew no way out that would conform to his hypothesis. Thus he felt compelled to concede:

> Indeed, we have here by way of exception (sic!) an example of agreement between Matthew and Luke as opposed to Mark in a

---

[1] δύο δύο.

passage which they hold in common with him; however, this should not interfere with our previous view of the synoptics' relationship to one another, since this congruity is unimportant and *sufficiently inexplicable* to be considered coincidental" (*Evangelische Geschichte*, Vol. 1, p. 401; author's italics).

This "coincidence" then took on special significance as a result of the fact that Weisse, while expounding on the tradition-hypothesis in an earlier context, had set forth a completely different evaluation of coincidence as a means of explanation. There he tells us:

Here, too, in order to explain this congruity, the assumption of a type of tradition has been used as a refuge. But this assumption itself contained the tacit *admission of a quite remarkable fortuitousness in this view; otherwise it obviously would have been more appropriate to appeal directly to the factual, chronological truth (Evangelische Geschichte*, Vol. 1, p. 71; author's italics).

But when it came to the fortuitousness that he himself had asserted, the important thing was not "to appeal directly to the factual, chronological truth" but, rather, not to let this "interfere with our previous view of the synoptics' relationship to one another."

This lack of real substance in the motivations which the founders of the Marcan hypothesis attribute to the Evangelists is one of the main objections one must raise against their psychologizing. Hence, Weisse, for want of a better reason, gets past his difficulty by accusing Luke of "negligence." We refer here to the so-called "Lucan omission," the entire continuous narrative Mk. 6:45-8:26, in which Mark runs parallel only with Matthew, but for which there is no equivalent in the Gospel of Luke. One could rightfully expect that Weisse would present not just a plausible but also a well-founded reason for Luke's alleged "omission." For as long as the reason why Luke made such an extensive omission consisting of two chapters is not made evident, there is a clear breach of the Marcan hypothesis. Yet Weisse explains it in a manner as surprising as it is banal:

Until the beginning of the alleged travel narrative (Lk 9:51), he (Luke) had indeed *generally followed Mark,* to be sure not without several insertions and also not without a very conspicuous gap (6:45-8:26), that was *probably caused by mere carelessness (at least no reason can be found that comes even close to explaining it sufficiently) (Evangelische Geschichte*, Vol. 1, p. 88; author's italics).

At this point one would like to remind Weisse of his own words cited above, "to appeal directly to the factual, chronological truth" instead of taking refuge in: "at least no reason can be found that comes even close to explaining it sufficiently"; for if only he had made it clear to himself that in the entire "Lucan omission" Mark coincides with *Matthew*, he would have been able to find a "reason that comes even close to explaining it sufficiently." In any case it would have been better for him to have looked for the fault in himself, instead of accusing Luke of "negligence."

But Matthew does not fare much better at Weisse's hands. Specifically, the pericope of the widow's mite can be found only in Luke and Mark (12:41-44 par Lk 21:104), but not in Matthew. Naturally, from the viewpoint of the Marcan hypothesis this is conspicuous and needs to be explained, especially since here we are dealing with a particularly beautiful pericope both in terms of form and of religious and ethical substance. Hence, from the standpoint of Weisse's source theory, this question arises: what prompted Matthew to omit this pericope which, according to the hypothesis, he must have read in Mark? Weisse's psychological explanation is the following:

> Mark, whom Luke also follows here with absolute exactitude, had assigned this place to it (the pericope) by association with the widows mentioned in the previous saying; *the author of the first Gospel seems to have forgotten it after interpolating the long speech* (Vol. I, p. 588; author's italics).

Not even Mark remains unscathed by Weisse's difficulties in finding psychological motives. In the passage describing the sending out of the disciples (Mk 6:6-13 par.) Matthew and Luke express the appointment of the apostles by Jesus with a simple "he sent out."[2] Mark, however, states "he began to send out"[3] (6:7). Weisse comments: "But one must admit that the misunderstanding appears to begin with *Mark, who frequently may not have listened very carefully* (to the narrations of Peter)" (Vol. I, p. 404; author's italics).

Now, to be sure, this is an astonishing admission for Weisse to make. It certainly is not much of a recommendation for the reliability of his main source, Mark, especially when he writes "who frequently may not have listened very carefully." Likewise, the proof from Petrine origin, which he endorses so explicitly, also appears to be somewhat affected as a result of these reflections cast on the reliability of the only star witness, Mark.

---

[2]ἀπέστειλεν.

[3]ἤρξατο αὐτοὺς ἀποστέλλειν.

Now one might be tempted to explain these examples as a manifestation of Christian Hermann Weisse's psychological uncertainty and bewilderment in finding motivations for his writers, but neither Wernle nor Holtzmann does much better. The problem lies, not with the person, but with the material, and hence with the impossibility of carrying through a complete proof from psychological reflection. Here, too, in the case of all three founders of the Marcan theory it becomes clear how much they are prisoners of their own hypothesis; for they are inescapably constrained by their own principle, which Wernle formulated as follows: "Or he (the Evangelist) read but intentionally omitted them. In that case there must be evidence indicating that he read them, *and reasons why he omitted them"* (See above, p. 102).

We will demonstrate this further with a few other examples:

Healing of the blind man in Jericho (Mk 10:45-53 par.).

In Mark and Luke we read of *one* blind man, who, in Mark, is given the name Bartimaeus. In Matthew, on the other hand, there are *two* unnamed blind men. There is a variant (Mt. 9:27-31) of this pericope; here too there are two nameless blind men who are healed by Jesus. *Wernle* comments:

> What is new in Matthew is the doubling of the number of blind men (for whom no names are given) and the touching of the eyes. The doubling might be explained simply as the throwing together (!) of the blind man in Bethsaida with the one in Jericho—if 9:27-31 were not an exact doublet there. *I can explain it only as an oversight on the part of the Evangelist.* He either wanted to anticipate together the two healings of the blind in Mark in his miracle cycle and *forgot later (c. 20) that he had already narrated them;* or, as is even more likely, he had narrated them first here (c. 20); and *only at the end while revising the book inserted them again after c. 9*—as he did with the deaf-mute –in order to have a full ten miracles (p. 169; author's italics).

A commentary on this is hardly necessary.

The second crowing of the cock.

In the interpolated story of Peter's denial, the cock crows only once in Matthew and Luke, but twice in Mark (14:69 and 72). *Wernle's* comments on this: "He (Luke) probably had not yet read anything in his copy of Mark about a second crowing of the cock."

That is what Wernle writes on page 33. On page 4f., however, it had sounded rather different when Wernle spoke of the "defective copy" of Mark which Eduard Reuss had assumed Luke used in his explanation of the "Lucan omission." (See above, p. 137). Wernle: "For these reasons, the hypothesis that a page was missing at the 'great gap' in Luke's copy of Mark becomes superfluous." If it is Wernle's opinion that Luke's copy of Mark said nothing about the second crowing of the cock, then, to be sure, the same is also valid for Matthew's copy of Mark, for here, too, the cock crows only once. Hence Matthew must also have used a "defective copy." Should not this double coincidence have given Wernle sufficient reason to review his source theory?

The calling of the first disciples.

In the passage describing the calling of the first disciples (Mk 1:16-20 par Mt 4:18-22) we read at the end of the pericope in Matthew: "Immediately they left the boat and their father and followed him" (Jesus). In Mark, on the other hand: "And they left their father Zebedee in the boat *with the hired servants*[4] and followed him." Holtzmann claimed, in accordance with the Marcan hypothesis, that Matthew omitted this additional material in Mark: ". . . so too in Mk 1:20 the hired servants helping with the torn nets of the three fishermen are wholly appropriate themselves *since the fishermen do not know how to mend nets" (Synopt. Evangelien*, p. 111; author's italics).

Now, if Holtzmann had given as the reason: "in order not to leave the old father alone with his work as a consequence of their abrupt departure," it would have been acceptable. His alternative explanation, however, is not exactly convincing; for they would have been the first fishermen in the world who "themselves . . . do not know how to mend nets." Moreover, Holtzmann has made a linguistic error here; for   καταρτίξειν   means "to put in order," as is done after every catch so as to ready the nets for the next sailing. In the entire pericope there is no more any mention of "repairing of nets" than there is of "torn nets."

Jesus' rejection in Nazareth.

Concerning Jesus' rejection in his native town (Mk 6:1-6 par Mt 13:53-58; cf. Lk 4:16-30), *Matthew* has the local people say of Jesus: "Is this not the carpenter's son?" Correspondingly, Luke has: "Is this not Joseph's son?" In contrast to that we read in *Mark:* "Is this not the carpenter, the son of Mary?"

Holtzmann asserts: "On the other hand, the other two authors object to the original word used by Mark   τέκτων   (carpenter), which in Matthew is how Jesus' father, and not Jesus himself, is portrayed" (*Synopt. Evangelien,* p. 52).

---

[4]μετὰ τῶν μισθωτῶν.

It is inconceivable why Matthew and Luke should have taken offense at the honorable profession of "carpenter." Mark certainly does not object to it, and evidently considers it respectable enough to attribute it even to Jesus himself.

On the other hand it can scarcely be doubted that *Mark* did object to the phrases "the carpenter's son" (Matthew) and "son of Joseph" (Luke). His formulation "the carpenter, the son of Mary"[5] cannot be understood at all in any different sense. It can only be Mark who transformed the son of Joseph into the son of Mary, since the reverse seems unlikely and Holtzmann's interpretation misguided. *In our opinion, we have here positive proof for the posteriority of Mark.*

The parable of the fig tree.

In the discourse on the return of Jesus, we read in Mark (13:28): "From the fig tree learn its lesson: as soon as its branch becomes tender and puts forth its leaves, you know that summer is near."

The Lucan parallel reads (21:29): "And he told them a parable: Look at the fig tree and all the trees; as soon as they come out in leaf, you see for yourselves and know that summer is already near."

Wernle explains the additional material in Luke as follows: "Luke adds to the fig tree 'and all the trees' (21:29) *since he anticipates readers who are perhaps unfamiliar with fig trees"(Synopt. Evangelien,* p. 13; author's italics).

The text of Mark in its entirety agrees verbatim with that of Matthew (24: 32). If one were to take Wernle's interpretation seriously, one would have to conclude from his logic that Matthew and Mark, conversely, anticipated readers "who were perhaps familiar with fig trees."

Trial before the Council.

Jesus' trial before the Council ends in Matthew and Mark with all its members judging Jesus to be deserving of death. In Luke this passage is missing. There we read (22:71-23:1): "And they said, 'What further testimony do we need? We have heard it ourselves from his own lips.' And the whole company of them arose and brought him before Pilate."

Wernle comments: "In his haste to abridge, Luke unfortunately forgot the main point, that a death sentence was passed on Jesus by the Sanhedrin" (p. 34).

---

[5] ὁ τέκτων, ὁ υἱὸς τῆς Μαρίας.

Now usually a death sentence is not exactly the kind of thing one "forgets," and especially not in "haste to abridge." But Wernle's regret over the matter is factually unfounded. Luke has the right version. The Sanhedrin was not authorized to pass a death sentence; only the Roman procurator was. Therefore, quite logically we read in Luke that they "arose and brought him before Pilate"—obviously with the intention of securing a death sentence from the latter.

It will also be worthwhile to trace the treatment of individual themes by all three founders of the Marcan hypothesis, taking note of the psychological motivations they reflect. We shall demonstrate by using two examples:

a) The cursing of the fig tree (Mt 21:18-29 par Mk 11:12-14, 20-21).

Matthew tells the story as a single incident: the withering of the fig tree follows immediately upon Jesus' words: "May no fruit ever come from you again!" In Mark, on the other hand, the event takes place in two stages. Jesus pronounces the curse on the way to Jerusalem, as in Matthew. Then he enters the city with the disciples and carries out the cleansing of the temple. Only on the next day, when he once more passes the fig tree with them, do they see that it has "withered away to its roots."

> *Weisse's* explanation:
>
> Hence it would appear that Mark divided the cursing of the fig tree and the fulfillment of the curse into two separate events in order to give the event special meaning, or for some similar reason. *It is obvious that in the first Gospel only the desire to achieve brevity led to the merging of the two events (Evangelische Geschichte,* Vol. I, p. 577; author's italics).
>
> *Holtzmann's* explanation:
>
> *At first Matthew wanted to pass over the story entirely; but when he came across it again (Λ Mk 11:20) he included it, to be sure, but in condensed form* by contracting the two parts of the event into one. Consequently, he also combined Jesus' first two days in Jerusalem, which are differentiated in A, into one day *(Synopt. Evangelium,* p. 198; author's italics).
>
> *Wernle's* explanation:
>
> *Luke leaves out the cursing of the fig tree because he regards it as a doublet of the parable of the fig tree, 13:6-9 (Synopt. Frage,* p. 6).

How strongly the three interpreters' psychological reasons differ from one another, and how problematical they are! Wernle's argument that Luke passed over the pericope because he saw in it a doublet of the parable of the fig tree is obviously unsound, for the two cannot be compared. One bears the form of a parable, while the other is reported as an actual event. Whether the Lucan form is the original one, and the others are to be regarded as distorted variants of it, is a completely different and unrelated question.

Weisse's explanation that Matthew "obviously" must have merged the two events suffers in view of the fact that the "obvious" problem in text criticism consists precisely in the alternative question: did Matthew condense, or did Mark divide and expand by trying to make the process of withering more or less understandable by interpolating a span of twenty-four hours? In the latter case, Mark's amplification "for it was not the season for figs" would have to be viewed as an explanatory supplement to the observation that the tree bore "nothing but leaves."

Holtzmann felt the same way, for he commented: " 'For it was not the season for figs'[6] does not compel us to assume that it is a supplement, however possible that may in fact be" (p. 91). He banished the doubts that were beginning to dawn on him about his own source theory by clearing away the obstacle to the hypothesis: "The more inexplicable it is, the more explicable its omission from Matthew" (p. 91).

This may sound somewhat sibylline, but it is keenly reasoned according to the Marcan hypothesis. Holtzmann insinuates here that he is not the only one who finds this passage incomprehensible in view of his source theory, but that it must have been equally so for Matthew. And precisely because the latter, too, found it inexplicable, it is all the more explicable that he omitted this passage, which was inexplicable to him.

Now Holtzmann's second contention—that Matthew had at first intended to pass over the entire story (precisely because of its first, incomprehensible part) but then changed his mind when he encountered the second part of the story, and then drew the two together—is nothing but tendentious conjecture about the reflections of the Evangelist. Thus armed, Holtzmann seeks to square the divergence between Mark's divided report and Matthew's uninterrupted story with his hypothesis.

b) The fleeing youth.

In the account of Jesus' arrest, which all three synoptic authors have in common, Mark alone adds a brief, famous report concerning the charming and realistic scene of the fleeing youth. Again and again there have been those who have wanted to believe that this was Mark himself, or at least to conclude that Mark personally was an eyewitness.

---

[6] ὁ γὰρ καιρὸς οὐκ ἦν σύκων.

Wilke called it an "interpolation"; Weisse interpreted its absence from Matthew and Luke as deliberate omission on the part of both. He described this passage as "insignificant in itself (and because of its insignificance omitted from the other two Gospels) but picturesque and characteristic" (*Evangelische Geschichte*, Vol. I, p. 449). At the same time he emphatically denied that Mark could have taken it from a different source: "[It is] a passage . . . which he surely would not have thought of explicitly adding—especially since he had omitted other much more important parts—if he had found the rest of the narrative already recorded somewhere else."

Weisse would have to know precisely what Mark would or "surely would not have thought of" doing. Here again we encounter a presumed knowledge about Mark's motives.

Holtzmann:

"[The] story of the youth who lost his robe [was] omitted by the others as imcomprehensible and 'unimportant' " (*Synop. Evangelien*, p. 108).

Holtzmann's characterization of the report as "unimportant" is synonymous with Weisse's "insignificant." But obviously, even this reason seemed to him too insignificant; thus he adds the word "incomprehensible." But why he declared this realistic description "incomprehensible" when even Weisse had termed it picturesque and characteristic, remains, indeed, incomprehensible. Neither its ideas nor its style is in the least bit obscure; Mark has sketched it for us quite vividly in just a few lines.

Wernle:

As will be recalled, Wernle had said very generally about Mark's presentation: "If ever a narrative presentation gave the impression of having its origin in the narration of an eyewitness, it is that of Mark" (*Synopt. Frage*, p. 204). As an "especially convincing" example of this he cites the fleeing youth:

> The brief passage about the youth in Jesus' entourage who fled at night from Gethsemane when he was seized by his shirt has all along given rise to the supposition that Mark here speaks of himself. It is the likeliest of all presumptions, even though it cannot be proved. The other Gospels have omitted this episode since it was meaningful only to one who was present (p. 204f.).

On this subject the following basic observation should be made. The problem here confronts all three founders of the Marcan hypothesis with the same two questions:

1) Why was this brief scene omitted by the other two Evangelists?

2) Why did *both* of them—who, according to the hypothesis, must have

read it in Mark—pass over it, independently and without knowledge of each other?

Weisse's and Holtzmann's answer to the first question ("insignificant" as well as "incomprehensible and unimportant") provides neither a sufficient nor a pertinent reason; for Weisse himself has already referred to the passage as "picturesque and characteristic." And so, indeed, it is, for this individual passage, this small but detailed portrayal of the fleeing youth who is seized by intruding soldiers, but then breaks loose leaving his chiton in their hands, brilliantly evokes a bit of the atmosphere of the turbulent scene during that nighttime raid. Why then should Matthew and Luke have omitted this passage if they had read it in Mark?

"Since it was meaningful only to the one who was present" says Wernle, and: "Mark here speaks of himself; it is the likeliest of all presumptions." Here the circle of errors within which Wernle argues becomes apparent. For why is it the most likely supposition? Because Mark himself was present; otherwise he would not have included this scene, since it was important only for someone who had been there. The only pertinent remark in Wernle's argumentation is the brief qualifying dependent clause: "even though it cannot be proved."

Moreover, one can prove the opposite of the assumption that the scene "was meaningful only for someone who had been there." For in the same context of this account of the arrest, Matthew and Luke report—in agreement with Mark—that someone from Jesus' entourage drew his sword and cut off the ear of the high priest's slave, and Luke is even able to report that it was the right ear (22:50). Following Wernle's logic, one would have to conclude from this that Matthew and Luke had also been present, because such passages were "meaningful only for someone who had been there." Hence according to Wernle's logic they could not have omitted the passage of the fleeing youth, for, indeed, they must have been eyewitnesses of the arrest scene—just as Mark had been, according to Wernle. And that would have to be especially true of the author of the Gospel of John, who tells us that it was Peter who drew the sword, and that the high priest's slave whose right ear he cut off (in agreement with Luke's report) was named Malchus (18:10). Thus there were probably plenty of eyewitnesses of Jesus' arrest, but whether the author of the Gospel of Mark was among them is not proved, at least not through Wernle's argumentation.

At this point the second problem becomes an issue. Wernle, of course, was confronted with more than the question: why did Matthew omit the scene of the fleeing youth? or why did Luke do so? Rather, the problem which he needed to solve is exactly the same as in the other 179 cases of extra material in

Mark that is not present in Matthew and Luke: Why did *both omit it, congruently, independently, and without knowledge of each other?* This is the fundamental synoptic problem that always confronts us anew and about which we have already exhaustively stated our viewpoint (see above, esp. p. 141f.).

As a preventive measure Wernle had already tried to save himself the trouble of explaining the coincidence of motivation of Matthew as well as Luke by declaring: "No wonder when these reflections coincided often enough." But this is no solution, and one cannot get out of it so easily. The duplication of testimony by two Evangelists, especially when it is as pervasive as it is in Matthew and Luke, cannot be invalidated by proof from psychological reflection, which in and of itself carries no weight to begin with. Weisse's "insignificance" and Holtzmann's "incomprehensibility and unimportance" discredit themselves since they obviously were brought forward only for lack of anything better. Similarly, Wernle's argument that both Matthew and Luke had no interest in the scene of the fleeing youth because they had not been eyewitnesses has been shown to be a misinterpretation.

But Wernle's treatment of motivation does point in a somewhat different direction, one more fundamental in character than those taken by Weisse and Holtzmann. For Wernle obviously felt that the strongly subjective character of the proof from psychological reflection was too unreliable and hence unsatisfactory; and therefore he looked for a more general and compelling way of settling the problem. Wernle's subsequent fundamental statement follows this train of thought:

> In general it is safe to say that the numerous omissions of detailed passages in the Marcan narrative can best be explained without assuming the use of each other's writings (by Matthew and Luke). What emerges here is simply the difference between the original writer (Mark) and his literary successors. To the latter a great abundance of minor comments are worthless and unimportant, comments which the first writer lovingly treasures. (How does Wernle know that?) Hence a number of names, such as Alphaeus, the father of Levi, the strange "Boanerges," Bartimaeus, Simon of Cyrene as the father of Alexander and Rufus, but also the Herodians and, finally, the youth who fled naked—none of these was any longer of interest to the second and third generations.... All these vivid, colorful notes, which let us recognize the first, fresh writer, were of no significance to the later writers and hence were omitted. The congruence of Matthew and Luke in omitting

certain passages shows clearly that the abridgement was
determined, not by the mere arbitrariness of one author, but
rather by general considerations conforming to certain rules
(*Synopt. Frage,* p. 58).

Thus Wernle had found the redeeming formula: "general considerations
conforming to certain rules" determined the "abridgement." If we are to give
this assertion tangible meaning, it can be understood only in the sense that
there must be some sort of historical or aesthetic-stylistic law which states that
the feeling for vividness diminishes in proportion to the distance from the
actual event. We have already demonstrated the untenability of this view in
our refutation of the proof from originality (see above, pp. 159-68).

Moreover, Wernle's assertion can be refuted on purely factual grounds.
We shall demonstrate this by using the example of the names which were no
longer of "interest to the second and third generation." In doing so we
certainly do not have in mind the list of names in the genealogy provided by
the first and third Evangelists, in which, according to Wernle, the second and
third generations should not have been interested (especially since they
diverge). But, long after Jesus' death, could there still have been an interest in
the names of Jesus' brothers, of whom James alone gained any prominence?
Matthew mentions them (13:55). And how contrary to the hypothesis that
Matthew mentions the name of the high priest Caiaphas (26:57) even though
the name does not appear in Mark, as well as the name of Archelaus as son of
Herod the Great (2:22).

And now consider Luke. He *alone* provides the following names:
Zechariah and Elizabeth (1:6), Augustus and Quirinius (2:1f.), Simeon (2:25)
and Anna (2:36), Tiberius and Lysanias (3:1), Annas (3:2), the Pharisee
Simon (7:40), Joanna and Chuza (8:3; 24:10), Susanna (8:3), Mary and
Martha (10:39), Zacchaeus (19:1), Cleopas (24:18). And then Wernle
seriously contends that the first and third Evangelists chose not to follow
Mark in giving the names of Alphaeus, Bartimaeus, as well as of Alexander
and Rufus because "none of these was any longer of interest to the second and
third generations"?

But Wernle does not limit himself to names alone in his effort to
demonstrate his "general considerations conforming to certain rules" for
abridgement, but goes even further:

> But the consciousness of the later writers, who were mindful only
> of important, didactic matters, also passes over the naive beauty
> and freshness of small, momentary depictions. How Jesus has pity
> on the leper and afterwards pushes the ritually still unclean one
> away with a vehement gesture; how the man with the palsy is

carried in by four men; how the disciples break a path for themselves through the grainfield; how Jesus glances back towards the Pharisees, full of anger and, at the same time, saddened over their hardness of heart. And then there are the numerical data: the pigs which numbered about two thousand; and the matter of whether the disciples should buy bread for the people at the cost of two hundred denarii. The drastic comparison: no fuller on earth can color anything as white as the clothes of the transfigured were. How Jesus takes the child in his arms; how he looks at the rich man with eyes full of love; how Jesus goes on ahead toward Jerusalem alone, while those following him are afraid; how the blind man, when called to Jesus, throws his cloak away, leaps up and comes to him; about the colt that was tied at the door outside on the street; how Pilate is at first surprised that Jesus has already died and releases the body only after making inquiries of the centurion; the fearful talk of the women on the way . . .

All these are touches, says Wernle, "which reveal to us the first, fresh narrator" and which "the consciousness of the later writers . . . passes over." Why? Because they were "mindful only of important, didactic matters."

Again, Wernle's assertion can be refuted on strictly factual grounds. The prehistory in Matthew and Luke will serve as a counter-example. In *Luke* we find an abundance of concrete passages: the foretelling of the birth of John the Baptist and Jesus; Mary's visit to Elizabeth, how she travels over the mountains and what is said of Elizabeth: when she heard Mary's greeting "the babe leaped in her womb." To this we may add the birth of John the Baptist with Zechariah's hymn of praise "Blessed be the Lord God of Israel"; the actual birth of Jesus when, in the "Katalyma," the travellers' inn, his parents could not find any other place for the child but the manger; the vivid scene with the shepherds in the field, keeping watch by night over their flock, and with the angel bathed in light from the glory of God. After that, the presentation of Christ in the temple with the touching figure of old Simeon: "Lord, now lettest thou thy servant depart in peace, according to thy word." And finally the report about the twelve-year-old Jesus in the temple, how he sits in the midst of the greatly astonished rabbis, authorities on the Scriptures, asking them questions—[7]"and all who heard him were amazed"(2:47)—while the worried parents search for him among relatives and acquaintances "a day's journey" away, how they then return and find him after three days in the

---

[7]ἐπερωτῶντα.

temple and his mother calls out: "Son, why have you treated us so? Behold, your father and I have been looking for you anxiously."

This is all full of concrete description and lively, vividly detailed passages. Is it any wonder, then, that these depictions belong to the most popular motifs of religious painting?

The same is true of *Matthew:* the appearance of the angel to Joseph in his dream; the Magi from the Orient who saw the star in the east and then came to seek the newborn king to pay him homage; the suspicious Herod who secretly summons and questions the Magi; the movement of the star ahead of them, "till it came to rest over the place where the child was;" the adoration itself, "opening their treasures" and presenting gifts to him: gold, frankincense, and myrrh; the second appearance of the angel to Joseph; the flight of the holy family to Egypt under cover of night; Herod's furious rage; the appearance of the angel to Joseph in Egypt with the order to return; the return home to the land of Israel; the fear of Herod's successor and the withdrawal to Nazareth.

Is that not also full of graphic observation and picturesque, detailed passages? Now one could object that all the cited examples stem from the prehistory, but that, in the main narrative concerning Jesus' activities and teachings (hence the part which Matthew and Luke have in common with Mark), these examples cannot be shown to the same extent. Yet even that can be refuted:

How vivid is the pericope of the centurion at Capernaum:

For I am a man under authority, with soldiers under me, and I say
to one, "Go," and he goes, and to another, "Come," and he comes,
and to my slave, "Do this," and he does it.

Or the Matthean pericope about the temple tax, where Jesus says to Simon Peter: "Go to the sea and cast a hook and take the first fish that comes up, and when you open its mouth you will find a shekel"? Likewise Peter's question: "Lord, how often shall my brother sin against me and I forgive him? As many as seven times?" And Jesus' answer: "I do not say to you seven times, but seventy times seven." Then the subsequent parable of the unfaithful servant: how his master commands that the slave be sold together with his wife and child and all that he had; how the servant throws himself on the ground in front of him and fervently implores: "Master, have patience with me, and I will pay you everything"; but how this same servant feels no pity at all for his fellow servant, but mercilessly has him thrown into prison and subsequently his Master indignantly tells him: "You wicked servant!"—and "in anger his master delivered him to the jailers . . ."

Correspondingly, in Luke: the village of the Samaritans which refuses to take in Jesus "because his face was turned toward Jerusalem." James and

John who ask Jesus: "Lord, do you want us to bid fire come down from heaven and consume them?" The parable of the good Samaritan: the priest saw the beaten man lying there nearly dead and "passed by." The Levite who came to the same place "saw him [and] passed by." Then the Samaritan "went to him and bound up his wounds, pouring on oil and wine; then he set him on his own beast and brought him to an inn, and took care of him." And, on the following day, "he took out two denarii" and gave them to the innkeeper with the order: "Take care of him!"

All this is so full of feeling for vivid description that the argumentation of Wernle and his predecessors Weisse and Holtzmann, claiming that the brief individual touches had "lost their significance for the first and third Evangelists," simply does not hold water. At the same time it demonstrates that the advocates of the Marcan hypothesis have not sufficiently tested the validity of their assertion against the available material.

In summary, we must conclude that there is nothing to Wernle's "general considerations conforming to certain rules"—nothing whatever. There is no law of abridgement. It can neither be substantiated in principle nor demonstrated factually—not even taking the Marcan hypothesis as a basis. And, indeed, it is precisely here that the fundamental problem lies, for the whole proof from psychological reflection represents an immense *petitio principii.* The pioneers of the Marcan hypothesis proceed from the assumption that the second Gospel served as the basis for the first and third. From this premise they pursue their train of thought in such a way as to represent their deviations from the Gospel of Mark as "alterations" of a positive or negative nature, which, accordingly, they interpret either as "additions" or as "omissions." On the basis of such preconceptions they then seek to trace Matthew's and Luke's thought processes as they think them possible or necessary within the framework of this hypothesis, and they strain their talent for conjecture in order to discover how these thought processes must have developed. And from their psychological findings they draw a conclusion about the correctness of the Marcan hypothesis and believe that they have proved it with a continuous proof from psychological reflection, proof that runs through all of the synoptic Gospels. The *circulus vitiosus* is closed.

And yet, their entire Sisyphean task was doomed to failure from the very beginning, for their premise was false. Thus the inevitable result was a whole anthology of misinterpretations. The enormous effort did not justify the outlay. The proof from psychological reflection became a labyrinth from which no one could escape. It represents the most painful chapter of the Marcan hypothesis, indeed the real tragedy in the scholarship of its pioneers.

We contend that it would have been better for them and for scholarship as such if their own subconscious yet often palpable knowledge—or at least presentiments—about the inadequacies of the proof from psychological reflection had moved them to reconsider the Marcan hypothesis in all its essentials.

Let us draw the final conclusion from our critical analysis of the "proofs" for the validity of the Marcan hypothesis. Not a single one of them has proved itself to be sound. They cannot be upheld, whether from a linguistic, stylistic, compositional, or even a psychological viewpoint. The same must be said of the "main proof" of the common narrative sequence, while the "fundamental" proof from Petrine origin is the least defensible of all.

Chapter XIII

Conclusion

In the first part of our investigation we have seen that the founders, the new founders and the consummators of the Marcan hypothesis had maneuvered it into a hopeless situation. In the second part we have refuted their "proofs" for it. Accordingly, we can state that the second Gospel does not possess priority over Matthew and Luke and was not their source. Therefore the result of our critical examination is that the Marcan hypothesis is false—false in its conception, execution, and conclusion.

What does it mean to say that a hypothesis is false?

In his *Einleitung in das Neue Testament* (1885), Holtzmann declared, in spite of his revocation: "At all events, the two-source theory offers the most probable solution to the synoptic problem" (p. 355).

Bornkamm supports the same point of view: "However one can hardly deny that it (the two-source theory) offers the *best* solution to the problem of synoptic sources in its main features" (*RGG³*, Vol. II, col. 755).

Wernle had been even more audacious:

> But it is certain that the extra-Marcan material common to Matthew and Luke cannot be explained in terms of a common lost source or by the use of [the writings of] one by the other. Rather, it is best explained by the freely flowing Marcan text and the freely reflecting relationship of both Evangelists to it. The history of the text calls our attention to the first explanation; the second emerges from the comparison of Luke to Mark. Every other

hypothesis is false because it is superfluous (*Synopt. Frage*, p. 61).

And Wilke, the most enthusiastic of all, had assured his readers: "For all eternity we affirm with hand and seal that our conclusion is the correct one" (*Urevangelist*, p. 684).

At this point the following fundamental observations must be made. There is no source hypothesis about the Gospels with whose help one cannot "explain" a great deal. Even the ur-gospel hypothesis was able to do so, although in intricately labyrinthine ways. A source hypothesis would not be advanced in the first place if it were not capable, more or less, of "solving" the synoptic problem. But, to be sure, there are degrees of correctness; however, the degrees of probability of a hypothesis are relatively insignificant where the decisive question of the complete explicability of the phenomena is at stake. As long as there are remainders which remain inexplicable, a theory is false because it is unable to confirm its validity in the final test against the factual realities of the text. There is only one single criterion for the absolute validity of a source hypothesis—it must "come out." And that means that it must be able to explain completely all the phenomena of the synoptic problem and that no questions remain unanswered.

How does the Marcan hypothesis fare in this respect? Let us examine the three different editions of *Die Religion in Geschichte und Gegenwart* from this viewpoint:

RGG[1]:

> Naturally the result which we have thus reached . . . is *not absolutely clear-cut* and convincing on all individual points. *Rather, various difficulties remain with respect to particular matters* . . . . But even among the historical narratives there is no pericope where Matthew and Luke do not agree against Mark at least in this or that detail. In a number of individual passages the narrative report of Matthew or of Luke again and again has given the impression of originality, even to researchers who in general maintain the priority of Mark (for example, the presentation in the pericope of the Canaanite woman appears to many to be more original in Matthew than in Mark). In other passages one cannot explain why or how Matthew and Luke—assuming that the Evangelist Mark was their source—arrived at their strongly deviating presentation. Why, for example, did Luke omit the entire passage Mk 6:45-8:26? *This is a question* to which no one has yet been able to give a certain answer (Vol. II, col. 705 Bousset; author's italics).

Similarly:

> One will have to be satisfied with the proof of general dependence, even if one *cannot conclusively deduce all the details;* and one will have to get used (!) to sometimes attributing many things to chance, arbitrariness, and the mood of the individual authors, whom one has to imagine neither as excessively dependent copiers of their sources nor as consistently superior editors. *At the same time it cannot be denied that acceptance of the Marcan hypothesis leaves unsolved difficulties in individual matters.* But here, too, one will generally *have to be content with a "we don't know."* It is enough that those uncertainties in particular matters are not so strong that they force us to revise the entire conception (col. 707 Bousset; author's italics).

RGG[2]:

> However, the main proofs that have been stated may be regarded as having established the two-source theory, *even if difficulties still remain and not every detail can be entirely explained.* To be sure, the fact that Matthew and Luke repeatedly concur against Mark in the rendering of the Lord's sayings and thereby display the better text, may be explained precisely in terms of the use of a second source. But the fact that they agree within the narrative not only in such major deviations as that represented by the omission of three special parts of Mark, but also in matters of detail in numerous smaller omissions, minor additions, transformations, and other changes, *gives rise to the question whether their basis was perhaps not our canonical Mark* at all, but rather a faithfully preserved "ur-Mark." Nevertheless, this assumption cannot be proved on the basis of synoptic comparisons. Rather, part of the mentioned concurrence of Matthew and Luke against Mark probably resulted from inevitable coincidence in the process of systematically abbreviating and stylistically improving the model. Above all there is no doubt that here the textual problem plays a role in higher criticism. Matthew and Luke did not read exactly the same Marcan text as the one we reconstructed from the earliest version available to us; thus they could very well render *their* Mark, even though they deviate from ours (sic!) (Vol. II, col. 425, Klostermann; author's italics).

RGG[3]:

> The two-source theory, too, *leaves numerous questions open on matters of detail.* . . . (Vol. II., col. 755, author's italics). The

sources that have been mentioned so far do not account for everything in the Gospels. After all, Mark contains a small quantity of special material (Mk 4:26-29; 7:32-37; 8:22-26). This circumstance, of course, cannot shake the thesis that Mark was used by Matthew and Luke. However, it does confirm the fact that the version of Mark that served as a basis for both other Gospels did not concur in all details, and was thus hardly identical to the second Gospel of our canon. The simple fact that in some passages Mark is paralleled by only one of the other Gospels compels us to assume that Matthew and Luke used variant texts of Mark. (Examples follow). If these examples demonstrate that the text of Mark underwent historical development even before the editorial changes by Matthew and Luke, then the special material and particularities of Mark which distinguish him from the other two . . . prove that his text also underwent subsequent historical changes (col. 756).

To be sure, this (the two-source theory) is capable of tracing back the synoptic sources and their elaboration only to a certain stage, not to the first beginnings; *in no case should it be understood in the sense of, as it were, a mathematical solution explaining all differentiations* (Vol. II, col. 756, Bornkamm; author's italics).

Can there be more convincing admissions that the Marcan hypothesis does not hold water than these testimonies by its exponents? All three join in feeling a certain uneasiness about the discrepancy between their advocacy of the Marcan hypothesis and the haunting consciousness of the inadequacy of their argumentation. *One can actually regard this attitude as characteristic of a generation of German New Testament scholars in the first half of our century.* And it was an appropriate expression of the general disposition—one can almost say, of their indisposition—when Erich Fascher wrote in 1924: "The two-source theory, about which we never were entirely happy . . . (*Die Formgeschichtliche Methode,* p. 233).

Since the time of its founding by Wilke and Weisse, the Marcan hypothesis had bequeathed questions about the synoptic problem which were not solved—because they could not be solved on its presuppositions. The question which therefore has forced itself upon us for a long time and now looms directly before us is: *how was it possible for the Marcan hypothesis to become established and then sweep everything before it in the previous century?*

We now turn to this problem.

Part III:

The Establishment and Dominance of the Marcan Hypothesis

Chapter XIV

The Ideological Background of the Marcan Hypothesis

The Marcan hypothesis is so demonstrably false that the question must be seriously raised: How was it possible for this source-theory to win such world-wide approval? The answer must be sought in the *ideological background*. And the solution to the riddle is: *David Friedrich Strauss.*

If there has ever been an explosive situation in the history of New Testament studies it was that caused by the appearance of Strauss' *Life of Jesus, Critically Examined* (1835). This impressed his contemporaries as a theological catastrophe which called everything into question. The thrill of "Hannibal-at-the-gates" stirred not only the professional world of scholarship but the Christian world as a whole. A hitherto unprecedented reaction set in, to disprove Strauss's fundamental thesis: "The Gospels contain not history, but myths!"

But whoever wished to refute Strauss had to be acuter than he and had to wield an equally keen blade—requirements not easily met. Thus his opponents preferred to strike at him indirectly, by endeavoring to disprove his source-theory. Now, as we have mentioned above, Strauss had not put forward his own source-theory, but had worked on the basis of the Griesbach hypothesis. As a consequence of this, the man who got his ears boxed— posthumously and fifty-five years after the appearance of his *Commentatio*— was Johann Jacob Griesbach.

In his critical analysis of the gospels Strauss had applied this basic principle: If the content is unacceptable, the sources must also be worthless—

and among "sources" he included the authorities adduced or quoted by the Evangelists. Now his opponents turned the tables and (with a substantial alteration of the notion of "source") established their own principle: If Strauss's source-theory is false, the content of his work—indeed, the whole of his argument—must also be false.

Accordingly, the storm against the Griesbach hypothesis—which had hitherto enjoyed the highest esteem—burst forth very suddenly, in the very year of the publication of Strauss's *Life of Jesus,* and continued with almost undiminished acrimony to the end of the century—with, moreover, a display of emotion which seems scarcely conceivable in the field of scientific source-criticism.

Karl Lachmann, indisputably one of the foremost scholars of his day, was the first to level heavy artillery at Griesbach. It is no longer possible today to determine whether his trenchant attack on Griesbach's source-hypothesis was occasioned directly by the publication of Strauss's work, but in any case it was the opening gun in the anti-Griesbach campaign and had the effect of a signal in both form and tone. We have already had several occasions to mention Lachman's essay, "De ordine narrationum in evangeliis synopticis," which appeared in *Theologische Studien und Kritiken* (1835) and which had such important consequences for the formulation of the Marcan hypothesis by C. H. Weisse. In this essay he adopted a position opposed to Griesbach's source-theory, as follows: "Multo autem minus probandi sunt . . . quibus placet Marcum esse ineptissimum desultorem, qui nunc taedio, modo cupiditate, tum neglegentia, denique vecordi studio inter evangelia Matthaei et Lucae incertus feratur et oberret. Nempe his quaedam Griesbachii disputatio sedulae subtilitatis specie inlusit, cum tamen minime ingeniosa sit, sed frigida tota et ieiuna" (p. 577)—"Much less, however, can one agree with those who deem it right to regard Mark as a very inept tight-rope walker, who now from weariness, now from capriciousness, now from negligence, and finally from blind eagerness swings back and forth between the Gospels of Matthew and Luke. These people have, to be sure, let themselves be deceived by a certain treatise by Griesbach, which gives the impression of careful and thorough scholarship; it is, nevertheless, anything but intelligent: it is quite trivial and devoid of content."

Still less restrained in his attacks on the Griesbach hypothesis was Christian Gottlob Wilke, in his *Urevangelist* (1838): "Mark would be thence, i.e., according to Griesbach) not an abbreviator, nor an epitomator, nor an excerptor, but—a castrator of the other texts; or how else should one describe someone who mutilates borrowed passages and mixes up what he had mutilated? Could such an idea be reconciled with the idea of a rational author? And could such an idea be expressed without accusing the prudent author of blithering and levity, whereas he far surpasses his fellow-authors in exactitude? What could have induced Mark to play fast and loose with expressions of his informants, or what could have caused him to make a mishmash of their words?" (p. 443).

The second founder of the Marcan hypothesis, C. H. Weisse, confined himself to expressing his full agreement with Lachmann and to saying that the latter had spoken very severely about the "accepted view among the majority of theologians" (i.e., the Griesbach hypothesis), but in no wise incorrectly, (*Evangelische Geschichte*, Vol. I, p. 39).

August Tholuck—"pious Tholuck," as he was called in the circles of the revivalist movement—took issue with the Griesbach hypothesis in minute detail in his work, *Die Glaubwürdigkeit der evangelischen Geschichte, zugleich eine Kritik des "Lebens Jesu" von Strauss, für theologische und nichttheologische Leser dargestellt* (1837). In this it is especially clear that he, by standing up for the Marcan hypothesis and by criticizing the Griesbach source-theory, means to strike at none other than *David Friedrich Strauss*: "It is true," he says, "that the view that the Gospel of Mark is only a mosaic of the first and third Gospels has won for itself not a few advocates, especially since Saunier came to the fore as an interpreter of Schleiermacher's lectures, and if D. Fr. Strauss is also of the opinion—on first impression—that Griesbach has 'proved' the matter, this is not to be marvelled at. Nevertheless, a more mature consideration will perhaps lead the more discerning reader to the opinion that it is rather the incorrectness of this hypothesis which has been 'proved' " (p. 248).

After this "device to win approval" and the appeal to the "discernment" which he concedes to Strauss, Tholuck takes pains on his own account to "prove" the Marcan hypothesis; to reduce Griesbach *ad absurdum*. He accomplishes this by the method of hyperbolic distortion with which the writings of Lachmann and Wilke have made us familiar:

> And such aimless wandering back and forth between the scrolls of his two predecessors (Lachmann. inter evangelia Matthaei et Lucae incertus feratur et oberret), copying a snippet now from the right, now from the left—should one have to expect such a procedure from any ancient author, much less from a man who had been as good a pupil of the apostles as Luke? It may be so. But how then is one supposed to explain the variation of expression which runs through the whole Gospel, which does not in two lines attach itself diplomatically to one of the predecessors? (p. 251) Further: And to what author should it occur, when excerpting another, to write *eisporeuontai* where the orginal has *katelthen*, to

write *sparaxan* for *rhipsan,* to substitute *ethambethesan* for
egeneto thambos, etc.? To a plagiarist, who doesn't want to have
his thievery noticed? To an English fop who has the cut of his
jacket altered because someone else has one like it? But such a
procedure would certainly not occur to a reasonable man (p. 252).

After this "conclusive argument" against Griesbach, Tholuck proceeds to
the practical application of it to achieve the real aim of his book, the
refutation of Strauss:

Thus enough has been said to show that, whether or not Dr.
Strauss has gone astray elsewhere, he has quite certainly done so
in regard to the Gospel of Mark. We can also scarcely believe
anything other than that this intelligent man will later retract or
radically modify this his opinion. However, we also cannot help
ourselves, we must admit it openly: his procedure with this Gospel
has been for us a new, convincing proof that the critic's results are
often the product of a dialectic which drives its subject now into
one corner, now into another, as a whip does to a spinning top (p.
266).

Here one sees objectivity already standing at a considerable distance, and
there is no longer any mention of an objective evaluation of the Griesbach
hypothesis.

A distinguished Catholic scholar also aligned himself with the anti-
Griesbach party: Johannes Kuhn, Professor of New Testament Studies in
Tübingen, who was reputed to be one of the most acute Catholic theologians
in Germany. He defined his position with respect to Strauss's identification
with the Griesbach source-theory in the following way:

If Strauss really imagines—relying on Griesbach and the
anatomical result of the synoptic comparison of the three first
Gospels—that Mark made use of his predecessors and patched
together his Gospel account, in much the same way that we cut the
three first Gospels to pieces in the Synopsis to facilitate our grasp
of the whole, then, to be sure, the account given by the Elder John
about our Mark is not so easy to sustain. But who in the world can
believe that Mark compiled his material in such a mechanical and
apparently unprecedented fashion? If one tries to imagine the
operation Mark would have had to perform, one will find it partly
absurd, and, for the rest, as good as impossible. If it were only an
uninspired mode of procedure which was being attributed to the
Evangelist here, we might count less on others agreeing with our
protest . . . but it is more than poor taste—and lack of inspiration,

which are being presupposed here" (*Leben Jesu, wissenschaftlich bearbeitet.* 1838 p. 33).

Kuhn now shows how, according to Griesbach's hypothesis, the Marcan Gospel must have originated. Where Lachmann had accused Griesbach of degrading Mark to a clumsy tight-rope walker, Kuhn blames him for reducing the Evangelist to an incompetent editor who assembled his material with scissors and paste:

> One would have to imagine that Mark had cut the two scrolls of Matthew and Luke up into little snippets, mixed these together in a pot, and produced his Gospel from this mixture. Or better, that he had taken a blank parchment, pasted the separate snippets of Matthew and Luke on it, and used this as a rough draft for manufacturing his own account (p. 34).

Now it might perhaps be possible to excuse these biased distortions of the Griesbach-Strauss thesis we have quoted by regarding them as derailments, so to speak, of rational thinking, to be understood as due to the first agitation over Strauss's revolutionary work and for this reason to be condoned. Now if this line of argument were correct, such expressions of prejudice would have had to cease after a while and been replaced by a calmer, objective critique of the Griesbach hypothesis.

The opposite is the case! Even twenty-five years later, in 1863, the "New Founder of the Marcan hypothesis," Heinrich Julius Holtzmann, seizes once again upon the most scurrilous expressions of Lachmann and Wilke in order to identify himself with them:

> One needs only to follow the hypothesis (i.e. Griesbach's) in detail once for a few steps to find Wilke's opinion justified: 'Mark would not have been an abbreviator, nor an epitomator, nor an excerptor, but a castrator . . . . What else could one call' him? Lachmann appropriately remarks in opposing such hypotheses, that our second Evangelist would be made out by them to be *ineptissimus desultor, qui nunc . . . oberrat.*

And now Holtzmann adds, on his own behalf, a further insult to the many that Griesbach is supposed to have directed at Mark: he alleges that Griesbach has accused Mark of intellectual plagiarism:

> If Mark had laid hands on the property of Matthew and Luke as the Griesbach hypothesis maintains, he would certainly offer his readers demonstrable contraband at one time or another (*Synopt. Evangelien,* p. 345f).

Now we move another twenty years further on to the most prominent representative and exponent of the Marcan thesis, *Bernhard Weiss*. If an emotionally calm and objective position with respect to the Griesbach hypothesis could be expected from anyone it would surely be from him. Should not the storm of criticism which raged against David Friedrich Strauss have abated now, ten years after his death?

In Bernhard Weiss's *Matthausevangelium (Meyers Kommentar* 1883[7]) we read:

> It is of course understandable that a form of criticism, which—by the nature of its philosophical presuppositions—sought to dissolve the substance of the Gospel tradition into a formless mass of legends, was interested in representing the rich historical detail, which our source (viz. Mark) contains and which offers the most tenacious resistance to this process of dissolution, *as a worthless retouching of a pretentious author;* and for this task the *Griesbach hypothesis,* which finds in our Gospel only an artfully adorned epitome with a certain appearance of originality, always provided a welcome apology. But in the face of an unprejudiced source-criticism these endeavors, which are based less on solid grounds than on witty affectation, can only come to naught (Vol. I, p. 50).

Accordingly, Bernhard Weiss's final opinion about the Griesbach hypothesis is as follows:

> In fact, the Griesbach hypothesis is the *sole unadulterated aberration in the history of source-criticism,* which in spite of some remarkable meanderings has succeeded nevertheless in discovering one or another facet of truth; this theory, on the other hand, has only hindered our reaching a clear understanding of the second Gospel—for a long time (p. 39f).

Now, the "unprejudiced source-criticism" which B. Weiss claims to practice is clearly not in very good condition. One senses that he is writing from a particular theological standpoint, and that though he says "Griesbach," he means David Friedrich Strauss.

One could proceed with this continuous vilification of the Griesbach hypothesis indefinitely, but we shall content ourselves with this selection, together with the positions taken in the articles in the three different editions of the *RGG* which have been mentioned above (p. 9f.), and which have the same purport. One marvels at the profusion of modifications of which a wilfully distorted description is capable: his opponents accused Griesbach of having degraded Mark to a clumsy tight-rope walker, of having debased him to a plagiarist, to a capricious fop, to a pot-mixer, a shredder of scrolls, a paster-together of snippets, to a castrator and muddler of the maimed, to an affected literary hack who added only worthless trappings to the work of his predecessors, to a slavish imitator and an incompetent excerptor . . .

And all this was repeated deliberately about Griesbach, who in his own research had excelled in noble impartiality and pure objectivity of scholarship. Nothing had been further from his mind than to write a *Life of Jesus* after the manner of Strauss's. But the anathemas of the conservative theology which were intended for Strauss struck Griesbach with equal or greater force: Griesbach would have had every reason, therefore, to cry out from his grave, "God preserve me from my friends!" The fact that Strauss took his source-theory as a point of departure cost Griesbach his scholarly reputation for a hundred and forty years. Those who wished to refute Strauss, the "great destroyer," flung themselves upon Griesbach and belabored him mercilessly.

The surprising, indeed shattering thing about the whole anti-Griesbach/Strauss campaign is just this: it does not seem to have crossed the mind of a single one of the jeering critics that the whole situation would be exactly reversed if their criticisms were justified. For the matter is not resolved by reproaching Griesbach for the ignominy he has heaped on Mark. Even if the satirical and caricaturing distortions are left aside, the facts they claim to describe still remain in their entirety, namely the peculiar relationship which exists between Mark and the other two Synoptic Gospels—and only the personalities involved would be exchanged!

Let us grant, for the sake of argument, that Griesbach's opponents were right: it was not Mark who made a selection from Matthew and Luke, but the other way round. What then? Then all the insults from which Griesbach's critics wished to exculpate Mark are now forcibly saddled on Matthew and Luke—and in double measure. Then it would be no longer Mark who should be described as "Desultor, Plagiarist, Castrator, or Compiler," but (1) Matthew and (2) Luke. And so, instead of one scoundrel, we would have two.

But this irresistible consequence of reversing the circumstances was, obviously, not clear to any of Griesbach's opponents in their unrestrained distortion of his basic thesis. It is astonishing enough, moreover, that the supporters of Griesbach resisted the obvious temptation to devise a satirical counter-parody to the exaggerated ironic presentation of their opponents and to repay them double with their own coin for what they had bestowed on Griesbach with biased points of view which were quite unworthy of them.

It was well, however, that Griesbach's partisans kept their arguments on an objective level. For the whole assault upon Griesbach, lasting as it did for more than a century, reveals a state of affairs which must be taken very seriously, namely this: that the proponents of the Marcan hypothesis made a systematic attempt to undermine the scholarly credibility of a source-theory which was distasteful to them—by incessantly disparaging the intellectual qualifications of their opponents.

It need hardly be said that in the field of source-criticism only the objective weight of arguments has any claim to validity if New Testament theology intends to be a scientific discipline. And it is quite unnecessary to point out that there is only one admissible way to refute a thesis or hypothesis with which one disagrees, and that is by marshalling the objective, valid counter-evidence. Irony, satire, and ridicule, however, prove less than nothing. They only permit the suspicion to arise that the Marcan hypothesis is anchored less in the reason than in the emotions. What was the main objection that C. H. Weisse made against Wilke? "Such a procedure is even more deplorable since it must unavoidably arouse suspicion among non-specialists and, even more, in those with evil intent; for if a hypothesis demands such acts of violence in order to be established, then such a hypothesis cannot possibly have a sound foundation."

Now it is natural to ask: Why, for Strauss's opponents, did sanctioning the *priority* of the Marcan Gospel matter so much? Two important theological considerations lay at the basis of their impassioned defense of Marcan priority:

1) Strauss, in agreement with Griesbach's source-theory, had regarded Mark as the last, chronologically, of the synoptic Gospels, and maintained that the "details" of Mark's account, his little expansions and illustrations (Griesbach: . . . paraphrastikos exprimere), were signs characteristic of an advanced mythologizing development, since such things would increase with the degree of distance from the facts of experience.

If, however, the adherents of Mark could succeed in proving the Marcan Gospel to be the *oldest* of the three synoptics and, more than this, to be *the source of the two others,* then Strauss's whole argumentation would fall at one stroke, and his assertion of the mythical character of the Gospels would thus be shown to be erroneous. And this means: Strauss's fundamental thesis would be overturned.

2) The Gospel of Mark was, in comparison with Matthew and Luke, relatively the freest from legendary material: it lacks the whole pre-history, the genealogy and the birth-narratives. The legendary, mythically embellished character of these was unmistakable. In addition it differs considerably from Matthew and Luke.

Above all, Mark has no "post-history"; it is the only one of the three synoptics to contain neither a resurrection narrative nor an ascension narrative; it ends at the empty tomb with the words, "For they were afraid." And there is no continuation . . .

To be sure this understanding of the matter was bound up with a presupposition: the conclusion of Mark (16:9-20) had to be regarded as spurious. Griesbach himself regarded the existing conclusion of Mark as spurious, and had called the sudden, unorganic breaking-off of the Gospel at Mk 16:8 a "clausulam abruptissimam" and added: "Omnibus incredibile videri debebat Marcum sic finivisse commentariolum suum." ("It ought to seem incredible to everyone that Mark finished his little narrative in this way.") For partisans of the Marcan hypothesis it was immediately made a point of principle that the conclusion of Mark was spurious, for only in this way could their anti-mythical (and therefore anti-Strauss) interpretation of the Marcan Gospel be carried through at all.

If now the oldest Gospel, as they declared Mark to be, was clearly to be regarded as maximally legend-free—at least in relation to the two others—then the Straussian thesis "not history, but myths" would be seen to be refuted and changed into its opposite: Not myth, but history!

Guided by these ideas the adherents of the Marcan hypothesis now persevered in their efforts to prove:

1) that the Apostle Peter was the authority and the immediate source of Mark,
2) that the *logia,* as a collection of the Lord's sayings, had been written down by the Apostle Matthew personally.

Thus New Testament research of the previous century believed it had guaranteed the existence of two exceptional *historical sources:* one first-hand apostolic source and another at second hand. And it was convinced that it could outline a historically accurate picture of the "historical Jesus" on the basis of these two authoritative sources.

With this rounded and self-contained hypothetical construction, the scholarly study of the Gospels did indeed answer to a requirement of faith in the theology of the last century, but at the same time it also departed from the indispensable basic principle of scholarship—which is to proceed without presuppositions and free from tendencies; and this means, in the present instance: to proceed without regard to some predetermined goal of faith. The Marcan hypothesis cannot make this claim. *It grew out of theological commitment. It is a theologumenon.*

Chapter XV

The Continuing Influence of the Marcan Hypothesis

The initial question of the preceding chapter was: How was it possible that this source-theory could attain such world-wide recognition? The key question of our last chapter must be: How could the predominance of the Marcan hypothesis continue—to this very day? A characteristic feature of this predominance was the fact that the proponents of the hypothesis obviously wanted it believed that general recognition constituted proof of validity.

And yet a certain qualification had to be made here. For if they boasted of this general recognition, they nevertheless were forced always to place a small, embarrassed "almost" before it. In fact, there was from the very beginning a counter-current, a group of antagonists who raised objections. It was, to be sure, quantitatively small but qualitatively impressive, and associated exclusively with famous names. The entire Second Tübingen School belonged to it; its members unanimously rejected the Marcan hypothesis. Only Ritschl defected and expounded his divergent standpoint in an essay in the *Theologische Jahrbücher* (1851, pp. 480-583) "Über den gegenwärtigen Stand der Kritik der synoptischen Evangelien." On that account Christian Hermann Weisse bestowed upon him the dubious commendation: "A younger pupil of this school who is striving for independence with capable vigor has openly turned toward it (the Marcan hypothesis)"(*Evangelienfrage*, p. 85).

David Friedrich Strauss, of course, had not established his own source theory but adopted the Griesbach theory as the basis for his investigation.

Even he expressed his view in detail on the question of sources for the first and only time—belatedly, indeed, too belatedly—in 1864 in his "Volksausgabe." At the same time he explicitly stated various arguments against the Marcan hypothesis.

The two-source theory really gained momentum only after the great Swabian scholars had died and their massive opposition had ceased. It coincided in time roughly with the appearance of Holtzmann's *Synoptische Evangelien* (1863). Ferdinand Christian Baur died in 1860, Albert Schwegler in 1857, David Friedrich Strauss in 1872. And Eduard Zeller, who had edited the *Theologische Jahrbücher,* the leading publication of the Tübingen scholars, had been forced to change over to philosophy, since he was refused a professorship at Tübingen and was not permitted to teach theology at Marburg. An unflinching old warrior from the Second Tübingen School— the only North-German among them—Adolf Hilgenfeld (1823-1907), continued to work in an almost rudimentary fashion into our century. Until the end of his life he neither wavered nor yielded in fighting a lonely battle against the Marcan hypothesis.

Also, the founder of a new and entirely different Tubingen School, Adolf Schlatter (1852-1938), proved to be a steadfast opponent of the two-source theory. "Father Schlatter," who was not only a pious man but also a good scholar, upheld the priority of Matthew to the very last. Hence he was held in ill repute as a "Biblicist."

Similarly, a New Testament scholar of the highest rank, Theodor von Zahn (1838-1933), known abroad as the personification of German thoroughness, took a position against the Marcan hypothesis. Hence his "progressive" opponents characterized him as a "conservative." And Heinrich Julius Holtzmann considered it appropriate to say of Zahn's supporters: "Behind the scholar stands a large herd of traditionalists and ignoramuses" ("Die Markushypothese in ihrer heutigen Gestalt," in: *Archiv für Religionswissenschaft,* 1907, p. 20).

Still, the two-source theory remained controversial in Germany until the First World War. It received its essential historical sanctioning only after the end of the war through "form criticism." The latter's founders, Martin Dibelius (*Formgeschichte des Evangeliums,* 1919; 1933[2]) and Rudolf Bultmann (*Geschichte der synoptischen Tradition,* 1921; 1957[3]) expressly adopted the two-source theory and based their argumentation upon it:

Dibelius:

The research of half a century has examined the origins of the Gospels from a certain standpoint. By virtue of its analytical method it has achieved a broadly acknowledged and, in its main features, a relatively sure result in the form of the so-called two-source theory: Matthew and Luke are both dependent upon Mark and, moreover, on a source which can be reconstructed from the Matthean and Lucan texts, the hypothetical collection Q (p. 8).

Bultmann:

The result of the synoptic comparison, the two-source theory, is not the only thing assumed here; rather, even the distinction between tradition and redaction cannot be made without critical analysis. Research in form criticism cannot possibly perform its task in opposition to literary criticism (p. 3).

Under the impact of the adoption of the two-source theory by the founders of form criticism, the misconception crept in from the very beginning that this was only a special modification, a particular "method," of the two-source theory. In any case, such a characterization was imparted to it from the beginning by its first reviewer and critic, Erich Fascher, in his work: *Die Formgeschichtliche Methode. Eine Darstellung und Kritik* (1924). Thus it came about that for a long time one spoke, in professional discussion, of agreement with the two-source theory "especially within the framework of form criticism."

However, in this one overlooked the fact that the two-source theory had undergone a change in function, and a reassessment and shifting of importance. *For form criticism was by no means an offshoot or a variation of the Marcan hypothesis*; rather, it was an essentially *new source-hypothesis* in the form of a "regression behind the Gospels." Earlier, such a regression had been seriously attempted only by the fathers of the written and above all the oral ur-gospel hypothesis, as well as by Schleiermacher in his Diegesis theory. Their intention had been to fill the vacuum between two poles: "the disciples' experience of Jesus" and "the writing down of this experience." It was this dark and empty space *before* the Gospels, a space unknown to us, that the originators of form criticism then sought to penetrate and illuminate.

In doing so they established a new *hypothetical theorem* which constitutes the essential principle of their analysis of sources, namely the "principle of small units." What is involved here is primarily a *pericope-theory.*

Dibelius:

The stories preserved in the synoptic Gospels . . . were transmitted at first as individual stories. (p. 175)

Bultmann:

The original elements of the synoptic Gospels (are) the individual fragments of saying and story (p. 3).

In order to be able to explore these assertions on the basis of literary criticism and textual analysis, they employed the method of redaction critical investigation which had received its classical statement in the ground-breaking work by *Karl Ludwig Schmidt* in the same year that Dibelius' *Formgeschichte* was published: *Der Rahmender Geschichte Jesu* (1919). In it Schmidt supports the same viewpoint as Dibelius and Bultmann:

> On the whole there is no life of Jesus in the sense of an unfolding life story, no chronological outline of the story of Jesus, but *only individual stories, pericopes set into a framework* (p. 317; author's italics).

Thus came into being the long-lasting marriage of form criticism and redaction criticism. It has been given an exhaustive general presentation in the unpublished dissertation of Joachim Rohde: *Formgeschichte und Redaktionsgeschichte in der Neutestamentlichen Forschung der Gegenwart* (Berlin, Humboldt University, 1962); West German abridged edition: *Die Redaktionsgeschichtliche Methode,* (1966); English translation of the latter: *Rediscovering the Teaching of the Evangelists,* (1968).

It is obvious, then, that the two-source theory had to undergo a substantial change of function once it was incorporated into form criticism and redaction criticism. They now had *two* source theories to offer, but of *different value.* The central, leading function here was assigned to the *pericope-theory.* The Marcan hypothesis suffered a devaluation, or revaluation—*it sank from the status of a fundamental hypothesis to that of an argumentative hypothesis.*

How did that happen? Because of their method of arguing from the history of the tradition and its forms, the founders of form criticism and redaction criticism could not ignore the synoptic question. Indeed, they constantly had to work with the mutual relationships of the first three Gospels for the purpose of argumentation, especially since they had excluded the Gospel of John from their deduction as not affected by form criticism. *In view of this they could not help but presume that there had to be a solution to the synoptic problem.* For lack of something better, they took the two-source theory as a basis. What other choice did they have, especially since the latter—although at this point it was not yet generally accepted—was nevertheless regarded as the "best" or "most likely" solution, or at least as the one "with which one could work"?

In this connection it is almost tragic to observe that the founders of form criticism themselves looked upon the Marcan hypothesis with skepticism, and with the uneasiness mentioned above ("with which we were never entirely happy"). This reserve becomes most obvious in the case of Dibelius when he speaks of the "in its main features *relatively* sure result" and of the *"hypothetical* collection Q." And Bultmann, too, had explicitly emphasized: *"He (Luke) does not take the Marcan outline as his basis"(Synopt. Tradition,* p. 135). To argue with this kind of evidence, to which the founders themselves were prepared to give only limited consent, and then with certain reservations, is precarious for any scholar.

Hence form criticism, too, was not spared the impact of this error; but it also resulted in positive repercussions for the Marcan hypothesis itself. For the main thesis of form criticism was based on the principle of small units which were to be seen as having been formed in the community: hence the proof from Petrine origin became meaningless, and consequently was widely regarded as antiquated. *Dibelius* writes in this sense: "Hence Mark, in the main part of his book, which deals with the life and works of Jesus, has joined together as he saw fit fragments of the *tradition preserved in the communities"* (p. 219; author's italics).

Bultmann said something similar: "In Mark one can still clearly recognize—and one sees it best in comparison with Luke—how the *oldest tradition* consisted of individual parts and that the continuity is secondary" (p. 362).

That the use of the two-source theory would lead form criticism into error was naturally unavoidable. It is also unmistakable. For reasons of space we will illustrate this with a single, striking example from Bultmann's argumentation. We have chosen for this purpose a section of his treatment of the inquiry into the origin and establishment of the whole Gospel, namely, his deduction of the "modification that the Marcan material underwent when it was revised by Matthew and Luke:"

> But the total view of Jesus' life is not portrayed in any essentially different way by Matthew than it is by Mark. To be sure, Matthew undertook a few transpositions in the Marcan outline, the most important of which is that he offers a combination of miracle stories (8:1-9:34) and to that end condenses separate and differently ordered stories from Mark (ch. 1-5). It is hardly a significant alteration that, for reasons which can no longer be ascertained with certainty, he passed over a few stories in Mark (1:21-28; 7:32-36; 8:22-26; 9:38-40; 12:41-44). Nor is it important that he often abbreviates Mark's stories by eliminating small, novelistic features. He is not always apt in doing this, as for example in 9:1-8 (the healing of the paralytic) where in consequence of omitting Mark 2:2, 4f., the words 'when Jesus saw their faith' in verse 2 is left unmotivated. Another example is 8:28-

34, where it is incomprehensible that the spirits flee from the two demoniacs into the whole herd of swine because the word "legion" (Mk 5:9) has been struck. Finally, there is 9:20-22, where the story of the woman with a hemorrhage has lost its main feature, her secret touching of Jesus' garment . . . . (*Geschichte der synoptischen Tradition*, 1921, p. 378).

On the basis of our argumentation it is obvious that the exact opposite of Bultmann's explanation is correct, and that one grasps the true state of affairs only by reversing his thesis point by point. His allegation that Matthew eliminated a few of Mark's "small, novelistic features" exhibits nothing other than the paraphrastic supplements, the small, distinct rays of light that Mark adds to the text of Matthew. With them he elucidates it and makes it more understandable. No wonder that Bultmann's false source theory has led him to burden Matthew with the priority of Mark, attributing to him "omissions" from the Marcan text that have made it partially "incomprehensible" or "unmotivated."

Of the Marcan stories that Matthew supposedly passed over, 7:32-36 (the healing of the deaf-mute) and 8:22-26 (the blind man of Bethsaida) are well known and are unique to Mark. Hence they are also missing from the Gospel of Luke. From the very beginning these two stories have constituted the *crux interpretum* of the representatives of the Marcan hypothesis; none of them has succeeded in offering an even slightly credible explanation of why Matthew and Luke, independently and without knowledge of each other, should both have omitted the two pericopes in mysterious, inexplicable concord. In the other pericopes Mk 1:21-28 (Jesus in the synagogue at Capernaum), 9:38-40 (the man casting out demons who did not follow Jesus), and 12:41-44 (the widow's mite) Mark follows Luke, in whose Gospel alone there are parallels to these stories. Here, too, the supporters of the two-source theory have moved heaven and earth, with the aid of their proof from psychological reflection, to explain why Matthew did not follow Mark here, although Luke allegedly did so in all three cases. Bultmann is somewhat more cautious, inasmuch as he avoids an explanation of this kind and satisfies himself by saying that Matthew omitted them "for reasons that can no longer be ascertained with certainty"—i.e., he does not know. In any case, this indirect admission was better than the conjecture that Bultmann added in a footnote: "Perhaps he did not read all of them in his Marcan text . . . ." (!)

Here it becomes instructively evident that exegetic uncertainty was not the only inevitable result of the adoption of the two-source theory by the founders of form criticism. Rather, their own evaluation in terms of form criticism of these "abridgements" that Matthew supposedly made in the Marcan text is shown to be faulty when Bultmann asserts:

As a result of such abridgements, the miracle stories have lost their purity of style, without, to be sure, being transformed into another genus in the process. Dibelius is of the opinion that they have been desecularized, christianized. I believe that it comes closer to the mark to say that they have been made less hellenistic. This redaction displays Matthew's Judeo-Christian style (p. 378).

Of course this controversy between Bultmann and Dibelius is superfluous. Matthew neither desecularized nor christianized. The "abridgements" were determined neither by hellenistic nor by Jewish-Christian influences. They are enlargements which Mark undertook in the Matthean text. Here, on the basis of individual examples, it becomes apparent that the Gospels of Matthew and Luke cannot be traced back, with the help of the Marcan hypothesis, to an ostensibly earlier stage of tradition in the Gospel of Mark. Moreover, it becomes equally obvious that in general, the attempt to track down the laws of form and tradition in the synoptic Gospels with the help of the two-source theory was doomed to failure from the start. These considerations verify what we stated in the first pages of this book, "that all statements about the Gospels and about Jesus which are based on an erroneous source-hypothesis must inevitably go astray." Form criticism made use of the two-source theory for purposes of developing its own argumentation. But if the two-source theory is wrong, it follows that the deductions of form criticism which emerged from the use of the Marcan hypothesis are also insupportable. Hence the assertion that the validity of the two-source theory has been confirmed by form criticism—an assertion which has been made over and over again for a long time, and most recently in 1973 by Josef Schmid in his "newly and completely revised" edition of the *Einleitung in das Neue Testament*—is also questionable. The *circulus vitiosus* that runs "The laws of form criticism and of the history of tradition, when applied to the Gospels, are confirmed by the two-source theory, and the validity of the two-source theory is confirmed by the results of research in form criticism" can in no way be reconciled with the findings contained in this study.

As a whole the adoption of the two-source theory by form criticism had a profound and far-reaching impact on historical research. For, to be sure, form criticism had not been generally recognized at all as a primary new source-hypothesis, and its argumentation by Dibelius and Bultmann as well as by Karl Ludwig Schmidt appealed explicitly to the two-source theory— even though the latter was only a means to an end for them. Hence this situation contributed to a broadening recognition of the two-source theory, in a sense as a secondary effect.

That such a relationship actually existed is confirmed by the fact that wherever form criticism found or gained support, the two-source theory was also recognized at the same time—and vice versa: whenever it failed to strike a responsive chord, the Marcan hypothesis fared accordingly. The first was the case in Catholic research, the second in English-speaking research.

In the course of the last fifty years the rapid and victorious advance of form criticism and the two-source theory within German Protestantism was followed by a similar development among Roman Catholics. It began slowly at first but then progressively gained ground in almost geometrical fashion in a Church that, through the centuries, traditionally had scarcely ever failed to uphold the priority of Matthew.

To be sure, a few individual Catholic New Testament scholars had earlier stood up for the Marcan hypothesis in opposition to Strauss' theory of myths. This was especially true of Johannes Kuhn with his *Leben Jesu, wissenschaftlich bearbeitet,* 1838 (see above, p. 230f.), and of J. Gehringer (*Synopt. Zusammenstellung der Texte der vier Evangelien,* 1842); both of whom were followed later by several others. But this opposition remained restricted to exceptions which the Catholic church officially disavowed. For only shortly before the First World War, Marcan priority was rejected as "unsubstantiated by any evidence based on tradition, or by historical argument" by the two decretals of the Pontifical Biblical Commission (June 19, 1911, and June 6, 1912). Instead, they emphasized the priority of the Gospel of Matthew, which was said to be "quoad substantiam"identical with the Aramaic original (*Enchiridion Biblicum,* p. 388-405). And in the same year (1912) the edition of Tillman's *Kommentar zur Heiligen Schrift des Neuen Testaments. Die drei älteren Evangelien* had to be withdrawn because of F. Maier's positive commentary on and attitude toward the two-source theory.

But in spite of the continuing prevalence of this official rejection, the two-source theory gradually gained approval and adherents in Catholic circles as well, under the influence of the kerygmatic attitude of form criticism. In 1930 Josef Schmid struck the decisive first blow with his inaugural dissertation *Matthäus und Lukas.* The same scholar was able to declare in the latest edition of his *Einleitung in das Neue Testament* (1973) that Catholic scholarship also recognizes the two-source theory as "generally, today, at least the best possible explanation of the synoptic problem" (p. 280).

It was prior to this that in 1943—in the midst of the bloodiest time of struggle in the Second World War—a sublime document of the timelessness of Gospel research, the Papal Encyclical "Divino afflante spiritu" of September 30, 1943, was published with the title "On the Timely

Advancement of Biblical Studies"—*De sacrorum bibliorum studiis opportune provehendis.*

It is not difficult to see that the word "timely" is not quite an adequate equivalent for "opportune," but goes beyond it. But it was in accordance with the sentiment of the German Catholic researchers who greeted this Encyclical as the long and greatly desired *Magna Carta* for freedom of scientific research into the Gospels. Nevertheless, with Vatican prudence the papal document said not a word about the two-source theory, but fundamentally recognized the rightful place of new research:

> Therefore those who are without exact knowledge of the status of Biblical studies unjustly maintain that the Catholic exegete of our day has nothing to add to what was achieved by Christian antiquity. On the contrary, our age has brought forth much that requires new investigation and new examination, providing the modern exegete with no small spur to ardent study.

Now it could only be a question of time until the way for form criticism, too, was essentially cleared. This occurred with the appearance of the *Instructio de historica Evangeliorum veritate* of the Pontifical Biblical Commission (April 21, 1964). In it form criticism is even mentioned by name: "Where it is appropriate, exegetes may lawfully investigate and evaluate sound elements in the method of form criticism in order to duly arrive at a fuller understanding of the Gospels" (*Bibl. Zeitschrift,* Vol. IX, p. 152).

These "sound elements", however, are confronted with a number of limiting "unacceptable philosophical and theological principles." Therefore we consider Josef Schmid's interpretation somewhat euphemistic when he says of form criticism: "Of late, an *Instructio* of the Pontifical Biblical Commission of April 21, 1964 has also declared it essentially correct" (*Einleitung in das Neue Testament,* 1973[6] p. 292).

It was then an almost inevitable consequence—one that was, in any case, hardly unexpected—of the very late adoption of the two-source theory by Catholic scholarship that it shared almost all the main errors and mistakes of Protestant scholarship. They have already been clarified on the basis of our expositions in the chapters dealing with proofs and therefore do not require further consideration here. In need of correction, however, are some statements which must be considered as untenable or simply false, even in the framework of the Marcan hypothesis—as, for example, when Wilke is named with Weisse as a founder of the two-source theory (Schmid/Wikenhauser, *Einleitung,* p. 279).

It is also an inversion of the actual historical facts when Josef Schmid claims:

> The fact that it (the two-source theory) did not immediately achieve due recognition must be blamed on David Friedrich Strauss' *Leben Jesu* (1835), which occupied historical research for a long time. Thus it came about that the success that the two scholars. had deserved was reaped only by the Göttingen orientalist H. G. A. Ewald (p. 279).

Schmid puts the cart before the horse here. For Wilke's *Urevangelist* and Weisse's *Evangelische Geschichte* were prompted precisely by Strauss' *Leben Jesu.* They were meant to be deliberate replies to his work and to refute the Griesbach hypothesis on which Strauss had based his study. Also, Josef Schmid would seem to have confused Wilke with Ewald, for the man who reaped the glory of "immortality"—as early as 1841, in fact, through Bruno Bauer—was of course precisely Wilke (and, to a lesser degree, Weisse). It certainly was not Ewald, whose pertinent works addressing the synoptic question did not actually appear until a decade later, i.e., in 1849-51. (See above, pp. 58, 61).

We have seen that in Catholic New Testament scholarship the recognition or non-recognition of the Marcan hypothesis was causally linked to the acceptance or rejection of the "method of form criticism" and its use of the two-source theory in advancing its arguments. The same phenomenon is apparent in the English-speaking world where form criticism found only minimal support, and encountered considerable resistance, from the very beginning. In like manner the two-source theory encountered no little skepticism and criticism . As late as 1959, Hans Conzelmann wrote:

> But outside of Germany we meet a closed front which refuses to recognize form criticism as a scholarly method. Rather, it is regarded as a matter for debate, should that be necessary, but there is in fact little inclination to do so since form criticism is regarded as a typical German overstatement; as the product of continental radicalism. The form critics are—seen from abroad— a small, somewhat peculiar sect, lacking in "common sense." Even those new Testament scholars who have adopted this method narrow it down to the formal classification of narrative forms, and dispute the assertion that an analysis based on form criticism can lead to judgements on historical authenticity. ("Zur Methode der Leben-Jesu-Forschung," in: *Zeitschrift für Theologie und Kirche,* 1959, Beiheft I, p. 7).

Although in the meantime some things have changed in this respect, this overwhelmingly negative attitude in the English-speaking world was nevertheless confirmed in 1970 by Laurentius Klein ("Anglikanische

Theologie im 20. Jahrhundert," in : *Bilanz der Theologie*, Vol. II, p. 135). As late as 1972 Hans Werner Braun wrote of the "widespread distrust among Anglo-Saxon New Testament scholars toward form criticism" ("Theologie und Geschichte in der Überlieferung vom Leben Jesu," in: *Evangelische Theologie*, Vol. 32 p. 128). Symptomatic of this reserved attitude among English-speaking scholars is the fact that Bultmann's main work on form criticism was not published in English translation until forty years after its first publication. At the same time, this was an indication that form criticism had gained ground there.

While in Germany critical scholarship on the Marcan hypothesis almost entirely ceased after the end of the First World War, the opposite was true of English-speaking research during the same period. It was English scholars who initially pointed out Christian Hermann Weisse's cardinal mistake (see above, pp. 143f., 153)—his "Lachmann fallacy" and his "schoolboyish error of elementary reasoning at the very base of the 'Two-Document-Hypothesis'" (B. C. Butler, *Two-Document-Hypothesis*). This Lachmann fallacy then became a major theme in English and American scholarship. N. H. Palmer belongs here: ("Lachmann's Argument" in: *New Testament Studies*, 13, 1966/7, p. 368 ff.), which was followed a year later by W. R. Farmer: ("The Lachmann-Fallacy") in *New Testament Studies*, 14, 1967/8, p. 441 ff.).

This essay was preceded by Farmer's main critical work of 1964: *The Synoptic Problem. A Critical Analysis*. Farmer begins his decisive chapter with the apt statement: "The synoptic problem is difficult, but not necessarily insoluble" (p. 199). The goal of his research is the following: "It is intended to encourage a serious reconsideration of a solution which was first formulated in the eighteenth century, flourished in the first half of the the nineteenth century, but which for the past one hundred years has been eclipsed by the two-document hypothesis" (p. 202).

This meant the resumption of the fundamental idea of the Griesbach hypothesis, which in Germany had been attacked in immoderate terms "for one hundred years." Perhaps we were indeed a little lacking in English "common sense."

The result of William R. Farmer's research is this: "*Mark wrote after Matthew and Luke and is dependent upon both*" (p. 202).

And yet Farmer was no more able to present proof for the partial dependence of Luke upon Matthew than Griesbach had been in his time—the latter had thematically limited such dependence to the two resurrection reports (see above, p. 5).

In general, one can say that there are indications in American scholarship of a renaissance of the Griesbach hypothesis, or at least of a new professional discussion about it. More than one hundred and fifty years after the first edition of Griesbach's *Commentatio*, a joint essay was published in the *Journal of Biblical Literature* by two American New Testament scholars, C. H. Talbert and E. V. McKnight, entitled "Can the Griesbach-Hypothesis be falsified?" (*Journal of Biblical Literature*, 91. 1972 p. 338-368). The stress here lies on the word "*Can.*" They attempt to refute Griesbach, "or at least cast doubt upon the Griesbach-Hypothesis."

Two years later George Wesley Buchanan answered them in the same Journal under the title: "Has the Griesbach-Hypothesis been falsified?" (*Journal of Biblical Literature*, 93. 1974 p.550-572). This time the stress lies on "*Has been?*" For Buchanan tries to refute the attempt at refutation made by the other two. The result of his critical analysis of their argumentation reads: "A careful study of this case against the Griesbach-Hypothesis suggests the verdict: *Not proved!*" (p. 572).

If this revival of discussion concerning the Griesbach hypothesis is a symptom of growing skepticism about the Marcan hypothesis, then the same had been no less true earlier of that phenomenon which Grant fittingly called "Multiple source Theories." These theories played a role in international professional discussion primarily as a result of B. H. Streeter's work *The Four Gospels* (1924), as well as of Vaganay's *Le Problème Synoptique* (1954), and similarly, on the German side, of Emanuel Hirsch's *Frühgeschichte des Evangeliums* (1940/41; 1951[2]) and Heinrich Helmbold's *Vorsynoptische Evangelien* (1953). Although these works are quite different from each other, they all nevertheless have their origin in the same critical attitude toward sources. That is to say that in principle they agree that the two-source theory from which they proceed does *not* suffice to explain the inherent problems of the synoptic Gospels but, rather, that it needs supplements. Indeed, the more or less manifold suggestions for improvement are not to be understood in any other way; they try only to settle the remaining unsolved questions by means of new additional subsidiary hypotheses until their main hypothesis "comes out."

The danger of an unintended ultimate effect hangs threateningly over all these "multiple sources theories," namely that a *system* of hypotheses is formed which—just as in the case of the written ur-gospel hypothesis— reduces itself *ad absurdum* through a multiplicity of auxiliary theories that are no longer acceptable. This was the case with Hirsch, with Helmbold, and with Vaganay, too. For if the inadequacy of the two-source theory was the point of departure for the multiple source theories, nothing was gained when, in the end, there was surfeit of *too* many sources.

In the search for these supplementary forms, a characteristic difference between German and Anglo-Saxon scholarship became evident. With its developed sense for the realities of the situation, the latter recognized that in structure as well as in essence, the Gospel of Luke constitutes a much more profitable place to look for signs favoring multiple source theories than the homogeneous, consistent Gospel of Mark. Thus the Anglo-Saxon scholars placed the search for early forms of the third Gospel distinctly in the foreground. This was true, not just of Streeter, but also of his predecessors and successors.

Since in German Gospel-research the Marcan gospel traditionally occupied the absolute key position, there had been a long-standing search—as the course of our demonstrations has shown—again and again for the "early forms" or the modalities of an earlier version of the second Gospel. Not satisfied with a "proto-Mark," one felt obliged to come up with a "deutero-Mark," a "trito-Mark," etc.—until the search had to be called off since, after all, it could not be continued *ad infinitum.*

Then, after the possibilities of stretching the "historical source Mark" were finally exhausted, and it had become clear that the battle to substantiate the two-source theory could be continued only with Q, research shifted to this much more flexible second source, and found in it a rich field for scholarly pursuits. For the ban, of course, had been lifted by Bernhard Weiss' arbitrary decree: "The sayings source also contained narratives" (see above, p. 121f).

Consequently the main emphasis of the argumentation shifted. To the extent that the Marcan source stagnated, source "Q" flourished. As a result, in the last decades, especially in the German-speaking realm, there has been an increase of Q-literature which Wernle himself could not even remotely have suspected when he formulated in 1899 the fateful words: "The—hypothetical—source is to be called 'Q.' " Thus this "hypothetical source" represents today the most controversial problem in Gospel-research. Scholarly literature on the New Testament displays an almost bewildering abundance of research-results, examinations, hypotheses, deductions, constructions, assertions, and presumptions; all related to the intensive inquiry into the nature of Q: into its form, scope, literary character, content, purpose, objective, theological tendency, author, place of origin, time of origin, its preliminary stages, its modifications, its relationship to Mark, its comparability to the Gospels (Evangelical document? half-gospel? full-gospel?), the definition of its contents (kerygmatic? didactic? catechetical?), its textual arrangement, its language (Aramaic? Greek?), its wording—in short, there is hardly a problem concerning Q which has not been raised and to which an answer could not be found in literature even though these answers are quite diverse and conflicting. Only one question remains unanswered: *Where is the literary evidence for Q?*

Here we have a division of minds: *pro et contra Q.* For the question about literary evidence is followed by another one: *Did a document having the characteristics of Q, so essential to the maintenance of the Marcan hypothesis, actually exist?*

This whole comprehensive problem of Q is presented in a form that is as concise as it is exhaustive by W. G. Kümmel in the seventeenth ("once more completely and newly revised") edition of his *Einleitung in das Neue Testament* (1973, p. 37-49). In it all of the champions as well as the adversaries of a written source Q are listed by name (§ 5, p. 22, n. 8; p. 38, n. 54 and 55). Thus today the advocates of both views oppose each other with utterly unyielding fronts—deeply at odds, opinion against opinion.

At this point the fundamental difference between the nineteenth and twentieth centuries in the history of the Marcan hypothesis becomes clear. The turning-point in its history is marked precisely by the next to the last year of the past century (1899) in which Wernle's *Synoptische Frage* was published. Until then the Gospel of Mark had been the dominant source in the argumentation because it was regarded as more flexible and more variable than the sayings source; previously—ever since Weisse had used Schleiermacher's definition of logion as the basis for his argumentation—that source had been regarded as a constant. Accordingly, one operated only with secondary forms, with earlier stages of the historical source Mark, while the pure form of the sayings source did not permit this; and at most could force one to retreat, as had been the case with Weisse.

But then Wernle pronounced his verdict on the ur-Mark theory, viz. that it was formulated "merely to alleviate the synoptic problem" (see above, p. 92), and with the same stroke of his pen renamed and transformed the sayings source into "Q." In doing so he became the actual spiritual and intellectual guide of the new phase of the Marcan hypothesis, which then in the early years of the new century, took its irresistible course after Q had received its inner, i.e., content-related authorization from the decree of Bernhard Weiss.

Hence, under the influence of the changes in circumstances of the Marcan hypothesis occasioned by Wernle and Weiss, the basis of proof of the two-source theory developed in a manner which was contrary to that of the preceding century, Q became dominant, since it proved itself to be exceedingly variable. On the other hand, the historical source Mark, whose flexibility was exhausted, and moreover negated, marked time and became fixed. Hence it is that even today in discussions of the Marcan hypothesis, all arguments adduced in favor of the historical source almost invariably still stem from the last century and have remained unchanged—without thereby having become any more correct. The elements of proof in favor of the sayings source, in contrast, originate in their overwhelming majority in our century.

This transformed relationship of the two basic factors in the Marcan hypothesis, the shifting of emphasis from Mark to Q, has manifested itself in the torpidly perseverant character of the Marcan proofs and in the progressively greater attention given to arguments based on Q. This shift in emphasis, together with the significant fact of the quantitative dissemination of the two-source theory, probably represents the essential characteristic of the continuing influence of the Marcan hypothesis in our century.

When one surveys the approximately 140-year history of the Marcan hypothesis in its overall development and looks back to the initial position of its founders and their argumentation from the perspective of modern research into the subject, one can say that, little by little, one argument after another crumbled away. In the majority of cases they discredited themselves through the inner development of the Marcan hypothesis; almost nothing is left of them. And it was precisely those fundamental elements essential to Marcan priority that were the first to be abandoned because they had become untenable.

What reputable scholar today still accepts the arguments for the Petrine origin of the second Gospel? The assertion could not withstand critical scrutiny. The fact that the Gospel of Matthew contains far more Petrine elements and a stronger emphasis on Petrine priority than does Mark was plainly conclusive and could not be reasoned away.

The other main support of the two-source theory, the proof from doublets, collapsed under its own weight as a result of the conclusion forced upon it by the historical development of the Marcan hypothesis: that not only mutual knowledge of both main sources had to be presumed, but also that reciprocal relationships must have existed, with the incorporation of saying material into the Marcan source and of historical, narrative elements into the sayings source. The careful separation between a purely narrative source and a purely sayings source, which, after all, had been the central assumption of the proof from doublets, broke down. Consequently the existence of "doublets" could not be used to draw conclusions about origins, (a) from a sayings source, and (b) from Mark.

The proof from language proved to be devoid of substance because it was derived from a fictitious, unreal, artificially constructed source which was utterly unconvincing. The proof from vividness was based on an assumption that was not only false but incapable of being substantiated by any aesthetic or stylistic law: that vividness of presentation is a characteristic of priority. In fact, it is *de facto* only a question of literary ability. The same is true of the proof from uniformity.

The proof from common narrative sequence, highly emphasized and stubbornly defended again and again by the founders of the Marcan hypothesis, was established on the basis of a *petitio principii* and a *circulus vitiosus*. It already presupposed what was still to be proved, and in its argumentation it resorted to what was undeniably an elementary error in logic.

And finally, the proof from psychological reflection reduced itself *ad absurdum* because of its subjective character and its inadmissible and scientifically unjustifiable presumption of knowledge, down to the last detail, about what motivated the Evangelists while they composed their works.

Referring back once more to our own initial position, i.e., to our summary of the general problems to be solved by the founders of the Marcan hypothesis (see above, pp. 9-22); and if one contrasts it to today's final position of the Marcan hypothesis at the end of its 140-year history by asking the question: "Did they succeed in overcoming this insurmountable mass of problems?"; the answer, naturally, can only be: quite the contrary! There are three main, distinctive features which can be traced as constant characteristics throughout the entire history of the Marcan hypothesis: dissatisfaction with the solution attained, the continuous compulsion to self-correction, and the fact that the source theory never "came out," no matter what efforts they invested in it. There was by no means a straight line of argumentation running through the 140 years of the history of the Marcan hypothesis. Rather, it was a continuing variation of possibilities and also of impossibilities, a constant shifting and wandering from one wrong path to the other. Its advocates constantly had to patch it up, toiling over it honestly—sometimes, also, a bit dishonestly—but in spite of every new approach and new beginning, the Marcan hypothesis refused to "come out," as little today as 140 years ago.

This becomes apparent once again on the Catholic side as well as on the Protestant side in the last two editions of *Einleitung in das Neue Testament*, as when Kümmel must admit, on the subject of the extensive omission of Marcan material in Luke: "The absence of Mark 6:45-8:26 is, of course, 'puzzling' " (*Einleitung*[17], p. 35), and of the special material in Mark: "Only the omission of the parable of the seed is inexplicable" (p. 30f.).

This attitude comes across even more strongly when Josef Schmid declares (with a deliberate attempt to minimize the problem): "The synoptic problem has left behind a few peripheral questions for which there are no answers, but which are insignificant in relation to what the two-source theory in fact wants to accomplish" (p. 289).

Now, Weisse and Holtzmann and the three different editions of the *RGG* as well had contended precisely the same thing. But it is not a matter of what a source theory *wants* to accomplish, but, rather, of what it *can* accomplish. The two-source theory leaves too many residual problems unsolved. And too many "marginal questions" amount finally to one central question; for Josef Schmid gets into trouble in view of the remaining unexplained residues of the Marcan hypothesis:

> A third class of agreements between Matthew and Luke remains to be mentioned, for which the explanations in terms of independent corrections and coincidental agreements of Matthew and Luke cannot be made to carry so much conviction. [Examples follow]. Of the various attempts to solve the problem posed by the agreements, one should mention—since both the ur-Mark hypothesis and the deutero-Mark hypothesis are to be ignored as useless—the attempt at a solution by Streeter (pp. 239-331), who points out that the text of the New Testament as we know it today may not have been at all accurately transmitted by tradition. Therefore it is quite possible that in particular passages one text was assimilated, either Luke's text to Matthew's or vice versa (p. 289).

Now, this is a consolation, but only— as Walther von der Vogelweide would say—"ein kleines trostelin." For one could obviously advance this very general argument in all textual passages. It is, however, not weighty enough to help a source theory of the historical significance of the Marcan hypothesis out of a hopeless situation.

Now, such a changing historical development as that of the Marcan hypothesis, so rich in variations and evolving in such contrasts, is in itself not a particularly good recommendation for a source theory. This is especially true in view of its frequent changes in position, its repeated advancements and retreats, and—in the end—its still unsatisfactory results. But the course of the Marcan hypothesis is so inconsistent that it almost contains within itself the seeds of self-refutation— simply because of its history.

It is therefore especially instructive to recapitulate here at the end of our examination the historical development of arguments in favor of the Marcan hypothesis, and once more conjure up a clear picture of the totality of the fundamental mistakes in their overwhelming abundance: how Weisse attempts in vain to disguise the non-logia elements of the extra-Marcan material common to Matthew and Luke as logia and thereby to incorporate them in his auxiliary "logia source" hypothesis. How he then finds himself compelled to retract his own views under the weight of Ewald's counter-arguments and instead invents an ur-Mark in order to accommodate there what he could not fit into the logia source, as well as much other material for which there was no place in his ur-Mark, such as Luke's special material about the "young man of Nain" and the "ministering women." How Holtzmann then feels obliged to correct Weisse's mistake and to extract these wrongly classified pericopes again, only to make his own far more ill-fated attempt by inventing a much more comprehensive ur-Mark and transforming it into a fictitious, historically unreal source; to this ur-Mark he not only assigns the canonical Mark but also all the parallel passages in Matthew and Luke and, in addition to that, even the abbreviated Sermon on the Mount on the pretense that Mark afterwards omitted it because it was "too long" for him. How Holtzmann then constructs the sayings source on the basis of the scattered logia material in the Lucan travel narrative while excluding the Sermon on the Mount; he claims that Matthew and Luke had taken those parts of their logia material that coincide with Mark, not from the discourse source, but from the travel narrative, thereby decisively decreasing the importance of the sayings source, allowing it to be eclipsed by Mark. How then Wernle on his part seeks to refute Holtzmann and declares the ur-Mark hypothesis to be untenable because it was advanced "merely to alleviate the synoptic problem." How he establishes the priority of Mark by neglecting the only possible synoptic method of comparison and instead drawing individual comparisons with both other synoptic Gospels, each time giving precedence to the second Gospel as the *tertium comparationis* and thereby painting a distorted picture of the overall synoptic relationship. How he then reevaluates and renames the logia source to Q and attributes to it a previous history and postulates no fewer than seven different modifications of Q. How finally he is forced to admit that Mark had knowledge of the sayings source but rigorously denies that the Evangelist used it, explaining that it already was in circulation in the community and: "The most important dominical sayings were memorized at that time by every Christian entering the community." How then Bernhard Weiss on his part refutes Christian Hermann Weisse's self-refutation concerning the non-dominical sayings attributed by Weiss to the sayings source; he views the other scholar's refutation as based on "prejudice" and annuls it, declaring officially: "The sayings source also contained narratives." How in subsequent discussions Q develops into a "half-Gospel" and is called a Gospel without a Passion story while Bernhard Weiss seeks to explain away this objection by declaring the pericope of Jesus' anointing, which he had attributed to Q, to be a substitute Passion. How Q quantitatively and qualitatively expands more and more until it assumes the dominant role in the two-source theory as a result of the stratified character that had been attributed to it in the meantime. How then the ur-Mark hypothesis is totally exhausted following Holtzmann's self-correction, and how finally the circle closes with C. H. Weisse's initial definition of the logia source: "We are convinced that everything that the two Evangelists have in common with each other, but not with Mark, is to be attributed to it" (see above, p. 51); and how this function of the sayings source, which Weisse could not maintain and hence again abandoned, is then taken over by Q so that subsequently A. E. J. Rawlinson declares accordingly in the *Encyclopaedia Britannica*: "It is in any case wiser to regard 'Q' as a mere symbol, a convenient designation for the non-Marcan material, which is common to Matthew and Luke" (1962, Vol. 10, p. 538).

When one surveys in retrospect this historical development of the Marcan hypothesis with its accumulation of mistakes, it takes the shape of a vast system of make-shift solutions, of a continuing series of experiments with and corrections to the hypothesis, of wrangling and maneuvering and unceasing argumentation and psychologizing.

With what result? With the result that the traveller, having followed its tortuous, labyrinthian paths this far, must conclude at the end, when with difficulty he has found his way out again, that the Marcan hypothesis has come back to the same point from which it originated 140 years ago.

Part IV:

Conclusion of the Study

We have now reached the point in our deduction where we should view our subject from a distance, detach ourselves from detailed source-critical analysis, and view the Marcan hypothesis as a whole in its theological context as a phenomenon in the history of ideas. For certainly one cannot do it justice if one regards it only as an object for detailed philological research, even though it had to prove its scientific validity and accordingly was promoted in this way even by its champions. But ultimately it must be correctly placed into the historical framework of its time. Only from this over-all perspective can it be adequately judged.

Hence, when we raised the question "How could the Marcan hypothesis have come into being in the first place?," we already had inquired into its ideological background. We had established that it can be understood only against the background of the great intellectual struggle of the previous century that was set in motion by the publication of David Friedrich Strauss' *Leben Jesu, kritisch bearbeitet.*

Of course, Strauss' main thesis that "the Gospels are myths rather than historical documents" caused all positive-minded gospel scholars to feel called to battle and to rise up and refute Strauss with one voice. As we have shown, the two-source theory was born under the influence of this anti-Strauss movement.

But this is not the whole story. Even more influential was the understandable concern of Strauss' antagonists not to limit themselves to negative arguments, to attempts at purely philological refutation. Rather, they wished to go beyond that to explode Strauss' theory of myths with elaborate, factual counterproof. Hence his opponents—and who was not one at that time?—strove fervently to derive an irreproachable, scientifically absolute and incontestable image of the historical Jesus from the Gospel of Mark.

The inevitable consequence of this was an event of extraordinary significance for the history of theology: the founding of historical Gospel-research—with the result that for a period of almost one hundred years it has enjoyed the dominant position in New Testament scholarship. There was a further result that was of still greater importance for the history of ideas. That was the growth and flourishing of research into the life of Jesus, which spread in almost geometrical progression and reached its high point at the beginning of our century—up to the advent of form criticism. It alone brought an end to historical research into the Gospels by declaring: the Gospels are not to be regarded as historical records but as documents of faith. Hence they are not to be appreciated historically but kerygmatically; for they do not render contemporary recollections of the disciples about Jesus, but constitute instead the deposit of post-historical experiences of Christ by the community of believers.

Form criticism was supported in this view by the fact that researchers into the life of Jesus, who had hoped to gain so much from their application of the Marcan hypothesis, did more to obscure than to illuminate the image of the historical Jesus.

There was also a second factor. What David Friedrich Strauss had especially emphasized as the main element of his critique of the Gospels in order to prove their negative character, their mythical quality, is exactly what was adopted, in a reverse sense and as a programmatic demand, by kerygmatic theology. It did so in order to be able to portray all the more clearly the Gospels' supratemporal substance of faith by liberating them from time-bound historical dross—by "demythologizing."

With this the anti-Strauss excitement had lost its meaning for Gospel-research and had disposed of itself in two respects; in the same way the Strauss-trauma of the previous century lost its influence; the theology of today no longer stands under this spell.

What conclusion about the Marcan hypothesis is to be drawn from this? "Our Marcan lions, young and old, may roar as much as they please . . . . " D. F. Strauss had written in the appendix of his critique of Schleiermacher's *Leben Jesu* (1865), after reading Holtzmann's *Synoptische Evangelien*. Now, one must concede that the founders of the Marcan hypothesis did indeed fight like lions for their cause. And they have—viewed from the perspective of their goal—fought a good fight; for what they wanted to accomplish was a great thought and was worth the pains of the noble: the historical image of Jesus.

Today this battle is antiquated, both for theology and for the history of ideas—and hence the same is also true of the Marcan hypothesis, which provided the source hypothesis on which to base historicist research into the Gospels—especially since the Marcan hypothesis is in any case philologically untenable. Even in an ideological respect it is now of only historical significance. The time, then, has come for us to terminate its anachronistic existence; instead, we should set it in the context of the history of Protestant Gospel-research and grant it an honorable place there as a major polemical hypothesis of historicist theology.

What consequences can be drawn from this with respect to the literary-critical ranking of Mark's Gospel in its synoptic setting? Was Griesbach right then? Now, in the exaggerated formulation that "The whole Gospel of Mark was taken from those of Matthew and Luke," he was not right. The second Gospel represents neither an excerpt nor a compilation from the first and third. But there can be no doubt about the temporal posteriority of the gospel of Mark. Thus, Henry Owen and Johann Jacob Griesbach correctly recognized that Matthew and Luke formed the textual basis for Mark. And Griesbach in fact proved this with a textual analysis carried out with philological precision.

However, that was not yet sufficient. For what neither David Friedrich Strauss nor the Second Tübingen School recognized is the fact that the Gospel of Mark represents a *new intellectual creation* of independent character. It was conceived from a different perspective than were Matthew and Luke, and it restricts itself solely to the presentation of the kerygmatic activity of Jesus, foregoing the legendary prehistory and posthistory. It is only in the light of this thematical limitation that the beginning of the Marcan Gospel can really be understood in its programmatical significance: "The beginning of the Gospel of Jesus Christ."[1]

The creatively distinctive thing about the second Gospel is the compositional transformation of the various subject-matter elements which it draws from Matthew and Luke on an irregular basis, changing freely from one to the other and which are then arranged into a new, uniform, short version, complete unto itself, of the "Gospel of Jesus Christ." The clarity and straightforwardness in his description of events, the easy intelligibility and

---

[1] Ἀρχὴ τοῦ εὐαγγελίου Ἰησοῦ Χριστοῦ.

vividness of his presentation make it the most accessible of all the Gospels and point in the direction of popular missionary work.

His tendency to revise with a nimble hand, his principle of frequently adding explanatory interpolations as well as the small rays of light which Mark likes to shed on specific matters (Griesbach's "periphrazein" and "periphrastikos exprimere"), the courage of the author in limiting his material quantitatively while qualitatively expanding the depiction of details—all of these characteristics stamp Mark as the pedagogue among the Evangelists. Precisely for that reason the Gospel named after him has, from the earliest time, played an especially favored role in teaching and religious instruction.

What new state of affairs has this change in synoptic priorities produced for Gospel research? First of all the Gospel of Mark must be reclassified. As an object for source criticism it now is of secondary significance. In its place, Matthew and Luke move up to the primary position.

Does that mean, then, that we now simply reverse the two-source theory and take up where Griesbach left off? That would be an incorrect assessment of the immediate effect of our criticism of the Marcan hypothesis. As an examination of the three synoptic Gospels' relationships to one another, it was its chief function to clarify certain fixed points in the Gospels' causal and temporal relationships in order to open the way for further research.

Today we know where Mark obtained his material. But now we are confronted with a much more difficult, more important, more comprehensive question, and that, to be sure, with increased forcefulness: *Where did Matthew and Luke get their material?* Not just their common elements, but also those that diverge and differ; not only the historical narratives, but also the whole logia complex, the discourses, the parables, the series of sayings, the lost individual sayings—in short, all of the material that they present—where did they get it? At this stage we can only answer negatively—contrary to the Marcan hypothesis: In any case, not from Mark and "Q"! But we cannot offer a positive answer; it is still an unsolved mystery.

Since our investigation restricted itself solely to the synoptic Gospels, we are left with the second major component of the Gospel problem: the Gospel of John with its entirely different set of traditions. And now the truly fundamental question about the Gospels looms before us: the question about the original sources of all the Gospels, not just of the synoptic Gospels, but also the Gospel of John. This is the real *"aenigma fundamentale evangeliorum"* whose clarification thus far has yet to be given a form which, in my opinion, will convey to us essential new insights.

In the last decades the view has been repeatedly advanced that further analytical investigation into the sources of the Gospels will not turn up any new knowledge. Accordingly, it was even claimed that an end ought to be made of literary critical research since "final results" had been achieved. As early as 1937 Kendrick Grobel wrote: "The twentieth century has added nothing to our knowledge about written sources of the synoptic Gospels. The literary investigations published so far also have only confirmed this statement" (*Formgeschichte und synoptische Quellenanalyse, Forschungen zur Literatur des Alten und Neuen Testaments.* N. F. 35, 1937).

From this interpretation P. Vielhauer drew the conclusion: "Critical work on the sources of the synoptic Gospels has in fact reached its end with the two-source theory" (*Theologische Literaturzeitung,* 80, 1955, p. 652).

And Josef Schmid endorsed this opinion in 1973: "Literary critical studies of the synoptic Gospels during the nineteenth and the beginning of the twentieth century have finally led to the realization that a certain end point has been reached; this is because it is bound by limits beyond which it cannot penetrate" (Schmid-Wikenhauser, *Einleitung,* p. 290).

Well, it is erroneous to believe that the study of Gospel sources can be regarded as already closed. On the contrary, it is entering a new phase in which an altered perspective provides us with a new viewpoint and a new evaluation. And that means that in Gospel research, we do not stand at the end point. We stand—so I believe—at a turning point.

Appendix

Minor additional details in Mark that extend beyond the text of Matthew and Luke, including passages where either Matthew or Luke is lacking.[1]

with text-critical notes by Charles E. Wolfe

(1)	1:1	ἀρχὴ τοῦ εὐαγγελίου ᾽Ιησοῦ Χριστοῦ
(2)	1:7	κύψας[2]
(3)	1:13	καὶ ἦν μετὰ τῶν θηρίων
(4)	1:15	καὶ πιστεύετε ἐν τῷ εὐαγγελίῳ
(5)	1:19	ὀλίγον[3]
(6)	1:20	μετὰ τῶν μισθωτῶν
(7)	1:29	καὶ ᾽Ανδρέου μετὰ ᾽Ιακώβου καὶ ᾽Ιωάννου.[4]
(8)	1:33	καὶ ἦν ὅλη ἡ πόλις ἐπισυνηγμένη πρὸς τὴν θύραν.
(9)	1:35	κἀκεῖ προσηύχετο.
(10)	1:36-37	καὶ κατεδίωξεν αὐτὸν Σίμων καὶ οἱ μετ᾽ αὐτοῦ, καὶ εὗρον αὐτόν καὶ λέγουσιν αὐτῷ ὅτι Πάντες ζητοῦσίν σε.
(11)	1:41	καὶ σπλαγχνισθεὶς[5]

---

[1]The text of the following 180 items is essentially that which is found in Kurt Aland (ed.), *Synopsis Quattuor Evangeliorum*. 8th Edition. Stuttgart: Württembergische Bibelanstalt, 1973). In these notes, symbols from that apparatus will be used for groupings of MSS.

Since the point is that this is additional material in Mark, variant readings will be noted if some MSS. lack the item or if some MSS. include it at a parallel passage. Variant readings within the additional material will not be noted unless they change the sense of the passage.

[2]Not found in D, Θ, and Old Latin.

[3] ℵ* has εκειθεν. This is the reading found at Matt 4:21. C, Koine, A, fam. 13, Latin have the conflate reading εκειθεν ολιγον. This suggests that assimilation from Matt 4:21 has occurred. B, D, W, some minuscules, and Old Latin have ολιγον. When the assimilation is considered, this is adequate textual support for the reading.

[4]και Ανδρεου is found in D and Old Latin at Lk 4:38.

[5]For σπλαγχνισθεις D, a, ff², and r¹ have οργισθεις. Many critics have accepted this as the more difficult reading in spite of its relatively weak MS. support. Since neither reading appears as a detail in Matt 8:3 or Lk 5:13, however, Stoldt's point is not affected.

(12)	1:43	καὶ ἐμβριμησάμενος αὐτῷ εὐθὺς ἐξέβαλεν αὐτόν
(13)	2:2	καὶ συνήχθησαν πολλοί, ὥστε μηκέτι χωρεῖν μηδὲ τὰ πρὸς τὴν θύραν, καὶ ἐλάλει αὐτοῖς τὸν λόγον
(14)	2:3	αἰρόμενον ὑπὸ τεσσάρων[6]
(15)	2:9	καὶ ἆρον τὸν κράβατόν σου[7]
(16)	2:13	καὶ (ἐξῆλθεν) πάλιν παρὰ τὴν θάλασσαν· καὶ πᾶς ὁ ὄχλος ἤρχετο πρὸς αὐτόν, καὶ ἐδίδασκεν αὐτούς[8]
(17)	2:14	τὸν τοῦ Ἀλφαίου[9]
(18)	2:15	ἦσαν γὰρ πολλοί, καὶ ἠκολούθουν αὐτῷ
(19)	2:16	ὅτι μετὰ τῶν τελωνῶν καὶ ἁμαρτωλῶν ἐσθίει[10]
(20)	2:18	καὶ ἦσαν οἱ μαθηταὶ Ἰωάννου καὶ οἱ Φαρισαῖοι νηστεύοντες[11]
(21)	2:19	ὅσον χρόνον ἔχουσιν τὸν νυμφίον μετ' αὐτῶν, οὐ δύνανται νηστεύειν[12]
(22)	2:23	ὁδὸν ποιεῖν[13]
(23)	2:25	ὅτε χρείαν ἔσχεν[14]
(24)	2:26	ἐπὶ Ἀβιαθὰρ ἀρχιερέως[15]

---

[6]This detail is lacking in W.

[7]W omits the phrase. The και is not found in C, D, 33, f, l, q, and Eus.

[8]Stoldt has placed εξηλθεν in ( ) to indicate that ℵ is also found in Lk 5:27. At Lk 5:27 D has και ελθων παλιν παρα την θαλασσαν τον επακολουθουντα αυτω οχλον εδιδασκεν.

[9]Found in D at Lk 5:27.

[10]There are textual variants relating to word order and the form of the verb, but the material as a whole is not omitted by the MSS. or included at the parallels.

[11]Koine, fam. 1, a, l, and some Bohairic have των Φαρισαιων. W has μαθηται των Φαρισαιων. These readings have probably been influenced by the phrasing later in the verse.

[12]Not found in D, W, fam. 1, 33, and Old Latin.

[13]Not found in D, W, and Old Latin.

[14]Not found in Sahidic.

[15]Not found in D, W, Old Latin, and Syr^. Since Abiathar was not the high priest at the time, these MSS have probably intentionally omitted the name. C, A, Θ, 074, fam. 1, and fam. 13 have του before Αβιαθαρ. This is generally considered to be a correction to permit the interpretation that it happened in the time of Abiathar, but not necessarily during his high priesthood. It is not found in the parallels.

(25)	2:27	τὸ σάββατον διὰ τὸν ἄνθρωπον ἐγένετο, καὶ οὐχ ὁ ἄνθρωπος διὰ τὸ σάββατον¹⁶
(26)	3:5	μετ᾽ ὀργῆς, συλλυπούμενος ἐπὶ τῇ πωρώσει τῆς καρδίας αὐτῶν¹⁷
(27)	3:6	μετὰ τῶν ῾Ηρῳδιανῶν
(28)	3:7	πρὸς τὴν θάλασσαν
(29)	3:8	καὶ ἀπὸ τῆς ᾽Ιδουμαίας¹⁸
(30)	3:9	καὶ εἶπεν τοῖς μαθηταῖς αὐτοῦ ἵνα πλοιάριον προσκαρτερῇ αὐτῷ διὰ τὸν ὄχλον, ἵνα μὴ θλίβωσιν αὐτόν
(31)	3:14-16 a	ἵνα ὦσιν μετ᾽ αὐτοῦ, καὶ ἵνα ἀποστέλλῃ αὐτοὺς κηρύσσειν καὶ ἔχειν ἐξουσίαν ἐκβάλλειν τὰ δαιμόνια· καὶ ἐποίησεν τοὺς δώδεκα,¹⁹
(32)	3:17	καὶ ἐπέθηκεν αὐτοῖς ὄνομα βοανηργές, ὅ ἔστιν υἱοὶ βροντῆς²⁰
(33)	3:22	καὶ οἱ γραμματεῖς οἱ ἀπὸ ῾Ιερουσολύμων καταβάντες
(34)	3:30	ὅτι ἔλεγον· πνεῦμα ἀκάθαρτον ἔχει.
(35)	3:34	καὶ περιβλεψάμενος τοὺς περὶ αὐτὸν κύκλῳ καθημένους
(36)	4:1	καὶ πάλιν ἤρξατο διδάσκειν
(37)	4:2-3a	καὶ ἔλεγεν αὐτοῖς ἐν τῇ διδαχῇ αὐτοῦ· ἀκούετε
(38)	4:7	καὶ καρπὸν οὐκ ἔδωκεν.
(39)	4:8	ἀναβαίνοντα καὶ αὐξυνόμενα
(40)	4:10	καὶ ὅτε ἐγένετο κατὰ μόνας
(41)	4:12 b	μήποτε ἐπιστρέψωσιν καὶ ἀφεθῇ αὐτοῖς²¹
(42)	4:13	οὐκ οἴδατε τὴν παραβολὴν ταύτην, καὶ πῶς πάσας τὰς παραβολὰς γνώσεσθε;

---

[16] Not found in D and Old Latin. και ουχ ο ανθρωπος δια το σαββατον is not found in W and Syr ˢ.

[17] W, b, c, and d do not have συλλυπουμενος. Instead of πωρωσει, 17 and 20 have πηρωσει; D, Old Latin, and Syr ˢ have νεκρωσει. At Lk 6:10 εν οργη is found in D, Θ, fam. 1, and Old Latin; fam. 13 has μετ οργης.

[18] Not found in ℵ*, Θ, fam. 1, c, and Syr ˢ.

[19] C², Koine, A, D, Θ, 0133, fam. 1, fam. 13, and Latin have, with minor disagreements, additional material in vs. 15. After εξουσιαν they have θεραπευειν τας νοσους και and then continue with εκβαλλειν. This is probably an assimilation from Matt 5:1.

[20] Found in D at Lk 6:14.

[21] D, Θ, 1, Old Latin, Syr ˢ⁻ᶜ, and Eus. have μηποτε επιστρεφωσιν at Matt 13:13.

(43)	4:23	εἴ τις ἔχει ὦτα ἀκούειν ἀκουέτω
(44)	4:34	κατ᾽ ἰδίαν δὲ τοῖς ἰδίοις μαθηταῖς ἐπέλυεν πάντα
(45)	4:35	καὶ λέγει αὐτοῖς ἐν ἐκείνῃ τῇ ἡμέρα ὀψίας γενομένης
(46)	4:36	καὶ ἀφέντες τὸν ὄχλον παραλαμβάνουσιν αὐτὸν ὡς ἦν ἐν τῷ πλοίῳ, καὶ ἄλλα πλοῖα ἦν μετ᾽ αὐτοῦ
(47)	4:38	ἐν τῇ πρύμνῃ ἐπὶ τὸ προσκεφάλαιον
(48)	4:39	σιώπα, πεφίμωσο
(49)	4:40	τί δειλοί ἐστε οὕτως;
(50)	5:5	καὶ διὰ παντὸς νυκτὸς καὶ ἡμέρας ἐν τοῖς μνήμασιν καὶ ἐν τοῖς ὄρεσιν ἦν κράζων καὶ κατακόπτων ἑαυτὸν λίθοις
(51)	5:6	ἀπὸ μακρόθεν ἔδραμεν[22]
(52)	5:13	ὡς δισχίλιοι
(53)	5:20 c	καὶ πάντες ἐθαύμαζον.
(54)	5:26-27 a	καὶ πολλὰ παθοῦσα ὑπὸ πολλῶν ἰατρῶν καὶ δαπανήσασα τὰ παρ᾽ αὐτῆς πάντα, καὶ μηδὲν ὠφεληθεῖσα ἀλλὰ μᾶλλον εἰς τὸ χεῖρον ἐλθοῦσα, ἀκούσασα τὰ περὶ τοῦ ᾽Ιησοῦ, ἐλθοῦσα ἐν τῷ ὄχλῳ[23]
(55)	5:29	καὶ ἔγνω τῷ σώματι ὅτι ἴαται ἀπὸ τῆς μάστιγος.
(56)	5:30	ἐπιστραφεὶς ἐν τῷ ὄχλῳ ἔλεγεν· τίς μου ἥψατο τῶν ἱματίων;[24]
(57)	5:34 b	καὶ ἴσθι ὑγιὴς ἀπὸ τῆς μάστιγός σου.
(58)	5:40 c	καὶ εἰσπορεύεται ὅπου ἦν τό παιδίον.
(59)	5:41	ταλιθὰ κοῦμ, ὅ ἐστιν μεθερμηνευόμενον
(60)	5:42	ἦν γὰρ ἐτῶν δώδεκα
(61)	6:2	καὶ γενομένου σαββάτου[25]
(62)	6:5-6 a	εἰ μὴ ὀλίγοις ἀρρώστοις ἐπιθεὶς τὰς χεῖρας ἐθεράπευσαν. καὶ ἐθαύμασεν

---

[22]απο is not found in A and W. W and Old Latin have προσεδραμεν.

[23]Part of the idea content, although not the exact language, appears in Lk 8:43. ℵ, Koine, A, W, Θ, fam. 1, fam. 13, Latin, Syr c-p i, and Bo. have: ιατροις προσαναλωσασα ολον τον βιον. This is not found in p75, B, D, Syr s, and Sa. The textual evidence for omitting the words is strong enough that Aland has relegated them to the apparatus. On the other hand, the UBS 3rd edition of Greek New Testament has allowed them to stand in the text because they look like a digest of Mk 5:26. See B. Metzer, Textual Commentary, p. 145.

[24]Syrc has επιστραφεις at Lk 8:45 and D has μου ηψατο.

[25]D and Old Latin have ημερα σαββατων. This may be an assimilation to the εν τη ημερα των σαββατων of Lk 4:16.

(63) 6:7   καὶ ἤρξατο αὐτοὺς ἀποστέλλειν δύο δύο

(64) 6:12-13   ἐκήρυξαν ἵνα μετανοῶσιν, καὶ δαιμόνια · πολλὰ ἐξέβαλλον, καὶ ἤλειφον ἐλαίῳ πολλοὺς ἀρρώστους (καὶ ἐθεράπευον)

(65) 6:14   ὁ βασιλεὺς

(66) 6:14   φανερὸν γὰρ ἐγένετο τὸ ὄνομα αὐτοῦ

(67) 6:17   ὅτι αὐτὴν ἐγάμησεν

(68) 6:19-20   ἡ δὲ Ἡρῳδιὰς ἐνεῖχεν αὐτῷ καὶ ἤθελεν αὐτὸν ἀποκτεῖναι, καὶ οὐκ ἠδύνατο· ὁ γὰρ Ἡρῴδης ἐφοβεῖτο τὸν Ἰωάννην, εἰδὼς αὐτὸν ἄνδρα δίκαιον καὶ ἅγιον, καὶ συνετήρει αὐτόν, καὶ ἀκούσας αὐτοῦ πολλὰ ἠπόρει, καὶ ἡδέως αὐτοῦ ἤκουεν.

(69) 6:21   καὶ γενομένης ἡμέρας εὐκαίρου ὅτε. . . . δεῖπνον ἐποίησεν τοῖς μεγιστᾶσιν αὐτοῦ καὶ τοῖς χιλιάρχοις καὶ τοῖς πρώτοις τῆς Γαλιλαίας

(70) 6:23   ἕως ἡμίσους τῆς βασιλείας μου

(71) 6:24   καὶ ἐξελθοῦσα εἶπεν τῇ (μητρὶ αὐτῆς·) τί αἰτήσωμαι

(72) 6:25   καὶ εἰσελθοῦσα εὐθὺς μετὰ σπουδῆς πρὸς τὸν βασιλέα ᾐτήσατο λέγουσα²⁶

(73) 6:26   οὐκ ἠθέλησεν ἀθετῆσαι αὐτήν

(74) 6:27   καὶ εὐθὺς ἀποστείλας ὁ βασιλεὺς σπεκουλάτορα ἐπέταξεν ἐνέγκαι τὴν κεφαλὴν αὐτοῦ²⁷

(75) 6:30   καὶ ὅσα ἐδίδαξαν²⁸

(76) 6:31   καὶ λέγει αὐτοῖς· δεῦτε ὑμεῖς αὐτοὶ κατ᾽ ἰδίαν εἰς ἔρημον τόπον καὶ ἀναπαύσασθε ὀλίγον. ἦσαν γὰρ οἱ ἐρχόμενοι καὶ οἱ ὑπάγοντες πολλοί, καὶ οὐδὲ φαγεῖν εὐκαίρουν.

(77) 6:37   καὶ λέγουσιν αὐτῷ· ἀπελθόντες ἀγοράσωμεν δηναρίων διακοσίων ἄρτους, καὶ δώσομεν αὐτοῖς φαγεῖν;

(78) 6:38   ὁ δὲ λέγει αὐτοῖς· πόσους ἔχετε ἄρτους; ὑπάγετε ἴδετε. καὶ γνόντες λέγουσιν·

(79) 6:39   συμπόσια συμπόσια ἐπὶ τῷ χλωρῷ (χόρτῳ)

---

²⁶ευθυς μετα σπουδης is not found in D and Old Latin.

In place of ητησατο λεγουσα D, Θ, fam. 1, Old Latin, and Syr ˢ⁻ᶜ have ειπεν. This is a common type of scribal substitution. Matt 14:8 has an ellipsis of the verb. D, W, and Old Latin supply the same ειπεν.

²⁷D, W, fam. 1, 565, 700, and Latin do not have ο βασιλευς.

²⁸ ℵ*, C*, W, fam. 1, and Latin do not have οσα. The entire phrase is found in A at Lk 9:10.

(80) 6:40   πρασιαὶ πρασιαὶ κατὰ ἑκατὸν καὶ κατὰ (πεντήκοντα)[29]

(81) 6:41 b   καὶ τοὺς δύο ἰχθύας ἐμέρισεν πᾶσιν

(82) 6:47 b   καὶ αὐτὸς. . . ἐπὶ τῆς γῆς

(83) 6:48 b   καὶ ἤθελεν παρελθεῖν αὐτούς

(84) 6:52   οὐ γὰρ συνῆκαν ἐπὶ τοῖς ἄρτοις, ἀλλ᾽ ἦν αὐτῶν ἡ καρδία πεπωρωμένη

(85) 7:2-4   καὶ ἰδόντες τινὰς τῶν μαθητῶν αὐτοῦ ὅτι κοιναῖς χέρσίν, τοῦτ᾽ ἔστιν ἀνίπτοις, ἐσθίουσιν τοὺς ἄρτους,--οἱ γὰρ φαρισαῖοι καὶ πάντες οἱ Ἰουδαῖοι ἐὰν μὴ πυγμῇ νίψωνται τὰς χεῖρας οὐκ ἐσθίουσιν, κρατοῦντες τὴν παράδοσιν τῶν πρεσβυτέρων, καὶ ἀπ᾽ ἀγορᾶς ἐὰν μὴ ῥαντίσωνται οὐκ ἐσθίουσιν, καὶ ἄλλα πολλά ἐστιν ἃ παρέλαβον κρατεῖν βαπτισμοὺς ποτηρίων καὶ ξεστῶν καὶ χαλκίων

(86) 7:8   ἀφέντες τὴν ἐντολὴν τοῦ θεοῦ κρατεῖτε τὴν παράδοσιν τῶν ἀνθρώπων[30]

(87) 7:13   καὶ παρόμοια τοιαῦτα πολλὰ ποιεῖτε[31]

(88) 7:18-19 οὐ δύναται αὐτὸν κοινῶσαι, ὅτι οὐκ εἰσπορεύεται αὐτοῦ εἰς τὴν καρδίαν. . . . καθαρίζων πάντα τὰ βρώματα

(89) 7:24   καὶ εἰσελθών εἰς οἰκίαν οὐδένα ἤθελεν γνῶναι

(90) 7:26   ἡ δὲ γυνὴ ἦν Ελληνίς, Συροφοινίκισσα τῷ γένει

(91) 8:3 b   καὶ τινες αὐτῶν ἀπὸ μακρόθεν ἥκασιν[32]

(92) 8:12   καὶ ἀναστενάξας τῷ πνεύματι αὐτοῦ λέγει

(93) 8:14   εἰ μὴ ἕνα ἄρτον οὐκ εἶχον μεθ᾽ ἑαυτῶν ἐν τῷ πλοίῳ

(94) 8:15   καὶ . . . Ἡρῴδου[33]

(95) 8:17-18 οὐδὲ συνίετε; πεπωρωμένην ἔχετε τὴν καρδίαν ὑμῶν; ὀφθαλμοὺς ἔχοντες οὐ βλέπετε, καὶ ὦτα ἔχοντες οὐκ ἀκούετε;

---

[29]p[45] does not have κατα εκατον και κατα πεντηκοντα. At Lk 10:14, Θ has εκατον και ανα πεντηκοντα.

[30]The entire verse is not found in Syr ⸲

[31]Not found in W.

[32]B, L, and Δ have ηκασιν. This is the reading selected for *The Greek New Testament*, Third Edition (United Bible Societies, 1975). The remaining MSS. have εισιν. This is the reading found in the Aland *Synopsis* and in the Nestle-Aland 25th edition. There is, however, no implication for Stoldt's argument.

[33]p[45], W, Θ, fam. 1, fam. 13, 565, i, k, and Sa. have των Ηρωδιανων. Since neither term is found in the parallels, however, Stoldt's argument is not affected.

(96)	8:27	ἐν τῇ ὁδῷ
(97)	8:32	καὶ παρρησίᾳ τὸν λόγον ἐλάλει
(98)	8:35	καὶ τοῦ εὐαγγελίου
(99)	9:1	καὶ ἔλεγεν αὐτοῖς
(100)	9:3	στίλβοντα (λευκὰ) λίαν, οἷα γναφεὺς ἐπὶ τῆς γῆς οὐ δύναται οὕτως λευκᾶναι[34]
(101)	9:10	καὶ τὸν λόγον ἐκράτησαν πρὸς ἑαυτοὺς συζητοῦντες τί ἐστιν τὸ ἐκ νεκρῶν ἀναστῆναι
(102)	9:14-16	γραμματεῖς συζητοῦντας πρὸς αὐτούς. καὶ εὐθὺς πᾶς ὁ ὄχλος ἰδόντες αὐτὸν ἐξεθαμβήθησαν, καὶ προστρέχοντες ἠσπάζοντο αὐτόν. καὶ ἐπηρώτησεν αὐτούς· τί συζητεῖτε πρὸς αὐτούς;
(103)	9:25 b	τὸ ἄλαλον καὶ κωφὸν πνεῦμα, ἐγὼ ἐπιτάσσω σοι, ἔξελθε ἐξ αὐτοῦ καὶ μηκέτι εἰσέλθῃς εἰς αὐτόν.
(104)	9:26-27	καὶ κράξας καὶ πολλὰ σπαράξας ἐξῆλθεν· καὶ ἐγένετο ὡσεὶ νεκρός, ὥστε τοὺς πολλοὺς λέγειν ὅτι ἀπέθανεν. ὁ δὲ Ἰησοῦς κρατήσας τῆς χειρὸς αὐτοῦ ἤγειρεν αὐτόν, καὶ ἀνέστη.
(105)	9:28	εἰς οἶκον
(106)	9:29	καὶ εἶπεν αὐτοῖς· τοῦτο τὸ γένος ἐν οὐδενὶ δύναται ἐξελθεῖν εἰ μὴ ἐν προσευχῇ[35]
(107)	9:33-34	καὶ ἦλθον εἰς Καφαρναούμ. καὶ ἐν τῇ οἰκίᾳ γενόμενος ἐπηρώτα αὐτούς· τί ἐν τῇ ὁδῷ διελογίζεσθε; οἱ δὲ ἐσιώπων· πρὸς ἀλλήλους γὰρ διελέχθησαν ἐν τῇ ὁδῷ
(108)	9:35	καὶ καθίσας ἐφώνησεν τοὺς δώδεκα καὶ λέγει αὐτοῖς

---

[34]Koine, A, D, fam. 13, 22, 33,118, Lat., Syr ˢ⁻ᵖ, Bo ᵖˡ have λιαν ως χιων. At Matt 17:2 D, Lat, Syr ᶜ, and Bo ᵖˡ have χιων instead of το φως. The figure occurs in Matt 28:3 of the clothing of the angel at the tomb. It is a natural figure, however, and it is hazardous to explain textual material on the basis of form critical conclusions.

X, a, n, and Syr ˢ do not have οια γναφευς επι της γης ου δυναται ουτως λευκαναι.

[35]This text is based upon B, א* k, Georg ᵖˡ, and Cl. The remaining MSS. have also και νηστεια. Metzger (Textual Commentary, p. 101) considers this to be a gloss which has found its way into most MSS. because of the increasing stress on the necessity of fasting.

At Matt 17:21, this verse. with minor differences, is found in א ᶜᵒʳʳ, C, Koine, D, W, fam. 1, fam. 13, Lat., Syr ᵖ, and Bo ᵖˡ. Since these MSS. also have και νηστεια, that may have influenced Mk 9:29. This material is found in representatives of all textual families and is lacking in other representatives of all textual families. The textual decision will be made upon probabilities of assimilation.

(109) 9:36	ἐναγκαλισάμενος
(110) 9:39	οὐδεὶς γάρ ἐστιν ὅς ποιήσει δύναμιν ἐπὶ τῷ ὀνόματί μου καὶ δυνήσεται ταχὺ κακολογῆσαί με
(111) 9:48	ὅπου ὁ σκώληξ αὐτῶν οὐ τελευτᾷ καὶ τὸ πῦρ οὐ σβέννυται
(112) 9:49	πᾶς γὰρ πυρὶ ἁλισθήσεται
(113) 9:50b	ἔχετε ἐν ἑαυτοῖς ἅλα καὶ εἰρηνεύετε ἐν ἀλλήλοις
(114) 10:10	καὶ εἰς τὴν οἰκίαν πάλιν οἱ μαθηταὶ περὶ τούτου ἐπηρώτων αὐτόν.
(115) 10:12	καὶ ἐὰν αὐτὴ ἀπολύσασα τὸν ἄνδρα αὐτῆς γαμήσῃ ἄλλον, μοιχᾶται[36]
(116) 10:16	καὶ ἐναγκαλισάμενος αὐτὰ κατευλόγει
(117) 10:17	καὶ ἐκπορευομένου αὐτοῦ. . . . καὶ γονυπετήσας
(118) 10:19	μὴ ἀποστερήσῃς[37]
(119) 10:20	διδάσκαλε
(120) 10:21a	ἐμβλέψας αὐτῷ ἠγάπησεν αὐτόν
(121) 10:24	οἱ δὲ μαθηταὶ ἐθαμβοῦντο ἐπὶ τοῖς λόγοις αὐτοῦ. ὁ δὲ Ἰησοῦς . . . . ἀποκριθεὶς (λέγει) αὐτοῖς· τέκνα, πῶς δύσκολόν ἐστιν εἰς τὴν βασιλείαν τοῦ θεοῦ εἰσελθεῖν
(122) 10:29	καὶ ἕνεκεν τοῦ εὐαγγελίου
(123) 10:32	καὶ ἦν προάγων αὐτοὺς ὁ᾽ Ἰησοῦς, καὶ ἐθαμβοῦντο, οἱ δὲ ἀκολουθοῦντες ἐφοβοῦντο
(124) 10:38b-39b	ἢ τὸ βάπτισμα ὃ ἐγω βαπτίζομαι βαπτισθῆναι; . . . . καὶ τὸ βάπτισμα ὃ ἐγὼ βαπτίζομαι βαπτισθήσεσθε[38]
(125) 10:46	ὁ υἱὸς Τιμαίου βαπτιμαῖος
(126) 10:49-50	καὶ φωνοῦσιν τὸν τυφλὸν λέγοντες αὐτῷ· θάρσει, ἔγειρε, φωνεῖ σε. ὁ δὲ ἀποβαλὼν τὸ ἱμάτιον αὐτοῦ ἀναπηδήσας ἦλθεν πρὸς τὸν ᾽Ιησοῦν.

---

[36]The additional material has the wife who divorces her husband committing adultery if she marries again. This is found at Lk 16:18, with some verbal differences. At Matt 19:9 the additional idea is found, with verbal differences, in most MSS. The shorter text is based upon ℵ, C³, D, L, Old Latin, Syr ˢ⁻ᶜ, and Sa.

[37]Not found in B*, W, Δ, Ψ, fam. 1, 700, and Syr ˢ. Scribal tendency would be towards omission, since it is not obviously one of the Ten Commandments, as are the others. It belongs here, therefore, as the more difficult reading. The MSS. have not inserted the phrase at the parallels.

[38]The additional material at the end of each verse is found also at Matt 20:22-23 in C, Koine, W, Δ, Φ, 0197, fam. 13, 118, 209, and Syr ᴾ.

(127)	10:52	ἐν τῇ ὁδῷ
(128)	11:4	δεδεμένον πρὸς θύραν ἔξω ἐπὶ τοῦ ἀμφόδου
(129)	11:11b	καὶ περιβλεψάμενος πάντα, ὀψὲ ἤδη οὔσης τῆς ὥρας
(130)	11:13b	ὁ γὰρ καιρὸς οὐκ ἦν σύκων
(131)	11:14b	καὶ ἤκουον οἱ μαθηταὶ αὐτοῦ
(132)	11:16	καὶ οὐκ ἤφιεν ἵνα τις διενέγκῃ σκεῦος διὰ τοῦ ἱεροῦ
(133)	11:17	πᾶσιν τοῖς ἔθνεσιν
(134)	11:23	ἀλλὰ πιστεύῃ ὅτι ὃ λαλεῖ γίνεται, ἔσται αὐτῷ
(135)	11:25	καὶ ὅταν στήκετε προσευχόμενοι
(136)	11:28	ἵνα ταῦτα ποιῇς;[39]
(137)	12:5b	καὶ πολλοὺς ἄλλους, οὓς μὲν δέροντες, οὓς δὲ ἀποκτέννοντες
(138)	12:6	ἔτι ἕνα εἶχεν, υἱὸν ἀγαπητόν
(139)	12:12b	καὶ ἀφέντες αὐτὸν ἀπῆλθον[40]
(140)	12:13	καὶ τῶν Ἡρῳδιανῶν
(141)	12:14	δῶμεν ἢ μὴ δῶμεν;[41]
(142)	12:15	ἵνα ἴδω
(143)	12:21	καὶ ἀπέθανεν μὴ καταλιπὼν σπέρμα[42]
(144)	12:27b	πολὺ πλανᾶσθε
(145)	12:28	καὶ προσελθὼν εἷς τῶν γραμματέων, ἀκούσας αὐτῶν συζητούντων, εἰδὼς ὅτι καλῶς ἀπεκρίθη
(146)	12:32-34	ὅτι εἷς ἐστιν καὶ οὐκ ἔστιν ἄλλος πλὴν αὐτοῦ· καὶ τὸ ἀγαπᾶν αὐτὸν ἐξ ὅλης τῆς καρδίας καὶ ἐξ ὅλης τῆς συνέσεως καὶ ἐξ ὅλης τῆς ἰσχύος, καὶ τὸ ἀγαπᾶν τὸν πλησίον ὡς ἑαυτὸν περισσότερόν ἐστιν πάντων τῶν ὁλοκαυτωμάτων καὶ θυσιῶν. καὶ ὁ Ἰησοῦς, ἰδὼν αὐτὸν ὅτι νουνεχῶς ἀπεκρίθη, εἶπεν αὐτῷ· οὐ μακρὰν εἶ ἀπὸ τῆς βασιλείας τοῦ θεοῦ.
(147)	12:37	καὶ ὁ πολὺς ὄχλος ἤκουεν αὐτοῦ ἡδέως
(148)	12:41	καὶ πολλοὶ πλούσιοι ἔβαλλον πολλά[43]

[39]Not found in W, Θ, 565, Old Latin, and Syr ᵖ.

[40]Not found in W.

[41]Not found in D and Old Latin.

[42]Koine, A, W, Γ, Δ, Θ, fam. 1, fam. 13, and Latin have the expansion at Lk 20:30. The verbal differences, however, relate to Lk 20:29 rather than to Mk 12:21.

[43]Not found in D. At Lk 21:1 πλουσίους occurs, although the grammatical construction is different. D has the word with the other MSS.

(149)	12:42	ὅ ἐστιν κοδράντης[44]
(150)	12:43	καὶ προσκαλεσάμενος τοὺς μαθητὰς αὐτοῦ
(151)	13:3	Πέτρος καὶ Ἰάκωβος καὶ Ἰωάννης καὶ Ἀνδρέας
(152)	13:34b	καὶ τῷ θυρωρῷ ἐνετείλατο ἵνα γρηγορῇ
(153)	13:35b-37	ἢ ὀψὲ μεσονύκτιον ἢ ἀλεκτοροφωνίας ἢ πρωΐ· μὴ ἐλθών ἐξαίφνης εὕρῃ ὑμᾶς καθεύδοντας. ὃ δὲ ὑμῖν λέγω, πᾶσιν λέγω, γρηγορεῖτε·
(154)	14:5	ἐπάνω δηναρίων τριακοσίων. . . . καὶ ἐνεβριμῶντο αὐτῇ.
(155)	14:6	ἄφετε αὐτήν
(156)	14:7	καὶ ὅταν θέλητε δύνασθε αὐτοῖς εὖ ποιῆσαι
(157)	14:8a	ὃ ἔσχεν ἐποίησεν
(158)	14:13a	καὶ ἀποστέλλει δύο τῶν μαθητῶν
(159)	14:30	(πρὶν ἤ) δὶς (ἀλέκτορα) φωνῆσαι[45]
(160)	14:36	ἀββὰ
(161)	14:40b	καὶ οὐκ ᾔδεισαν τί ἀποκριθῶσιν αὐτῷ
(162)	14:44	καὶ ἀπάγετε ἀσφαλῶς
(163)	14:54	θερμαινόμενος πρὸς τὸ φῶς[46]
(164)	14:56b	καὶ ἴσαι αἱ μαρτυρίαι οὐκ ἦσαν
(165)	14:59	καὶ οὐδὲ οὕτως ἴση ἦν ἡ μαρτυρία αὐτῶν
(166)	14:65	καὶ οἱ ὑπηρέται ῥαπίσμασιν αὐτὸν ἔλαβον.[47]
(167)	14:68	καὶ ἀλέκτωρ ἐφώνησεν[48]

---

[44]Found in D at Lk 21:2. A singular reading has a low probability of being correct, and therefore this should be attributed to the common process of textual assimilation in the Gospels.

[45]Not found in ℵ, C*, D, W, Θ, and Old Latin. These MSS., therefore, agree essentially with Matt 26:34. Since Matthew was the most popular of the Gospels during the scribal period, assimilation of a purely textual nature tended to be in the direction of Matthew.

[46]Fam. 1 and Syr ˢ do not have πρὸς τὸ φῶς. At Lk 22:55 D has θερμαινομενος.

[47]D does not have και οι υπηρεται.

[48]Found in C, Koine, A, D, Γ, Δ, Θ, 067, fam. 1, fam. 13, 33, Latin, and Syr ᵖ⁻ʰ. Not found in B, ℵ, L, W, Ψ*, c, and Syrˢ. Metzger (*Textual Commentary, pp. 115-116*) noted impressive MSS. support on either side. The insertion can be explained as an attempt to fulfill the prophecy of verse 30, and in this case would not be a part of the original text. This is the decision made by Aland in the *Synopsis* and Nestle's 25th edition, which place it in the apparatus. On the other hand, it might have been removed in order to create agreement with the parallels. This is apparently the decision made by Stoldt. The *Greek New Testament* has placed it in the text, but enclosed in brackets, and identified with the sign for the lowest probability.

(168) 14:72   ἐκ δευτέρου (ἀλέκτωρ ἐφώνησεν)⁴⁹

(169) 15:8   καὶ ἀναβάς ὁ ὄχλος ἤρξατο αἰτεῖσθαι καθὼς ἐποίει αὐτοῖς

(170) 15:21   τὸν πατέρα ᾿Αλεξάνδρου καὶ ᾿Ρούφου

(171) 15:24   τίς τί ἄρῃ⁵⁰

(172) 15:25   ἦν δὲ ὥρα τρίτη καὶ ἐσταύρωσαν αὐτόν

(173) 15:29   οὐὰ⁵¹

(174) 15:41   καὶ ἄλλαι πολλαὶ αἱ συναναβᾶσαι αὐτῷ εἰς᾿Ιεροσόλυμα

(175) 15:43   τολμήσας

(176) 15:44-45   ὁ δὲ Πιλᾶτος ἐθαύμασεν εἰ ἤδη τέθνηκεν, καὶ προσκαλεσάμενος τὸν κεντυρίωνα ἐπηρώτησεν αὐτὸν εἰ πάλαι ἀπέθανεν· καὶ γνοὺς ἀπὸ τοῦ κεντυρίωνος ἐδωρήσατο τὸ πτῶμα τῷ ᾿Ιωσήφ.

(177) 16:1   ἠγόρασαν ἀρώματα ἵνα ἐλθοῦσαι ἀλείψωσιν αὐτόν⁵²

(178) 16:3   καὶ ἔλεγον πρὸς ἑαυτάς· τίς ἀποκυλίσει ἡμῖν τὸν λίθον ἐκ τῆς θύρας τοῦ μνημείου;⁵³

(179) 16:4b   ἦν γὰρ μέγας σφόδρα

(180) 16:8   ἔφυγον (ἀπὸ τοῦ μνημείου) εἶχεν γὰρ αὐτὰς᾿τρόμος καὶ ἔκστασις· καὶ οὐδενὶ οὐδὲν εἶπαν· ἐφοβοῦντο γαρ.

---

⁴⁹Not found in ℵ , C*, L, and c. These MSS. do not have the material in verse 68, and therefore they agree with Matt. 26:74 and Lk 22:60. Such weak MSS. support, combined with assimilation to parallel accounts, gives a high probability that the words belong in the text.

⁵⁰Not found in D, 157, Old Latin, and Syr ˢ .

⁵¹Found also at Matt 27:40 in D, M, Δ, Θ, fam. 13, Latin, Syr. ʰ⁻ᵖᵃˡ ', and Eusebius.

⁵²Θ and 565 have πορευθεισαι ητοιμασαν instead of ηγορασαν. This is an assimilation to Lk 23:56.

⁵³At Lk 24:1 this material is found in D, 0124, c, and Sa.

Minor additional details in both Matthew and Luke that extend beyond Mark

	MK	MT	LK	
(1)	1:5	3:5	3:3	πᾶσα ἡ περίχωρος τοῦ 'Ιορδάνου
(2)	1:8	3:12	3:16	καὶ πυρί[54]
(3)	1:40	8:2	5:12	κύριε[55]
(4)	2:3	9:2	5:18	ἐπὶ κλίνης[56]
(5)	2:12	9:7	5:25	ἀπῆλθεν εἰς τὸν οἶκον αὐτοῦ
(6)	2:23	12:1	6:1	ἐσθίειν
(7)	2:26	12:4	6:4	μόνοι (ἱερεῖς)
(8)	3:5	12:13	6:10	σου (τὴν χεῖρα)[57]
(9)	4:10	13:11	8:10	γνῶναι (τὰ μυστήρια)
(10)	4:15	13:19	8:12	καρδίᾳ[58]
(11)	4:36	8:23	8:22	ἐμβαίνειν εἰς τὸ πλοῖον
(12)	4:36	8:23	8:22	οἱ μαθηταὶ αὐτοῦ
(13)	4:38	8:25	8:24	προσελθόντες
(14)	5:27	9:20	8:44	τοῦ κρασπέδου[59]

---

[54] At Mk 1:8 the material is found in P, Sa [pt], and Hipp.

[55] B, W, Θ, Old Latin, Sa., and Bo [pt] have the word at Mk 1:40. Variation in the αυτω and οτι, however, lessens the importance of the evidence.

[56] At Mk 2:3 W has εν κραβαττω.

[57] At Mk 3:5 the word is found in ‌‌א, C, A, D, W Θ, fam. 1, fam. 13, Latin, Syr [s-p], Sa., and Bo. B, E, and a few later uncials can counter such evidence only on the assumption that the shorter text is more likely to be correct, since this is a logical insertion, and upon the assumption of assimilation from the parallels.

[58] At Mk 4:15 the word with the preposition εν (as in Matthew), but in the plural, is found in Koine, D, Θ, 0133, and Old Latin. A has the exact phrase which is found in Luke. Syr [s-p] has the preposition εις (as in Mark). It is not found in B, W, and fam. 13. The variation in prepositions suggests assimilation to the parallels.

[59] D, Old Latin, and Marcion do not have the detail at Lk 8:44 and fam. 13 has it at Mk 5:27.

(15)	6:7	10:1	9:1	καὶ θεραπεύειν νόσους
(16)	6:44	14:21	9:14	ὡσεὶ (πεντακισχίλιοι)[60]
(17)	9:2	17:2	9:29	τὸ πρόσωπον
(18)	9:7	17:5	9:34	αὐτοῦ λαλοῦντος (Lk: αὐτοῦ λέγοντος)
(19)	9:19	17:17	9:41	καὶ διεστραμμένη[61]
(20)	9:19	17:17	9:41	ὧδε[62]
(21)	10:22	19:22	18:23	ἀκούσας
(22)	10:26	19:25	18:26	ἀκούσαντες
(23)	11:27	21:23	20:1	διδάσκοντος (Matt: διδάσκοντι)[63]
(24)	12:3	21:35	20:10	οἱ γεωργοί[64]
(25)	12:7	21:38	20:14	ἰδόντες αὐτόν (Matt: τὸν υἱόν)[65]
(26)	12:12	21:45	20:16	οἱ ἀρχιερεῖς
(27)	12:12	21:45	20:16	ἀκούσαντες
(28)	12:28	22:36	10:25	διδάσκαλε[66]
(29)	12:28	22:35	10:25	πειράζων (Lk: ἐκπειράζων)
(30)	12:38	23:1	20:45	τοῖς μαθηταῖς
(31)	13:19	24:21	21:23	μεγάλη
(32)	14:37	26:40	22:45	πρὸς τοὺς μαθητάς
(33)	14:62	26:64	22:69	ἀπ᾽ ἄρτι (Lk: ἀπὸ τοῦ νῦν)
(34)	14:65	26:68	22:64	τίς ἐστιν ὁ παίσας σε;[67]
(35)	14:72	26:75	22:62	ἐξελθὼν ἔξω ἔκλαυσεν πικρῶς[68]

[60]There is confusion in the MSS. At Mk 6:44 ωσει is found in fam. 1 and ως is found in ℵ, Θ, 565, and 700. At Matt 14:21 the word is not found in W, 0106, and Old Latin while D, Δ, Θ, 067, and 33 have ως. At Lk 9:14 the word is not found in q, Syr ˢ⁻ᶜ, and Bo. while ως is found in D, a, e, and f.

[61]Found in p⁴⁵, W, and fam. 13 at Mk 9:19.

[62]Not found in D, and rⁱ at Lk 9:41

[63]Not found in 7, Old Latin, Syr ˢ⁻ᶜ, and Or ᵖᵗ at Matt 21:23.

[64]Not found in D, Latin, Syr ˢ⁻ᶜ at Lk 20:10.

[65] ℵ* and M do not have αυτον at Lk 20:14.

[66]Not found in D at Lk 10:25. At Mk 12:28 the word occurs in D and Old Latin.

[67]Found in U, W, X, Ψ, and fam. 13 at Mk 14:65.

[68]Not found in 0171 and Old Latin at Lk 22:62.

Concurrence of Matthew and Luke
in expressions and wording,
contrary to Mark

		MK	MT	LK
(1)	1:10	σχίζεσθαι[69]		ἀνεῳχθῆναι
(2)	1:10	εἰς αὐτόν[70]		ἐπ᾿ αὐτόν[71]
(3)	1:13	σατανᾶς[72]		διάβολος[73]
(4)	2:9	ὕπαγε[74]		περιπάτει
(5)	2:12	ἐξίστασθαι[75]	φοβηθῆναι	πλησθῆναι φόβου
(6)	2:16	ὅτι[76]		διὰ τί
(7)	2:21	ἐπιράπτειν[77]		ἐπιβάλλειν

---

[69]D, Latin, and Georgian have ηνοιγμενους, in agreement with the verb common to Matt and Lk.

[70] ℵ Koine, A, W, Θ, fam. 1, and Or. have επ αυτον. The combination of B, D, and fam. 13 and the principle of the different reading from the parallels is adequate justification for the reading.

[71]D has εις αυτον at Lk 3:22.

[72]Θ has διαβολου.

[73]243, e, and Syr ˢ have σατανα at Lk 4:2.

[74]There is considerable confusion in the MSS. concerning the verb. περιπατει occurs at Matt 9:5 and Lk 5:23. At Mk 2:9 it is found in B, C, Koine, A, W, Θ, fam. 1, fam. 13, and Vulg. This is extremely strong support. υπαγε is found in ℵ, D, and 0130. The principle of the different reading, however, has less force because the verb is found in verse 11 and can therefore be explained as scribal harmonization within the account.

Matt 9:6 agrees with Mk 2:11 in the use of υπαγε. Lk 5:24, however, has πορευου and this has probably influenced the reading of ℵ* at Matt 9:6.

[75]There is some confusion in the MSS. C, Koine, and Θ have εθαυμασαν at Matt 9:8 and this is reflected in θαμβου in D* at Lk 5:26 and in θαυμαζειν in W at Mk 2:12.

[76]There is confusion in the MSS. at Mk 2:16. B, C, and Bo ᵖˡ have οτι. Koine, A, fam. 1, and fam. 13 have τι οτι. Θ and Syr ᴾ have τι. ℵ, D, W, Latin, Sa., and Bo ᵖˡ have δια τι. Since the text at Matt 9:11 and Lk 5:30 is firm, the variants may be considered as due to assimilation and the "most different" reading accepted.

[77]D and W have επισυρραπτει.

(8)	2:26	σὺν αὐτῷ[78]		μετ' αὐτοῦ
(9)	3:1	ἐξηραμμένη (χεῖρ)[79]		ξηρά (χεῖρ)
(10)	4:41	ἐφοβήθησαν	ἐθαύμασαν	φοβηθέντα ἐθαύμασαν[80]
(11)	5:14	ἐλθεῖν	ἄπελθεῖν	ἐξελθεῖν[81]
(12)	5:27	ἐλθεῖν		προσελθεῖν
(13)	6:11	χοῦς		κονιορτός
(14)	6:32	ἀπελθεῖν	ἀναχωρεῖν	ὑποχωρεῖν
(15)	6:43	πληρώματα	τὸ περισσεῦον	τὸ περισσεῦσαν[82]
(16)	8:31	ὑπὸ (τῶν πρεσβυτέρων)[83]		ἀπὸ (τῶν πρεσβυτέρων)
(17)	8:34	ἀκολουθεῖν ὀπίσω	ἐλθεῖν ὀπίσω	ἔρχεσθαι ὀπίσω[84]
(18)	9:18	ἰσχύειν[85]		δύνασθαι
(19)	10:51	ῥαββουνί[86]		κύριε
(20)	11:2	φέρειν[87]		ἀγάγειν
(21)	12:15	φέρειν	ἐπιδεῖξαι	δεῖξαι[88]
(22)	12:18	ἔρχεσθαι πρός		προσελθεῖν
(23)	12:22	ἔσχατον		ὕστερον
(24)	12:37	λέγειν		καλεῖν[89]

---

[78]D, W, and Θ have μετ αυτου.

[79]D and W have ξηραν.

[80]ℵ has οι δε φοβηθεντες.

[81]D has παραγενομενων at Lk 8:35.

[82]D, W, and fam.13 have το περισσευμα at Lk 9:17.

[83]At Mk 8:31 Koine, Λ, W*, Γ, Δ, and Θ have απο. At Matt 16.21 D has υπο and at Lk 9:22 D and fam. 1 have υπο.

[84]At Lk 9:23 ℵ corr, Koine, Γ, and Δ have ελθειν.

[85]W has ηδυνηθησαν.

[86]D and Old Latin have κυριε ραββι. 1241, k, q, Syr P, and Bo pt have ραββι. 409 has κυριε.

[87]There is confusion in the MSS. At Mk 11:2 Koine, A, D, W, Γ, Θ, Φ, fam. 1, fam. 13, and 157 have αγαγετε while at Mk 11:7 ηγαγον is found in Koine, A, D, Γ, Φ, 0133, 157, 565, and 700 while ℵ* , C, W, Θ, fam. 1, and fam. 13 have αγουσιν.

[88]At Lk 20:24 επιδειξατε is found in C, Koine, Γ, Δ, and fam. 1.

[89]D has λεγει at Lk 20:44.

(25)	14:11	εὐκαίρως	εὐκαιρίαν
(26)	14:36	ἀλλά--ἀλλά	πλήν--ἀλλά
(27)	14:47	παίειν	πατάσσειν
(28)	14:47	ὠτάριον	ὠτίου (Lk: 22:51)
(29)	14:53	συνέρχεσθαι	συναχθῆναι (Lk: 22:66)
(30)	15:1	ἀποφερεῖν (ἀπήνεγκαν)[90]	ἀπαγεῖν (Lk: ἄγειν)
(31)	15:20	ἐξάγειν[91]	ἀπάγειν
(32)	15:39	κεντυρίων	ἑκατόνταρχος (Lk: ἑκαρτοντάρχης)
(33)	15:43	εἰσελθεῖν πρὸς (τὸν Πιλᾶτον)[92]	προσελθεῖν (τῷ Πιλάτῳ)
(34)	15:46	ἐνειλεῖν	ἐντυλίσσειν
(35)	8:31	μετὰ τρεῖς ἡμέρας ἀναστῆναι[93]	τῇ τρίτῃ ἡμέρᾳ ἐγερθῆναι

---

[90]C, D, G, W, Θ, fam. 1, 565, 700, Old Latin, and Or. have απηγαγον.

[91]A has αγουσιν.

[92]D has ηλθεν.

[93]There is confusion in the MSS. D and Old Latin have some form of μετα τρεις ημερας at both Matt 16:21 and Lk 9:22, where Marcion is also cited for the reading. At Mk 8:31 τη τριτη ημερα is found in W, fam. 1, fam. 13, 33, 579, and Syr [s-p].

Concurrence of Matthew and Luke in
diverging from Mark's word form

		MK	MT	LK
(1)	2:22	εἰ δὲ μή		εἰ δὲ μή γε[94]
(2)	4:3	ἐξῆλθεν ὁ σπείρων σπεῖραι[95]		ἐξῆλθεν ὁ σπείρων τοῦ σπεῖραι
(3)	4:9	ὅς ἔχει ὦτα[96]		ὁ ἔχων ὦτα
(4)	4:11	τὸ μυστήριον (τῆς βασιλείας)		τὰ μυστήρια (τῆς βασιλείας)[97]
(5)	4:41	ὁ ἄνεμος ὑπακούει αὐτῷ[98]		οἱ ἄνεμοι ὑπακούουσιν αὐτῷ
(6)	6:7	προσκαλεῖται[99]	προσκαλεσάμενος	συγκαλεσάμενος
(7)	6:7	ἐδίδου[100]		ἔδωκεν
(8)	8:36	ὠφελεῖν[101]		ὠφελεῖσθαι
(9)	9:14	ἐλθόντες[102]		ἐλθόντων

[94]B does not have the γε at Matt 9:17.

[95]At Mk 4:3 the articular infinitive is found in ℵ corr, C, Koine, A, Θ, 0133, fam. 1, and fam. 13 while the infinitive itself is not found in D and Bo pt.

[96]ℵ corr, C², Koine, A, W, Θ, 0133, fam. 1, and fam. 13 have ο εχων ωτα. This may be understood as assimilation to Matt 13:9 and Lk 8:8, since the MSS. do not show the reverse influence.

[97]Old Latin, Cl, and Iren lat have the singular at Matt 13:11 and the Latin has the singular at Lk 8:10.

[98]D, W, Θ, ℵ corr, fam. 1, and Old Latin have οι ανεμοι. D, Koine, A, W, Θ, and 0133 have the plural verb. ℵ does not have και υπακουουσιν αυτω at Lk 8:25.

[99]D, 565, and Old Latin have προσκαλεσαμενος.

[100]W has εδωκεν and D, 565, c, e, and ff² have δους.

[101]The variants fall within the grammatical categories except for ωφελει at Lk 9:25, which is found in ℵ, C, and D.

[102]The principal variant is ελθων, found in Mk 9:14 in C, Koine, A, D, N, Γ, Θ, fam. 1, fam. 13, Latin, Syr s-p, and Bo. and at Matt 17:14 in D and Latin.

(10)	9:31	παραδίδοται	μέλλει παραδίδοσθαι
(11)	10:20	ἐφυλαξάμην[103]	ἐφύλαξα
(12)	10:28	ἠκολουθήσαμεν[104]	
(13)	11:1	ἐγγίζουσιν[105]	ἤγγισαν ἤγγισεν
(14)	11:1	ἀποστέλλει[106]	ἀπέστειλεν
(15)	11:2	λύσατε[107]	λύσαντες
(16)	11:3	εἴπατε	ἐρεῖτε
(17)	11:8	εἰς τὴν ὁδόν	ἐν τῇ ὁδῷ[108]
(18)	12:17	ἐξεθαύμαζον[109]	ἐθαύμασαν
(19)	13:2	καταλυθῇ	καταλυθήσεται
(20)	13:25	αἱ δυνάμεις αἱ ἐν τοῖς οὐρανοῖς[110]	αἱ δυνάμεις τῶν οὐρανῶν
(21)	14:10	᾽Ισκαριώθ[111]	᾽Ισκαριώτης
(22)	15:14	σταύρωσον	σταυρωθήτω σταυρωθῆναι[112]

---

[103]There is confusion in the MSS. εφυλαζαμην is found at Matt 19:20 in C, Koine, W, Δ, Φ, fam. 13, 118, and 209 and at Lk 18:21 in Koine, D, W, Γ, Δ, fam. 13, and 131. εφυλαξα is found at Mk 10:20 in A, D, and Cl. and εποιησα occurs in fam. 1, 565, and Syr ˢ.

[104]The aorist is found in ℵ, Koine, A Γ, Δ, Θ, Φ, Ψ, fam. 1, fam. 13, and Cl. The distribution of text types in B, C, D, and W, however, adequately supports the perfect.

[105]The imperfect ηγγιζεν is found in D, Old Latin, Syr ᵖ, and Bo ᵖᵗ but the aorists are confined in the MSS. to Matt 21:1 and Lk 19:28, although there is variation between singular and plural.

[106]F, H, 1, Old Latin, Syr ˢ⁻ᵖ, Sa., and Bo. have απεστειλεν while C has επεμψεν.

[107]Koine, A, D, W, Γ, Θ, Φ, fam. 1, fam. 13, and 157 have λυσαντες. This may be considered as assimilation to Matt 21:2 and Lk 19:30, since the MSS. do not reflect the reverse influence.

[108]Not found in D and 229 at Lk 19:36.

[109]D ᶜᵒʳʳ., L, Δ, Θ, 565, and 892 have εθαυμαζον while C, Koine, A, W, Γ, Φ, fam. 1, and fam. 13 have εθαυμασαν.

[110]D, Old Latin, Syr ˢ⁻ᵖ, Sa ᵖᵗ, and Bo. read αι δυναμεις των ουρανων. At Lk 21:26 D and Old Latin reveal the opposite tendency with αι δυναμεις αι εν τω ουρανω.

[111]Koine, A, W, Γ, Δ, Φ, fam. 1, and fam. 13 have Ισκαριωτης. D, Latin, and Syr ˢ⁻ᵖ have Σκαριωτης, which they also have at Matt. 26:14.

[112]At Lk 23:23 B has σταυρωσαι.

Bibliography

Bauer, Bruno: *Kritik der evangelischen Geschichte der Synoptiker* 3 Vols. 1841/42. Abr.: *Synoptiker.*

Baur, Ferdinand Christian: *Rezension von C. H. Wiesses „Evangelischer Geschichte,"* in: *Jahrbücher für wissenschaftliche Kritik.* 1839, 161ff.

Bengel, Johann Albrecht: *Gnomon Novi Testamenti.* 1972. Abr.: *Gnomon.*

Buchanan, George Wesley: "Has the Griesbach-Hypothesis been falsified?," in: *Journal of Biblical Literature* 93, 1974.

Bultmann, Rudolf: *Die Geschichte der synoptischen Tradition.* 1921, 1970[8]. Abr.: *Synopt. Tradition.*

Butler, B.C.: *The Originality of St. Matthew. A critique of the Two-Document-Hypothesis.* 1951. Abr.: *Two-Document-Hypothesis.*

Conzelmann, Hans: *Zur Methode der Leben-Jesu-Forschung,* in: *Zeitschrift für Theologie und Kirche.* 1959, Beiheft 1.

Dibelius, Martin: *Die Formgeschichte des Evangeliums.* 1919, 1933[2], 1959[3]. Abr.: *Formgeschichte.*

Eichhorn, Johann Gottfried: *Über die drei ersten Evangelisten,* in: *Eichhorns Allg. Bibliothek der Biblischen Literatur.* 1794.

Enchiridion Biblicum. Documenta Ecclesiastica Sacram Scripturam spectantia. Naples and Rome 1927, 1954[3].

Ewald, Heinrich Georg August: *Jahrbücher der biblischen Wissenschaft.* 1849ff Abr.: *Jahrbücher.*

—— *Die drei ersten Evangelien, übersetzt und erklärt.* 1850. Abr.: *Drei Evangelien.*

Farmer, William R.: *The Synoptic Problem: A Critical Analysis.* 1964. Abr.: *Synoptic Problem.*

—— "The Lachmann-Fallacy," in: *New Testament Studies* 14, 1967/8. Abr.: *Lachmann-Fallacy.*

Fritzsche, Karl August Friedrich: *Matthaeus recensuit et cum commentariis perpetuis.* Leipzig, 1826.

—— (ed.) *Marcus recensuit et cum commentariis perpetuis.* Leipzig 1830.

Gersdorf, Gotthelf: *Beispiele zur Sprach-Charakteristik der Schriftsteller des Neuen Testaments, eine Sammlung meist neuer Bemerkungen.* 1816

Gieseler, Carl Ludwig: *Historisch-kritischer Versuch über die Entstehung und die frühesten Schicksale der schriftlichen Evangelien.* 1818.

Griesbach, Johann Jacob: *Synopsis Evangeliorum Matthaei, Marci et Lucae una cum iis Joannis pericopis, quae omnino cum caeterorum Evangelistarum narrationibus, conferendae sunt.* Halle 1776, 1797[2], 1822[4].

—— *Commentatio, qua Marci Evangelium totum e Matthaei et Lucae commentariis decerptum esse monstratur.* Jena 1789. 90. Abr.: *Commentatio.*

—— *Paschatos Solemnia pie celebranda civibus indicit Academia Jenensis: Inquiritur in fontes, unde Evangelistae suas de resurrectione Domini narrationes hauserint.* Jena 1783. Abr.: *Resurrectio Domini.*

Grobel, Kendrick: *Formgeschichte und synoptische Quellenanalyse,* in: *Forschungen zur Literatur des Alten und Neuen Testaments* N.F. 35. 1937.

Harnack, Adolf v.: *Spruche und Reden Jesu.* 1907.

Helmbold, Heinrich: *Vorsynoptische Evangelien.* 1953.

Herder, Johann Gottfried: *Vom Erlöser der Menschen. Nach unseren drei ersten Evangelien . . . Nebst einer Regel der Zusammenstimmung unserer Evangelien aus ihrer Entstehung und Ordnung.* 1796/7. Abr.: *Erlöser der Menschen.*

Hirsch, Emanuel: *Frühgeschichte des Evangeliums.* 1940/1, 1951².

Holtzmann, Heinrich Julius: *Die synoptischen Evangelien.* 1863. Abr.: *Synopt. Evangelien.*

—— *Lehrbuch der historischen Einleitung in das Neue Testament.* 1885, 1892³. Abr.: *Einleitung. N.T.*

—— *Die Marcus-Kontroverse in ihrer heutigen Gestalt,* in: *Archiv für Religionswissenschaft.* 1907.

Jülicher, Adolf: *Einleitung in das Neue Testament.* 1894; New edition with E. Fascher. 1931⁷. Abr.: Julicher/ Fascher *Einleitung.*

Koppe, Johann Benjamin: *Marcus non Epitomator Matthaei.* 1782, 1789².

Kuhn, Johannes: *Leben Jesu, wissenschaftlich bearbeitet.* 1838. Abr.: *L.J.*

Kümmel, Werner Georg: *Einleitung in das Neue Testament, 17. wiederum völlig neu bearbeitete Auflage der Einl. in d. N.T. von Paul Feine und Johannes Behm.* 1973. Abr.: *Eintung¹⁷.*

Lachmann, Karl: *De ordine narrationum in evangeliis synopticis,* in: *Theologische Studien und Kritiken.* 1835. Abr.: *De ordine narrationum.*

Lohmeyer, Ernst: *Das Evangelium nach Markus (Meyers Kommentar).* 1967¹⁷.

—— *Matthäus (Meyers Kommentar).* 1967⁴.

Marsh, Herbert: *Abhandlung über die Entstehung und Abfassung unserer ersten drei Evangelien.* 1803.

Owen, Henry: *Observations on the four Gospels.* London 1764. Abr.: *Observations.*

Palmer, N.H.: "Lachmann's Argument," in: *New Testament Studies.* 1966/7.

Papal Encyclical "De sacrorum bibliorum studiis opportune provehendis," 1943.

Papias-Fragment: *Eusebius hist. eccl.* III 39; II 1 284. 290f. Harnack/Gebhardt: *Patrum apostolicorum opera ed. maj.* I:2, 1878²; E. Preuschen: *Antilegomena.* 1905². Abr.: *Papiasfragment.*

Rawlinson, A.E.J.: "Q," in: *Encyclopaedia Britannica* Vol. 10, 1962, p. 538.

Die Religion in Geschichte und Gegenwart. 1909-13, 1927-32², 1957-65³.Abr.: *RGG¹·²·³.*

Reuss, Eduard: *Geschichte der Heiligen Schriften Neuen Testaments.* 1842, 1852².

Rohde, Joachim: *Formgeschichte und Redaktionsgeschichte in der Neutestamentlichen Forschung der Gegenwart.* Dissertation, Humboldt University, East Berlin, 1962. West German abridged ed.: *Die redaktionsgeschichtliche Methode.* 1966.

Schleiermacher, Friedrich: *Über die Zeugnisse des Papias von unsern beiden ersten Evangelisten,* in: *Theologische Studien und Kritiken.* 1832. Abr.: *Über Papias.*

Schmid, Josef: *Einleitung in das Neue Testament, völlig neubearbeitete Auflage von*

Alfred Wikenhauser. 1973[6]. Abr.: Schmid-Wikenhauser: *Einleitung*.

Schmidt, Karl Ludwig: *Der Rahmen der Geschichte Jesu*. 1919.

Schwegler, Albert: *Rezension von Wilkes " Urevangelist,"* in: *Tubinger Theologische Jahrbücher*, Vol. II, 1843.

Schweitzer, Albert: *Geschichte der Leben-Jesu-Forschung*. 1913, 1951. Abr: *L.-J.-Forschung*.

Soden, Hermann, Frh. v.: *Die wichtigsten Fragen im Leben Jesu*. 1904.

Storr, Gottlob Christian: *De fonte evangeliorum Matthaei et Lucae*. 1794.

—— *Über den Zweck der evangelischen Geschichte*. 1810[2].

Strauss, David Friedrich: *Das Leben Jesu, kritisch bearbeitet*. 2 Vols. 1835, 1838-39[3], 1840[4]. Abr.: *Leben Jesu [1,3,4]*.

—— *Das Leben Jesu für das deutsche Volk bearbeitet*. 1864. Abr.: *Volksausgabe*.

—— *Der Christus des Glaubens und der Jesus der Geschichte: Eine Kritik des Schleiermacherschen Lebens Jesu*. 1865.

Streeter, B.H.: *The four Gospels*. 1924, 1940[4].

Talbert, C.H. und E.B. Knight: "Can the Griesbach-Hypothesis be falsified?," in: *Journal of Biblical Literature* 91. 1972.

Tholuck, August: *Die Glaubwürdigkeit der evangelischen Geschichte, zugleich eine Kritik des "Leben Jesu" von Strauss, für theologische und nichttheologische Leser dargestellt*. 1837.

Vaganay, Léon: *Le Problème Synoptique*. 1954.

Weiss, Bernhard: *Leben Jesu*. 1882, 1902[4].

—— *Matthäus (Meyers Kommentar)*. 1911[10].

—— *Markus (Meyers Kommentar)*. 1901[9].

—— *Lukas (Meyers Kommentar)*. 1909[9].

—— *Die Quellen der synoptischen Überlieferung*. 1908.

—— *Die Quellen des Lukasevangeliums*. 1907

Weiss, Johannes: *Das älteste Evangelium*. 1903.

—— *Die Predigt vom Reiche Gottes*. 1900[2].

Weisse, Christian Hermann: *Die evangelische Geschichte, kritisch und philosophisch bearbeitet*. 1838. Abr.: *Evangelische Geschichte*.

—— *Die Evangelienfrage in ihrem geganwärtigen Stadium*. 1856. Abr.: *Evangelienfrage*.

—— *Rezension von Wilkes "Urevangelist"*, in: *Berliner Jahrbücher für Wissenschaftliche Kritik*. 1838.

Wellhausen, Julius: *Einleitung in die drei ersten Evangelien*. 1905.

Wernle, Paul: *Die synoptische Frage*. 1899 Abr.: *Synopt. Frage*.

Wilke, Christian Gottlob: *Der Urevangelist oder exegetisch-kritische Untersuchung über das Verwandtschaftsverhältnis der drei ersten Evangelien*. 1838. Abr.: *Urevangelist*.

Wrede, William: *Das Messiasgeheimnis in den Evangelien*. 1901, 1913[2]. Abr.: *Messiasgeheimnis*.

Indexes

Edwin D. Johnston

Author

Subject

Scripture